This is one of the most interesting and original books yet written on Druidry. It approaches each aspect of the Druid tradition from an intensely personal viewpoint, informed by considerable experience, and has something significant to say about each. The sections on deities, magic, and meditation are especially thoughtful and valuable.

—Professor Ronald Hutton, Bristol University, author of *Blood and Mistletoe*

A truly remarkable work. With great care and sensitivity, Hughes has crafted an accessible and deeply insightful guide to the spiritual path of Druidry, steeped in the rich and diverse heritage of the Celtic world....It is Hughes's extraordinary approach to Druidry sets this work apart from all others on the subject—an approach that he is uniquely qualified to take as a native Welsh speaker, scholar, and founder of the Anglesey Druid Order. Drawing upon the wisdom of his ancestors, Hughes's words are infused with the creative spark of Awen that has empowered him to breathe new life into ancient tradition.... It is an exceptional resource for scholars, students, and practitioners alike, and a testament to the enduring power and relevance of Druidic wisdom.

—Jhenah Telyndru, founder of the Sisterhood of Avalon and author of *The Ninefold Way of Avalon*

Against the background of his Welsh culture, Kristoffer inspires, without being prescriptive, the reader to forge their own path forward, yet not leaving out the challenges and pitfalls that every path faces. Hughes's deep knowledge of the way of the Druids and his honesty about his own personal trials equips the reader not only with a plethora of insights and advice, but also with usable techniques to master real life.

—Christian Brunner, author of *Mountain Magic*

A mighty, rich tome of a book, flowing with Awen and packed to the brim with lore and practical tips for exploring and developing your own druid practice.... Kris's wealth of personal experience and impeccable research are combined to produce a guide that is both a reliable and trusted source and a delight to read. The pages dance with Kris's usual charm and the ease with which he guides the reader into deeper spiritual terrain.... This is a fantastic and exceptional guide to Druidry for the twenty-first century.

—Danu Forest, traditional seer, wisewoman,
and author of *Wild Magic*

Inspired by the Welsh myths and his native Welsh language, Kristoffer Hughes combines his unique personal experience and wisdom with scholarship to offer you profound insights and guidance as you explore the world of Druidry.

—Eimear Burke, Chosen Chief of the
Order of Bards, Ovates and Druids

The Book of Druidry is a verb and not a noun. While one will read this book (noun) about the oh-so-many-things that are Druidry, one will work through this book (verb) and become the Druid one is learning about. This is a cornucopia of history, practice, and devotion which will carry the reader through the breath of Druidry, masterfully guided by Kristoffer. Enjoy the journey!

—Jean (Drum) Pagano, Archdruid ADF

The cosmology outlined within these pages paints a picture of an animate, intelligent universe. The connections Hughes makes with the historical, scientific, and spiritual worlds opens many doors in understanding and leads the spirit to wisdom. The joy with which Kristoffer describes this world is beautiful, and his infectious humor and erudite wit show that this path is both powerful and profound.

—Sian Sibley, author of *Unveiling the Green*
and director of the Welsh Occult Conference

This book is a guiding light in both broad daylight and darkness. I was enveloped in a meaningful embrace, my hand always held in my quest to further fulfill a deep yearning for a connection with this land, myself, and

Druidry. Hughes is a true teacher. He possesses a breathtaking depth of practice and knowledge in Druidry, and his flair for beautifully articulating all he has learned and lived is unequivocable magic.

—Carys Eleri, Welsh actress, author of the shortlisted
Welsh Book of 2022, *Dod Nôl at fy Nghoed*

Deeply rooted in the sacred landscapes of Wales ... this work by Kristoffer Hughes presents a multi-layered approach to Druidry, which is an important resource that combines spirituality, art, and science into a comprehensive framework.... The book is an excellent companion for those interested in the healing arts as well as ritual and ceremony. It offers a broad understanding of different approaches and perspectives in connection with formulas that help create a foundation for focus and learning for both those new to this field of study as well as those already seasoned in creative magical practices.

—Francis Joy, PhD, author of *Sámi Shamanism, Cosmology, and
Art as Systems of Embedded Knowledge*

In ancient times, the Isle of Anglesey was a center of Druid learning and wisdom. In our time, it is again. With *The Book of Druidry*, Kristoffer Hughes—Chief of the Anglesey Druid Order—presents an introduction to modern Druidry that is grounded in what we know of the ancients, in the heritage of Celtic culture, and in the wisdom of contemporary nature spirituality. It guides the reader through the foundations of Druidry and their application in our lives here and now.

—John Beckett, Druid and author of *The Path of Paganism*

This book is not only a comprehensive guide to a working, living method of practicing modern Druidry, but also an insight into Hughes's native Celtic culture. Through mythological and bardic wisdom, this book gifts us an accessible insight to a nourishing spiritual path inspired by the arcane myths, legends, and poems of the past, whilst being firmly rooted in what we need in the here and now. Hughes has once again produced a divinely touched work that will surely inspire a new generation of Druids.

—Mhara Starling, author of *Welsh Witchcraft*

THE BOOK OF
DRUIDRY

About the Author

Kristoffer Hughes (Wales) is Chief of the Anglesey Druid Order, a Mount Haemus Scholar, and a member of the Order of Bards, Ovates and Druids. He is a teacher, writer, workshop leader, and guest speaker at Pagan conferences, camps, and festivals throughout the United Kingdom, Europe, and North America. Hughes worked professionally for His Majesty's Coroner for over thirty years. He is a Welsh language television presenter and actor. He's the author of *From the Cauldron Born, The Book of Celtic Magic, As the Last Leaf Falls* (previously titled *The Journey into Spirit*), and *Cerridwen,* as well as the creator of both the *Celtic Tarot* and the *Yuletide Tarot*.

THE BOOK OF
DRUIDRY

A Complete Introduction to the
Magic & Wisdom of the Celtic Mysteries

KRISTOFFER HUGHES

Llewellyn Publications
WOODBURY, MINNESOTA

FIRST EDITION
Second Printing, 2023

Book design by Rebecca Zins
Cover design by Kevin R. Brown
Line art by Llewellyn Art Department

Llewellyn is a registered trademark of Llewellyn Worldwide Ltd.

Library of Congress Cataloging-In-Publication Data
Names: Hughes, Kristoffer, author.
Title: The book of Druidry : a complete introduction to the magic & wisdom
   of the Celtic mysteries / Kristoffer Hughes.
Description: Woodbury, Minnesota : Llewellyn Publications, [2023] |
   Includes bibliographical references and index. | Summary: "Author and
   Druid Kristoffer Hughes presents a beginner guide to Druidry that covers
   what it is, where it comes from, and why it's an important and
   fulfilling spirituality. Hughes shares how to be a practicing Druid,
   Druidry's deep roots in history, its evolution into modern times, and
   ethical and environmental considerations, as well as many ways to
   explore prayer, meditation, ritual, and journaling to further engage
   with the world as a Druid"-- Provided by publisher.
Identifiers: LCCN 2023006594 (print) | LCCN 2023006595 (ebook) | ISBN
   9780738768878 (paperback) | ISBN 9780738769097 (ebook)
Subjects: LCSH: Druids and druidism.
Classification: LCC BL910 .H845 2023 (print) | LCC BL910 (ebook) | DDC
   299/.16--dc23/eng/20230510
LC record available at https://lccn.loc.gov/2023006594
LC ebook record available at https://lccn.loc.gov/2023006595

Llewellyn Publications
A Division of Llewellyn Worldwide Ltd.
2143 Wooddale Drive
Woodbury MN 55125-2989

www.llewellyn.com

PRINTED IN THE UNITED STATES OF AMERICA

CONTENTS

CONTENTS

PREFACE

WHAT IS A Druid? Can someone be a Druid today? What does a Druid do? What is the point of being a Druid?

In my thirty years of being a practitioner of modern Druidry, the four questions above distill the essence of inquiry that I receive the most often. In this book my aim is to address and expand on those four fundamental questions.

My mission is to provide the absolute beginner with a picture of modern Druidry, where it came from, how it developed and evolved into its current form, and why it is relevant in the twenty-first century as a valid and vibrant spiritual practise. This book will also provide you with the tools for practising Druidry and the various avenues and options available for you to further your progression as a Druid. For those who are familiar with Druidry or are currently practising Druidry, this book has something to offer you in re-examining some of the tradition's principles and practises.

In the pages that follow, I shall explore the four questions given above from the perspective of a practicing Druid, and by doing so I shall delve into the history of Druidry from the ancient past until more recent times. This will provide you with a snapshot of who the ancient Druids were and why we choose to adopt that particular name to describe a current spiritual practise.

Of the four questions above, the most startling and often jarring is "What is the point of being a Druid?" It is the one that caused me to stop and consider the very relevancy of a spiritual tradition that often brings to mind a gathering of bearded white men in white robes at Stonehenge. A quick internet search with the phrase "modern Druidry" results in anything but bearded men in white at ancient sites. The result will yield a picture of diversity, with few bearded, white-robed men in sight. Druidry is vibrant and energetic; it is a tradition that bridges the chasm between the secular and the spiritual, the scholarly and the visionary. It is a tradition that has magic as its beating heart. It is the language of trees and holds within it the treasures of indigenous languages and cultures past, present, and future. This book will serve as a testament to the "point" of Druidry.

Druidry or Druidism?

The term *Druidry* will be used throughout this book, which is differentiated from Druidism. Druidism—a term most often used in academia—can be taken to be a reference to the ancient Druids or to a vague notion of what Druidry may have been. The -ry suffix in English indicates something that one does; in a similar fashion that carpentry is something a woodworker does, Druidry is something that a Druid does. This book will explore and expand on what exactly a Druid might do.

Today, Druidry is an authentic and thriving spiritual tradition. Its roots are in the deep past, yet its expression is the epitome of modernity and progression. While Druidry is inspired by the past, it does not serve to re-create it but rather to seed the wisdom of a new tradition that is trailblazing a path into the future. An often-used criticism aimed at modern Druidry is that we do not know what the ancient Druids did and therefore we cannot be Druids. This misses the point and function of modern Druidry as a new and vibrant spirituality that is a product of several centuries of influence. Apostolic succession to the ancient Druids is neither desired nor a requirement; the term Druid means something quite different today than it did in ancient times. In its modern sense, as this book will serve to demonstrate, we are approximately 300 years old, give or take a few years. We stand on the shoulders of giants who inspired a new Druidry that is relevant to a new world. In the pages that follow, I will strive to explore the nature of who we are and who we are inspired by.

Any amount of information on the Druids and the baffling array of Druidic opportunities can be found online with a tap of a finger. But for one's spirit to be moved into deepening a connection with the world of Druidry, inspiration is required. We have a name for this particular kind of inspiration, a Welsh word: Awen, pronounced *AH-when*. This is the blessed, holy breath that blows through the entire universe and causes all of creation to spring forth in its wake. It is the prickling of the skin that we feel when we are moved or when something tugs at our heartstrings. This book can only truly be a reflection of my personal journey, for one of the most important aspects of my journey is to inspire others to find their way into the grove of the Druids. This book also stands as testament to the wider Druid community that I am a part of and that serves to inspire me.

Who Am I?

With that in mind, I should tell you something of who I am and why I am writing this book. I was born several decades ago in the small village of Llanberis, nestled in a deep valley at the foothills of Yr Wyddfa (Snowdon), the tallest mountain in Wales and England. I was raised by an entirely Welsh-speaking family and attended a Welsh-speaking school. The ideas of modern Druidry and its expression are inspired by Celtic culture, with one of those cultures being Welsh. Much of what is apparent in Druidry was a part of my upbringing; myths, legends, and stories of magical worlds and heroes occupied my imagination from when I was an infant. They were always there as a vital aspect of my heritage and culture. After exploring the dominant religion of Britain, Christianity, I left to seek something that would quench a thirst in me that the church was incapable of satisfying. What I needed was all around me; I had gone looking in all the wrong places for what I required to quench my spiritual thirst. It was held in the land itself.

As I matured, I found that a Pagan spiritual path was what sang to my heart and spirit. Druidry in Wales is a vibrant and current expression from both a secular and a spiritual perspective; therefore, it was natural that I was to be drawn towards its streams of inspiration. My first language is Welsh, or Cymraeg. I think and dream in Welsh, and English is very much my second and learned language. Wales lacked a Pagan Druid group that would encourage my learning and development, so I took it upon myself to establish the Anglesey Druid Order (Urdd Derwyddon Môn) in the year 2000. Anglesey (Ynys Môn) was the ancestral chief seat of the Iron Age Druids, attacked by Rome in the latter half of the first century of the Common Era. I am the current head of that order, which provides in-person and virtual training within the Welsh Druid tradition.

In addition, I completed further Druid training with the Order of Bards, Ovates and Druids, and I graduated as a Druid from that mystery school. I have written several books that are adjacent to Druidry, but this is my first book that explores the tradition itself. From the offset it must be stated that the Druidry I practise, teach, and write about is not the only version of the tradition. Druidry has many influences coloured by language and culture; for some Druids, their focus may be inspired by Ireland and the Irish language, while others are drawn towards Scotland or Brittany and their respective cultural expressions. While we are a common family group, there are linguistic differences; some are siblings, and some are cousins. Many Druids are comfortable taking inspiration from a variety of sources and may incorporate Welsh and Irish teachings into their practise as well as wider Indo-European influences. Others may be drawn to only one expression. As a native Welsh person, my perspective is wholly Welsh and will form the backbone of this book. Upon its completion you may find yourself wanting to explore how the other Celtic languages and cultures might contribute to your practise, and you will find some resources and suggestions for that at the conclusion of this book.

By sharing my understanding of Druidry—and, by proxy, my practise of it—my sincerest hope is that you will be inspired to further your studies and progression through the dappled paths of the Druid forest.

Wales and Welsh vs. Cymru and Cymry

The terms *Wales* and *Welsh* are commonly understood to refer to the peoples that inhabit the western promontory of mainland Britain, an area where a non-English-based language is spoken. The term *Welsh* is an Anglo-Saxon word that refers indiscriminately to the early inhabitants of Britain as foreigners.[1] The Germanic tribes used the term to describe the Celts and Britons or anyone who was a non-Germanic foreigner. The Welsh, therefore, are essentially described as foreigners in their own land. In the Welsh language, the inhabitants of Wales are called the *Cymry* and the land itself *Cymru.* These words are derived from the Brythonic word *combrogi,* meaning "fellow countrymen." In recent years there has been a move by Welsh language campaigners to refer to the language solely as *Cymraeg* and the land as *Cymru*, without reinforcing the concept that we are foreigners in our own land. The move is slow but progressive. In that spirit, throughout this book you will sometimes happen across the words that we choose to describe ourselves, our language, and culture; these will be used interchangeably with

---

1 "Welsh," Online Etymology Dictionary, accessed July 12, 2022, https://www.etymonline.com/word/welsh.

the terms *Welsh* or *Wales*. *Cymru* refers to the country itself, *Cymraeg* is the term for the language, and *Cymry* refers to its inhabitants.

How to Use This Book

This book presents the history and practise of Druidry from ancient times, across two thousand years to the present. It emphasises the reader's vitality by placing you as the central figure in this story. This is achieved by examining your attraction to Druidry, and to do this you will be using mythological tools such as journaling prompts and the internalisation of mythological principles throughout this book. The main portion of the book is information that focuses on the whys and hows of Druid practises. This contains information on natural science, magic, energy, meditation, prayer, and ritual, to name but a few. The final chapters offer you a handful of rituals and practises for you to try and maybe incorporate into your Druidry.

My aim is to offer you a foundation in Druid theory and practise that comes directly from my experience of it, but know also that this is merely the tip of the iceberg. Druidry has a depth that cannot possibly be covered in one tome. Consider this book to be a letter from me to you, offering you advice and guidance from someone who has been there. When I started on this path so many decades ago, no single book existed that covered such varied subjects as meditation, gods and goddesses, magic, history, and so forth. Here I have written the book that I wanted to read when I first embarked on this journey. There are exercises contained in this book; I encourage you to do as many of them as you can to assimilate the experience into practise.

The Sacred Art of Journaling

While this book is the perspective and journey of me, the author, it is also your journey; hand in hand, we can travel through the dappled groves of Druidry together. In doing so, it is important that you document your journey and the thoughts that arise along the way. Having a journal to accompany any journey is a wonderful addition to recording the process of exploration. At times it can be cumbersome and a nuisance to have to find that journal again and reflect on a particular and poignant part at the beginning of a journey. With this in mind, this book will double as your journal. There are spaces herein for you to record thoughts and ideas, rituals and activities, without the need to think *I should have brought my journal.* For me, books are companions, and I have always been one of those people who continuously writes notes in the margins of books (much to the horror of some, I can imagine)! Some of the profoundest insights I have gleaned have risen from what is known as marginalia—comments and scribbles by unknown hands in the margins and blank spaces of books.

While generally we know who authored a book, we may never know who commented in the marginalia, but there is a tantalising magic that excites me whenever I come across them. In this book I encourage you to write directly onto the spaces offered to you. To prevent bleed-through of ink, I recommend a lovely pencil, perhaps one that you purchase or select specifically for this task. By doing so, this book—which may collect dust on your bookshelf in years and years to come—will always act as a record of your initial journey onto the groves of Druidry, a treasure that you may reflect upon.

When we externalise our thoughts and put them onto paper or into a digital format, our relationship with the experience is heightened. Taking time out of one's day to journal is not only of benefit to your mental health but is a time-honoured function of magical practise.

This practise begins right here as I ask you to answer some questions. It is traditional in Druidry that a series of questions are asked of the seeker to probe and stir their thoughts as they journey. At this stage you may not be able to fully articulate your answers, but I suggest that you have a go. If this is your first time exploring Druidry, your answers might be brief.

· · · · · ·

☞ *I think a Druid is...*

....

....

....

☞ *Can someone be a Druid in the modern world?*

....

....

....

☞ *This is what I think a Druid does...*

. . . .

. . . .

. . . .

☞ *The function of a Druid is...*

. . . .

. . . .

. . . .

At the end of this book, the same questions will be asked
of you to discover how your perception may have altered.

* * * * * *

My hope is that by coming along on the journey of my Druidry, you may see a reflection of your own explorations. This is the power of inspiration, and it lies at the heart of the Druid tradition. Let us go together into the heart of the Druid forest.

INTRODUCTION

THERE IS AN old Welsh proverb that says *Dod yn ôl at fy nghoed*, which literally translates as "To come back to my trees." When used in conversation, it is taken to mean that one has returned to a balanced state of mind or rediscovered one's center. Nobody knows for sure where or when this proverb originated, but in Welsh culture it carries the sense of an ancient wisdom, one that is often connected to the Druids of the deep past. It evokes a feeling that the self is intimately connected to trees, and that they in turn have the ability to guide and teach us the wonders and mysteries of life. When we return to the trees, something remarkable happens: we discover who we are, who we were meant to be, and how we can express that to the world at large. But to say this is to imply that we have somehow wandered away from the trees; what does that mean?

As you hold this proverb in mind—to come back to my trees—consider that at the center of the Druid tradition is the concept of the world tree, or the tree of life. Some may refer to this metaphorical tree as the axis mundi, the center point, the pillar between that which is above and that which is below. In the Welsh tradition it is called the *Coeden y Bydoedd*, the tree of all worlds. It is not a single species but the wondrous expression of all trees that have ever existed. We can visualize this tree and its roots as they reach down deep into the earth or metaphorically into the underworld; the trunk is here in the present and its branches reach into the heavens. It is the point of origin, the place from where all things emerged and extended. You can imagine it as an enormous tree standing in a grove within a forest. We come from this tree; it is the point from which we enter the world and then steadily move into the surrounding forest. The proverb captures a deeper meaning: that as we emerge from the great tree, a moment of magic happens where the spirit is influenced by a combination of numerous trees forming the ingredients that will create the unique expression of your life. No two combinations are ever in the same order; they are unique. They are your trees of origin.

Excited and ready for adventure, the spirit rushes forward and into the surrounding forest that forms the grove's edges; this becomes the point of division where we might easily forget the world tree's magic. For many people, the experience of the center has become diminished by their constant wanderings in the surrounding forest of life. When we wander too far from the center, it is easy to lose one's way—to not see the forest for the trees, to become lost in the woods. This can very easily cause us to lose track of our center, of our point of origin and the reason why we are here in the first place. Druidry is the craft of finding and then reclaiming your center, to come back to your trees—not in a manner that diminishes or denigrates the wonders of the forest of life itself, not in a sense where we must vanquish or somehow remove ourselves from the experience of living. On the contrary: Druidry is the craft of being fully immersed in life while rediscovering and not losing sight of our center.

This is easier said than done, for the world is full of perils and wonder, dangers and treasure. The experience of life on this earth is varied and rich and riddled with the joys and the sadness that all humans encounter as they traverse the wheel of life. The beauty of Druidry and its practice is that it serves to direct our attention to the function and purpose of life as an expression of the creative force of the universe itself. It does so by one of the most powerful symbols that humankind has continuously utilized to express mystery: a tree.

When we are born into this world, we are still firmly attached to the world tree, but as time progresses and we discover our individuality, we become acutely aware of *I* and *other*. Slowly but surely, we move from the center and outwards into the experience of life, and in doing so many will eventually embark on a journey to discover exactly who they are. Druidry is the call of the world tree that reminds you of who you are. Its practice and crafting return you to the familiar roots of the world tree, where you discover the unique expression of your life's purpose and the inherent wisdom that lies within you.

Druidry serves to return you to the point at which your story becomes pertinent and you discover the unique purpose of your own personal Awen—your superpower. That word may appear provocative, grand even, and yet it truly is the function of the craft of

Druidry. Your own talents and skills are elements of the universe's creative force expressing itself through your human life. Your superpower may be in your ability to express that creativity through poetry or music or song; you may be drawn to write or spurred into action as an activist or a powerful organizer. Or your superpower might be your ability to be the best parent that you can be or your ability to listen intently to others. Your superpower is your Awen. Druidry helps you find that power and then express it in a manner that reflects the truth that your life and your living is an extension of the same power that gave rise to planets and suns and distant galaxies and the smallest of creatures that live on our planet. You are an embodiment of mystery, and through you the universe can learn much about itself. This is the function and purpose of Druidry: *dod yn ôl at fy nghoed*—to come back to your trees.

Spiritual traditions and religions have been constant companions in the experience of humanity, and they have arisen because of an inherent need: the desire to find meaning. I do not believe that in a wholly rationalized universe we will have a world populated by content and happy people. An entirely logocentric world—one without mythos, or beliefs—would be a cold and hard place, an unfeeling world of facts and statistics. Logos is the prevailing force in human society, and yet we crave and long for its counterpart—mythos. Logos rules the world of facts; it is calculated, rational; it believes it knows what is right and wrong and seeks to maintain the status quo. It helps us explain the world around us in scientific and quantifiable ways that make sense and are sensible. Facts are, after all, the truth—right? Unfortunately, no. We can individually or collectively manipulate the facts to substantiate a claim or strengthen an agenda. "Facts" provide gravitas and an air of indisputable organization.

In contrast, mythos provides a narrative that encourages us to explore how we feel and what we imagine. It is entirely subjective and cannot be quantified by facts and figures. It is the realm of deep imagination, the magic behind and between the words of a story. It is compelling and provides a window through which we can perceive the potential magic in the world and our place within it. Logos and mythos are not diametrically opposed; they are two sides of the same coin. Druidry is the craft of building the bridge between those two concepts, not favoring one over the other.

Druidry is the craft of learning and knowing the right protocols that enable the Druid and those that they inspire to find a way back to their trees. A Druid understands on a profoundly deep level that any part of us can return to the center. This place where we return to our trees is not a fixed destination, it is within you all the time; any part of us can become the center. The practice of Druidry serves to create and facilitate the rituals that are necessary to bring us to an awareness of the center, to bring the eternal and the mysterious into the present and into the now. When we do this, we consciously exist within the miraculous; this is the power of Druidry, a power that will be expressed to you throughout the coming chapters.

Dod yn ôl at fy nghoed—to come back to my trees; this is the truth that Druids strive towards, and the wisdom that results from returning to your center has the ability to enchant the world. We are never truly lost in the forests of life, for the entire forest is a metaphor for communication and relationship; we might lose our sense of direction and become temporarily blinded to the center, but we can always find our way. Scientifically we understand that the forest communicates via a vast mycelial network, the wood wide web. Each strand of that web is connected to the center, to the world tree. Druidry is the art and craft of finding the networks that return us to the trees of our making. It does this through the lens of the Celtic cultural continuum, finding the webs of connection between the here and now and the deep past. Druids weave the webs that connect us to the center, and as we weave, we become immersed in the wonders of the world around us, but not so distracted that we lose sight of the world tree. In that weaving Druids grow into their wisdom, and in that wisdom they serve the world and its inhabitants, and from that wisdom they illuminate the paths in the forest that lead to the world tree. Druids are the enchanters that the world so desperately needs. I wrote this book to offer you the tools and knowledge necessary for you to become the enchanter.

Druidry brings to my life the most meaning, significance, and beauty. It is a joyous path. At every turn in the forest of its treasures, one is met with the sagacity of the past, the wonder of the present, and the hope of a future that is steeped in inspiration, magic, and wisdom. Druidry transforms my anxieties into joy, and it has the potential to do the same for you. It is a path of inspiration and wisdom that was old when the world was new. It is a magical craft that has the potential to completely change your life.

So let us return through the forest to the trees of our making, and there make magic that made the world...

DRUIDRY: THE LANGUAGE OF TREES

PRIOR TO UNPACKING the meaning of Druidry itself, we must consider the use of the word *Druid*, what it means, and whether we can glean any inspiration from that meaning. In etymological terms, *Druid* can be taken to have two distinct meanings, which may at first glance appear to be at odds with one another. However, by closely examining the word, it is evident that its linguistic history is complex and indicative of a word that was in use for centuries by different languages who shared a common root. As the word evolved, it became further muddled by the ulterior motives and opinions of the authors who used it. If I start as close to the present as possible, it can be deduced that that the English word *Druid* is borrowed from the Old French *druide*, which in itself is a borrowing from the Latin *druides*. In turn, this is a development of the Gaulish *Druides* from the Celtic compound *dru-wid*, meaning "a strong seer." That is a lot of words borrowed from several sources, which implies that the term was in common use within the structure of the languages mentioned. It is unclear what precisely the Druids were able to see strongly—perhaps it relates to their ability to see beyond the limitations of ordinary sight and possibly it hints at a supernatural quality that they beheld.

The implication of strength or strongness appears to be an evolution of a much older source for the term found in the Old Celtic word *derwos,* meaning "true." In turn, this arose from the Proto-Indo-European term for tree, *deru*, which also carries the meaning of "solid" or "steadfast."[2] It is unclear if *deru* referred specifically to the oak; this may have been conflated by the Roman classical author Pliny the Elder, who directly associated the Druids with the Greek word for oak.[3] The suffix *wid* was also taken to mean "to know." *Wid* also carries connotations of "to see" and is connected with words that express sagacity or wisdom.[4] Hypothetically it is connected to the Sanskrit *veda*, meaning "I know."[5] From this it has long been deduced that the term Druid has its root meaning in "they who know the trees/oak," with the added potential for the term *strong* or *steadfast* to be included in the mix. That is a fair amount of information from a single five-letter word. It also tells us that the term was in linguistic circulation over a vast period of time and meant different things to different peoples, but what of the Druids themselves?

There is no evidence to suggest that the term was used by the Druids, but the origin of the word certainly has its roots in the Indo-European languages that were current at the time. The predominantly Roman classical authors certainly used the term to describe a religious priest caste of the Celtic peoples of Gaul and the British Isles. If we look to the insular British Celtic language now called *Cymraeg* (Welsh), which itself evolved from the Common Brittonic language of Britain, we will find the equivalent of Druid to be *derwydd* (singular) and *derwyddon* (plural). This word can be examined in two different ways, with each yielding a similar result. Firstly, the term can be seen to contain two syllables, *der* and *wydd*; the *der* component is related to Old Welsh *dâr*, meaning "oak," and the *wydd* has similar connotations to the *wid* that we saw earlier. This term is intimately connected to other Celtic languages, with versions of it evident in Cornish, Breton, and Irish. Figuratively, *dar* means "a foremost warrior, leader, or mighty lord." Here we can see cognate comparisons with *dru* in its meaning as "strong" or "to have strength," perhaps an indication of the strength or majesty of the oak in general. We can see from this breakdown that in Cymraeg, the term means "to be oak-wise, or oak-knowing."

---

2 "*Deru-," Online Etymology Dictionary, accessed July 12, 2022, https://www.etymonline.com/word/*deru-.

3 Aldhouse-Green, *Caesar's Druids*, 38.

4 Barnhart, *Chambers Dictionary of Etymology*, 304.

5 "Druid," Online Etymology Dictionary, accessed July 12, 2022, https://www.etymonline.com/word/druid.

The second interpretation is to consider that the *wydd* suffix is a mutation of *gwydd,* which in the plural would be *gwyddon*. According to the *Dictionary of the Welsh Language*, this term is also taken to mean a person of learning, a Druid, or magician, but simultaneously it is connected with witch and sorcerer and woodland deities.[6] As the language evolved and attitudes towards the magical changed, the term *gwyddon* was to become associated with powerful women who were denigrated as monsters, giantesses, and hags. This provides an interesting hint at the fact that the word *derwydd* may contain within it a vast array of meaning that connects those individuals to natural magical forces and expresses the strength or a knowing that comes specifically from the oak tree. To the elite and influential of late medieval Wales, these were problematic. Linguistically, the term cannot easily be separated from the craft of the Druid as a magician and the witch as a practitioner of folk magic. Later in this book you will discover other similarities and a common origin for modern Druidry and Witchcraft and Wicca.

Taking all the above into account, I translate the term *Druid* and *Derwydd* to mean "oak-wise." As this book progresses, various factors will go into the making of that oak wisdom and how it is emulated in the individual Druid. In all cases throughout this book, the terms *Druid* and *Druidry* are capitalised.

Alas, no records remain to tell us what the Druids might have called themselves, but there are clues hidden in medieval Welsh poetry that belong to a lineage of Bards within the Welsh Bardic tradition (*Y Traddodiad Barddol Cymraeg*). This tradition contains a baffling array of manuscripts, books, and a vast collection of poetry spanning from between the seventh and ninth centuries to the present time. One of these collections is given the title the Book of Taliesin. Taliesin is the prototypic and chief Bard of the Welsh Bardic tradition whose spirit continues to be venerated today. Taliesin, whose name means "radiant brow," was the transformed child of the witch goddess Cerridwen.[7] One of the poems attributed to this figure has a curious line within it that offers a tantalising clue that may hint at what the Druids called themselves. It is found in a poem called *Buarth Beirdd*, which can be translated to mean "the poets' enclosure" or "the poets' corner." The poem concerns itself with Bardic prowess and satirically condemns

---

6 Bevan and Donovan, *Geiriadur Prifysgol Cymru*, 1752–1754.
7 See my book *Cerridwen: Celtic Goddess of Inspiration*.

those of lesser Bardic ability than the Taliesin figure. In it we find this line: *Wyf dur, wyf dryw, wyf syw, wyf saer* or "I am hard, I am a Druid, I am a sage, I am a craftworker."[8]

There is a lot going on in these two short lines, and while its unpacking can be achieved linguistically, the Bardic tradition allows and encourages visionary insight, allowing the universal creative force, the Awen, to fill in the gaps. You will notice a repetition of the word *wyf,* which means "I am." The second word we see is *dur,* which is a reference to steel, but it is used figuratively in the Cymraeg language to describe someone who has the hardness or the strength of steel. This is not an alien concept; as previously explored, the significance of hard strength is contained within the early words for Druid. The second term is perhaps the most interesting—*dryw*—for in modern Cymraeg this term means "wren" and "Druid" simultaneously. In many modern translations, this term is often taken to mean "prophet" or "seer," both qualities resident in the Druid. Celtic scholar Marged Haycock translated this word to mean "wizard,"[9] while Gwyneth Lewis and Rowan Williams interpret it as "shaman."[10] In all cases there is an agreement that the term is magical or metaphysical. *Dryw* has similar cognates in the Irish, with some scholars assuming the Cymraeg version borrows from the Irish. The Cymraeg material has not been extensively translated to English owing mostly to the lack of expert philologists with a deep knowledge of the language. Therefore, during the late nineteenth and early twentieth centuries, there was an erroneous academic tendency that suggested Cymraeg simply borrowed words and concepts from the Irish.

The word *dryw* and its association with the smallest of British birds, the wren, is particularly interesting owing to the bird's position in folklore. Long considered the king of all birds in most parts of Europe, with its small body and huge voice, the wren has been associated with magic and enchantment for countless centuries.[11] Why the smallest bird would be associated with the Druids is lost to us; we can only assume. Perhaps the tenacity of the wren, its expert construction skills, and its pure voice were qualities that were admired and emulated by people. A Cymraeg folksong makes a comparison between man and wren by saying *dryw bach ydy'r gwr* (the man is a small wren).[12] The Christmas traditions of St. Stephens Day and boxing or killing the wren and parad-

---

8   Haycock, *Legendary Poems,* 79; my translation.
9   Haycock, *Legendary Poems,* 79.
10 Lewis and Williams, *The Book of Taliesin,* 40.
11 Muller, *The Irish Wren Tales,* 131.
12 https://www.youtube.com/watch?v=Ph0Xzoz7L5o.

ing its body around the community is both macabre and fascinating. This small bird is firmly entrenched in European folklore; therefore, did it have some connection to the ancient Druids, and is the poem of Taliesin alluding to this? We will, of course, never know, but there is a possibility that maybe the Druids of the old world used this term to describe themselves.

Taliesin goes on to describe their function as a sage (*syw*) and then as a craftworker (*saer*); however, the term *saer* refers to carpentry and woodwork, with the theme of woods and trees featuring once more in relation to Druids.[13] In this short verse we can glean much inspiration that seems to reflect the qualities of those who are oak-wise. Is it possibly capturing some echo of the old Druids? What it does demonstrate is that as soon as one takes to scratching the surface, we can come to all manners of conclusions, some of which are interesting and worthy of pursuit. Some conclusions have been entirely erroneous but are mostly due to modern writers not having the linguistic capabilities of examining the source material. When we do look to original materials, we must employ caution, and throughout this book if opinions and interpretations are offered from my perspective, I will always inform you how or why I have reached that conclusion. As a native first language Cymraeg person, I have certain skills to examine the source material.

What can be deduced with some certainty is the Druids' association with trees. This connection is simultaneously physical and metaphorical. There are classical accounts of the Druids harvesting the sacred mistletoe from the oak; it is said that they gathered in groves deep in the forests to cut the cherished herb and gather it in a white cloth. Mythology, legends, and poetry suggest that the trees were also metaphors for the human condition and acted as teachers; this principle will weave in and out of this book as it progresses. If Druidry is the language of trees, one of its branches is mythology; therefore, for much in this book to make sense, we must take a closer look at this branch of the tree.

---

13 I prefer the gender-neutral definition of they/them/it here because we all have the capacity to be Taliesin.

Branches of Myth and Story

In the tradition of Druidry, mythology, legends, and stories are the strings that tie the past, present, and future one to the other. They speak of an inner landscape that sings in unison with the outer landscape. History is that which is recounted and told by the victor, by the conqueror; it often comes with a good dash of ulterior motive, agenda, and propaganda. Mythology, on the other hand, is the history of the heart—of a people in love with the land. Often dismissed as innocent, futile, or just plain old stories, they often belie a mystery and a continuation of tradition—the power of words in story.

Nonthreatening and often perceived as silly pastimes, so much of the wisdom of our ancestors have been preserved in story, myth, and legend. They flew beneath the radar of scrutiny, but so much truth can be found within a seemingly innocent tale. Myths and legends are the foundations of spiritual traditions and religions; they arise from the heart of humankind to make sense of the world and their place within it. Generally, mythology narrates actions or events that do not have a foundation in historical fact. They usually recount the tales of mythical creatures, monsters, gods, and goddesses. Legends, on the other hand, may have a seed of truth or be based on an actual event that has since been embellished and decorated. Stories are the seeds of both myth and legend that we tell to describe them and are often beautifully exaggerated to embellish them with drama and tension. But at the heart of all three definitions, there is invariably a connection to mythology, and by proxy to land and culture.

Myths and legends are indicative of our journey to find meaning in life and living through the search for truth, meaning, significance, and transcendence, and we find them in every single culture on earth. However, myths do not teach us the meaning of life; that is not their function or point. Instead they provide us with keys to experiencing life with lucidity by being present and fully here. The fourth-century Roman emperor Julian the Apostate was famed to have said, "To conceal the truth by means of myth prevents the contempt of the foolish and compels the good to practise philosophy."[14] They do this through a sequence of symbols and narratives that sing to one's psychic and cultural constitution. The archetypes within myths are born of the cauldron of mystery and are representative of our greatest spiritual ideals; they act as allies, guiding us to understand and know the spiritual potential of being human and of total immersion in

---

14 Julian the Apostate, trans. Wilmer C. Wright, "Oration 7 to the Cynic Heracleios" in *The Complete Works of Julian the Apostate*, 204.

life and mysteries of the spirit. Myths define and express the relationship of humankind with the land. They are often locality specific, yet many capture a universal truth and strain of thought that is often like those in far-flung reaches of the globe. Contact with other cultures is not a prerequisite to common mythological motifs; they seem to have a global human quality to them. According to early twentieth-century occultist Dion Fortune, we possess a psychic constitution, and myths act as keys that open our subtle senses; hence the premise that people are drawn to certain myths and legends, not because they are pretty and entertaining, but because they match the individual's psychic constitution.[15]

The myths of Cymru reflect a landscape that was old when they were first written down; they capture the stories of the old Brittonic gods under new names that reflect the evolution of language. They concern themselves with the lives of humankind and express the deities' desire to form relationships with them. Modern Celtic scholars are of the opinion that hidden in the myths of Cymru are the religious pantheons of Celtic Britain.[16] Fundamental to the expression of Druidry in the Cymraeg tradition is a collection of myths called the four branches of the Mabinogi. The term *Mabinogi* may mean something along the lines of "the tales of youth"; it may also contain elements pertaining to the divine Celtic child Mabon. These tales have existed in written form for nearly a thousand years, but the consensus amongst academics is that while their composition is young, it is likely they contain elements that pertain to the Paganism of the pre-Christian era.[17] In her seminal work on the Mabinogi, Sioned Davies claims that the actions of the tales are in the Pagan past and that the characters inhabiting them have cognates in the ancient Celtic world. She makes a comparison example between Lleu of the fourth branch of the Mabinogi as cognate with the Celtic god Lugus, and that Rhiannon of the first, second, and third branches is cognate with the earlier figure of Epona,[18] who is also related to the Celtic Great Queen Rigantona. However, in their written form they are overlaid with the detail of the mediaeval era that they inhabited, and it is probable that that audience did not fully understand their significance as inhabitants of an earlier mythological landscape.

---

15 Fortune, *The Mystical Qabalah*, 10–13.
16 Brynley Roberts, introduction to Ifans and Ifans, *Y Mabinogion*, xiii.
17 Williams, *Pedeir Ceinc y Mabinogi*, xxiii.
18 Davies, *The Mabinogion*, xxv.

The Mabinogi collection has become the cornerstone of applied mythology in many currents of modern Druidry. While they may have their roots in the ancient Celtic world and their philosophies, they are also wonderfully modern. If their original position in time was during the Iron Age and towards the time when the Romans occupied the British Isles, then they have been a thousand years in the making before they were preserved onto parchment. During that time, names changed to reflect the new language of Old and then Middle Welsh. Taking all of this into consideration, it is important to note that the gods and goddesses herein and the names we use for them come from Cymraeg and are best identified today as Cymraeg or Welsh deities. Mythology preserved the attributes of mythological figures, but it did so in a way that carried them through time; when they arrived in the Middle Ages, they had been on long sojourns throughout Britain and sometimes onto the European continent. What they hold is a magic centuries in the making. From the visionary perspective of a modern Druid, the myths are vehicles that carried the wisdom of the Old World into the modern. In doing so they provided a means by which the future could adopt a new pantheon that has its genes in the deep past but is made fresh for a new world.

The Mabinogi[19] collection is preserved in their entirety in two manuscripts; the first is called the White Book of Rhydderch and the second, the Red Book of Hergest. However, neither of these books is believed to contain the original text, but rather later copies of them. It is believed that the myths were in circulation, literally and orally, for generations before they found their way into the white and red books. Many of the themes contained within the myths are referenced in earlier poetry. The Mabinogi(on) contains eleven tales in total, and within them are two subcategories: the first is called the four branches and the second, the three romances. They are interspersed by individual standalone myths.

In chronological order, the tales appear as follows:

> 1: Culhwch ac Olwen
>
> 2: Pwyll Prince of Dyfed (first branch)
>
> 3: Branwen (second branch)
>
> 4: Manawydan (third branch)

---

19 The term *Mabinogion* is sometimes used but is generally a reference to all eleven tales of the collection; the four branches are the Mabinogi proper.

5: Math (fourth branch)

6: Lludd and Llefelys

7: Lady of the Fountain (first romance)

8: Peredur (second romance)

9: Gereint (third romance)

10: The Dream of Macsen Wledig

11: The Dream of Rhonabwy

For the purposes of this book, any reference to mythology will primarily be in relation to the four branches as listed above. It is important that you see the landscape that they inhabited in its chronological entirety. The four branches are the perfect springboard for exploring the Druid mysteries, and there are plenty of books on the market that explore them from the perspective of modern Pagans as well as academic tomes that delve into their linguistic and cultural value. If you are unfamiliar with them, I would advise that you read or listen to the four branches. I suggest the translation in written form by Sioned Davies, published by the Oxford University Press, and called *The Mabinogion*, and that by scholar Will Parker, whose translation of the four branches is available freely online.[20] If you prefer to listen to the tales, the Pagan musician and Druid Damh the Bard has recorded the Mabinogi as individual albums.[21] For the Druid, the beauty of the myths swims between the visionary and the scholarly, never favouring one over the other. Within them we perceive seeds of wisdom.

The concept of tales containing deeper meaning is an old one. Countless cultures across the world have used storytelling as a way of conveying cherished ideas, philosophies, and beliefs. The characters of the four branches are not just people; they represent deific function as well as the human condition. As Druids we can connect to one or the other, or indeed both. Concealed within them are hidden meanings, and often these are difficult to discover or are lost in translation. Sometimes no explanation is given for the magical events that unfold, as if the audience of the time was expected to understand them. They contain within them a concept that the character of Pwyll in the first branch calls an *ystyr hyd*, or "a magical meaning." To find this meaning, we must travel

20 http://www.mabinogi.net/translations.htm.
21 https://paganmusic.bandcamp.com.

beyond the words on parchment and into the landscape itself, and Druidry offers keys to access myth in a way that is profoundly transformative.

Mythology is a sacred and elemental landscape that is simultaneously mystical and timeless. It exists just adjacent to our own reality and hints at special places where the weaving of that world and this one is thin and permeable. Bards and Druids have long since understood this and have often retreated from the mundanity of this world to experience the deep magic of the mythological world. For the Druid, storytelling, ritual, and vision-journeys enable us to explore the land of myth, which utterly transforms our relationship with them. When myth moves from simple storytelling to a key to explore mystery, we are forever changed by its power.

The ancient Druids may have left us a legacy of wisdom through channels of myth; in turn, they have become legends that are continuously embellished by imagination. There will come a point where the Druids of the current time will also become legendary; it is a cycle that perpetuates itself, and it does so for the love and meaning of myth. It is inseparable from the function of modern Druidry; to explore and work with myth is to learn to know ourselves. Myth can often call us to an awakened state of spiritual awareness. With that in mind, let us now turn to the mechanism that stirred your spirit to explore the mystical.

PWYLL AND THE
CALL OF WILD AWAKENING

BEFORE WE EMBARK on discovering the foundations of Druidry in a historical sense, it is important that we consider the nature of *your* foundation. While this book strives to give you a general Druidic background to theory and practise, any practical or contemplative application must begin with you, for this is essentially your journey into Druidry. This tradition is a sequence of stories and myths that are interwoven like intricate Celtic knotwork; while it contains the ancient narratives of those who influenced the rise of modern Druidry, the story of the individual Druid is just as important. So, we begin by finding your first steps in the landscape of Druidry. To do this, we must take a closer look at your inner landscape in conjunction with a mythological landscape.

Druidry is a call to action; it is the physical and spiritual embodiment of a calling from the hidden and subtle places of this world, from the liminal spaces that lie betwixt and between your senses. It starts with a whisper, and invariably that whisper rises from the subtle and unseen places to tease the ear and the spirit of the potential Druid. I imagine that the majority if not all Druids that practise today experienced a moment that I like to call the wild awakening: a point in life where the boundaries of what is real, fantastical, whimsical, and magical fracture and blur. It is a moment that almost holds its breath with the anticipation of change and transformation—a tingle across the skin causing goose pimples as one perceives something other; neck hairs that stand to attention as something other passes one's perception. It is a moment when the extraordinary reaches out from the ordinary and the world can never be seen in quite the same way again.

The call of wild awakening is often subtle and quiet—a moment in time that causes one's perception of one's place in the world to shift ever so slightly, for one to find themselves suddenly and inexorably beside themselves, seeing the world through a different lens coloured by the wonder of magic. For many it is a great eureka moment as they listen to an inspiring podcast or a presentation, or it may be words from the pages of a book rising to tease and tantalise the spirit.

For some the call arises from the powers of nature herself. The whispers of leaves moving gently in the breeze has been given a romantic term in the English language: psithurism. It describes the chatter of trees as they interact with the world about them. Many become aware of this chatter, of a living principle hid within the natural world that may have not been wholly apparent only moments before. A silent grove in the dead of night, where moonlight casts a silver glow on branches and leaves. A silence— too much of a silence for the space not to have been filled with activity only seconds before. Invariably something, a single moment, causes a great change in the heart, where one hears a different song with new lyrics that call one to explore a new world.

Our call of wild awakening is akin to a mundane walk in the park when suddenly an unknown voice whispers from over one's shoulder and says "*Pssst*—wake up! Look around you!" and suddenly, as if with new eyes, the world and its colours appear slightly different. In one manner or another, I imagine most magical practitioners or those called to explore the edges of spiritual expression have experienced this seminal moment, when seemingly nothing can or would ever be the same again.

It is tempting to consider that spirituality is a one-way street where the seeker goes about seeking and the search begins and progresses along a highway that may or may not have a defined destination. But this would be foolhardy, for matters of the spirit are rarely if ever a one-way street but a bustling highway of two-way traffic with influences coming and going from both directions. The call to wild awakening causes one to become aware of this traffic and the nature of those who share the highway with you. We would be naïve to consider that the call originates exclusively from an intrinsic source. Any form of spiritualty is a fusion of intrinsic influences, or those that happen within our own hearts and bodies and minds, and extrinsic influences, or those that happen outside of our own bodily or energetic fields of experience.

Although we appear to wander autonomously through the world and the experience of life, it is easy to succumb to the illusion that we are all that matters. In Western society and culture, so much emphasis is placed on the value of individuality that we can easily perceive ourselves to be islands in a vast ocean. This can lead to a profound sense of isolation or a belief that we are the centre of everything and life revolves around us. However, as the sixteenth-century poet John Donne wrote in his *Devotions Upon Emergent Occasions*, no man is an island:

> No man is an island, entire of itself; every man is a piece of the continent, a part of the main; if a clod be washed away by the sea, Europe is the less, as well as if a promontory were, as well as if a manor of thy friend's or of thine own were; any man's death diminishes me, because I am involved in mankind, and therefore never send to know for whom the bell tolls; it tolls for thee.[22]

I vividly recall listening to that poem being narrated by my English literature teacher in school, and it struck me as powerful even as a naïve teenager with little interest in anything other than the tumult of adolescent hormones. It moved me to look about the class and notice how others had responded to this piece of Bardic magic. Unmoved and untouched, I was seemingly alone in a moment of wild awakening that tugged at something within me. For you see, these moments can keep happening, calling to us, sometimes as a whisper so quiet, so subtle, that one barely hears a thing, to a shout that causes one to startle and jump, leaving one discombobulated and wondering what on earth just happened. They are precious moments that seek to inform us we are not alone; other forces are at play in our universe of wonder and magic, and we are not an island within its vastness. Instead, we are essential cogs in its mechanisms of awareness and expression, where our eyes act as windows that enable the universe to see itself.

I have had many of these moments of wild awakening, too many to correctly jot in my journals, and yet each one has added something to my becoming what I would eventually call a Druid. I recall another moment where the voice of an ancestor in my ears and the pull of the ocean acted as one to obliterate my perception of myself being an

---

22 "Meditation XVII" in *The Works of John Donne*, http://www.luminarium.org/sevenlit /donne/meditation17.php.

isolated island. The voice of the ancestor was the mystic and metaphysical philosopher Alan Watts, who had long since died; the poor recording of his voice played through a tape inserted into an old Sony Walkman, the kind of early portable device that played a cassette tape through wired headphones.

I stood on the rocky shore of the western coast of the island of Anglesey, the briny spray from the Irish Sea tickled my lips and blasted my face, leaving the skin feeling fresh and new. Alan's dulcet and wise tones peeled through my ears. I do not recall what Alan said verbatim, but the sentiment of what he said that day has never entirely left me. In it he described how everyone here on earth is something that the universe in its entirety is doing—not dreaming about or thinking about but doing in the true sense of the term. We are something it is doing in a similar manner that a single wave upon the countenance of the ocean is something that the ocean is doing in its entirety. The wave is not separate to that which it emerges from. When that single wave traverses across the expanse of sea and nears the edges of the land, it swells. It carries within it the flotsam and jetsam of the seas—all the things that it has gathered in its experience of being a wave. The rocks draw nearer and nearer until eventually that wave crashes upon them. The sound is deafening as a roar arises from the edges of the wave now torn into a billion pieces and a trillion bubbles, each one carrying that wave's experience and memory.

Is that wave's existence negated because it was torn into infinity and cast into land and sea and sky? Is the ocean itself less of a thing because of the loss of that one wave? No. It is infinitely more because of the unique experience of that wave. It is said that water has memory; it recalls all the things it has encountered and all the life forms it has passed through, retaining that memory until it is reunited with the wholeness of the ocean. That wave and all its particles and atoms was something that the ocean was doing. In the same manner, you are something that the universe is doing, right here and right now. It was another call of wild awakening wherein that moment utterly and completely transformed the way I perceived myself in the mechanism of the universe. I was no longer that single grain of sand on the beach; I was a part of the entire landscape.

That call of wild awakening shattered my existential fears. In a moment I lost my fear of death and the anxiety of the unknown. It all happened in moments, with a set of headphones, an old cassette tape, and words of wisdom from the past. This was a fusion of extrinsic and intrinsic influences coalescing into a single moment to whisper in my ear, "*Pssstt*—wake up! Look around you!" I recall feeling somewhat teary and profoundly moved, and I felt compelled somehow to thank the ocean, but how does one hug the sea? I succumbed instead to simply touching the wetness of the rocks that were caressed and kissed by the sea and simply being in a moment of gratitude. I would later learn that Druidry is, in fact, a way by which we hug the land, sea, and sky.

The Cautious Consideration of Wisdom

On that day it felt as if something had called me, something other than the ordinary mundanity of the everyday world. I was suddenly reminded of a sequence of events that happened in the corpus of Welsh mythology and forms a cornerstone of inspiration in many modern Druid traditions. In the first branch of the Mabinogi, we are introduced to Pwyll, the prince of Dyfed, and through him we can experience something of ourselves. Seeing that name—Pwyll—may immediately break you out in a cold sweat, but I ask that you do not allow the apparent alienness of another language to put you off; they are in truth simply sounds, and with a little practise anyone can master them.

Pwyll is a personal noun, but within this name lies a world of wonder and secrets and magic. It is approximately pronounced by saying the word *poo* followed by a very short *ee* sound before operating the spitfire mechanisms of your mouth and uttering the Welsh letter *ll*. This is formed by placing the tip of your tongue behind your upper two front teeth and exhaling voicelessly out through your cheeks. Fear not; it comes with practice, and nobody is going to demand that you sound fluent at first attempt. In addition to the odd written description of what these words sound like, you will also find a link in the footnote below to a YouTube channel where you can hear me saying the words.[23]

Do not worry or fret at this point if you are unfamiliar with this body of work. As we journey through the chapters of this book, you will find yourself become more and more acquainted with the myths that sing to the heart of the Druid tradition. For now, relevant to this current discourse, a short description of Pwyll's adventures is necessary.

Pwyll has an initially unsettling encounter with otherworldly forces and eventually goes on to be consort to the Welsh goddess of sovereignty, Rhiannon. Here are the opening lines of this myth, translated from the original Welsh by me:

---

23 Enter "Anglesey Druid Order" into the search function of YouTube.

Pwyll, prince of Dyfed, was lord over the seven regions of Dyfed (located in southeast Wales). And one day he was at Arberth, one of his main courts, and it came into his desires and mind to go hunting. And the region of his realm he chose to hunt was Glyn Cuch. He set forth that night from Arberth...Early the next day he arose and came to the grove of Glyn Cuch to unleash his dogs into the forest. He blew his horn and began to muster the hunt and went after his dogs, but in doing so he was separated from his hunting companions. As he listened for the cry of his pack, he heard the cry of a different pack. He could see a clearing in the forest, and as his own pack was reaching the edge of the clearing, he saw a stag in front of the other pack...Then Pwyll looked at the colour of the pack. Of all the hounds he had seen in this world, he had never seen dogs of this colour—they were a gleaming shining white, and their ears were red.[24]

Pwyll goes on to encounter a king from the indigenous Celtic otherworld called Annwfn, and a lifetime of adventures and trials begins for the prince. *Annwfn* can be translated to mean "the not-world," or the unfathomable depths; in some English-language books, it can also be written as Annwn. The entire meeting takes place deep in the forest, in a magical grove where Pwyll is called to return to the trees.

In this paragraph from the first branch of the Mabinogi we encounter the fallible Prince Pwyll. His name belies a mystery that swims within the body of Welsh myth. The names afforded the characters of our mythology are not simply nouns, but aspects of the human condition that we all share. The name Pwyll carries a plethora of meanings that includes deliberation, consideration, care, caution, discretion, prudence, wisdom, patience, understanding, intelligence, perception, judgement, mind, reason, sense, and sanity, to name but a few. All of those captured in a single word—Pwyll. Within the myths Pwyll is presented to the audience as a male prince, and yet the name Pwyll is both a masculine and feminine noun, a common quality in many Welsh nouns that transcend the limitations of gender. Pwyll is presented as male for the function of storytelling alone; Pwyll's attributes transcend this and are indicative of qualities inherent in the human condition. As a verb, Pwyll is something that we do when we deliberate, consider, and care in an active sense. It is important that this notion is understood for mythological assimilation to occur. The myths reflect not only the qualities and attributes of the fabled prince but also his ideals, challenges, and tribulations. The nature of Pwyll's lessons is foretold in the meaning of the name.

24 From *The White Book Mabinogion*, edited by J. Gwenogfryn Evans; my translation.

Pertinent to the purpose of this discourse, we must look for the most significant occurrence in the paragraph offered to you previously. In the various classes I teach on Druidry, I ask those present to ponder the significant moment that occurred in Pwyll's eventual encounter with the otherworld. For some it is the moment he is separated from his companions, and for others it is the moment when he sees the otherworldly hounds with their white coats and red ears. Both are significant in their own rights, and yet the most powerful moment in the entire myth is found in the first few sentences: *And one day he was at Arberth, one of his main courts, and it came into his desires and mind to go hunting.*

It came into his desires and mind. Some works of the Mabinogi translate this sequence to say *it came into his heart and mind*; the sentiment is similar in that something called to the feeling part of his person and the landscape of his mind to go hunting. In the original language, the word translated here as "desire" is *bryd,* meaning disposition, desire, intent, aim, purpose, will, resolution, mind. Pwyll did not act upon a whim but was moved both emotionally and logically to go hunting upon that particular day. It was his moment of wild awakening, where he was summoned by the powers of the otherworld to enter the forest of mystery. These external forces invoked him to move towards the experience of them. Without this call to the heart and mind, to will and reason, to emotion and logic, the entire sequence of mythological allegories and events would not have taken place. It is the foundation of myth: the first stirring, the moment when the hero is taken on a quest that will forever transform their life's course. It is the moment of separation.

Myths are often perceived as innocent stories, and yet in the Druid traditions myths are so much more, for they reflect our desire through the centuries to find and glean meaning. They reflect the human condition to understand and assimilate the experience of this life into expression. They address the existential crises of humankind and the myriad of tribulations and trials that we may face. Stories reflect the truth of humankind's experience, and within them we can see our own unique faces staring back at us. In essence, Pwyll is not an individual who lived in the distant past; Pwyll is the experience of your Pwyll qualities, which we will focus on at the end of this chapter. To see oneself in the pages of myth is to embark on a journey into self. In essence, a myth is something that never took place in the annals of history but is something that happens all the time.

So, let us stop here momentarily and give pause to the qualities of Pwyll that reside within you and consider their functionality and importance to your journey. As previously stated, the name Pwyll has a plethora of meanings; some are similar in nature to their counterparts. I have selected seven of these meanings for further exploration.

When we utilise mythological methodologies for exploring the foundations and expression of spirituality, we simultaneously move into the currents that gave rise to those myths. When we stand within those currents, we are no longer simple observers or readers but active participants in the magic of myth. When we perceive and examine the qualities of our personalities and persona in tune with the archetypes that decorate the mythological landscape, something incredible happens: the myth becomes something that happens to you and something that you "do." The myth ceases to be entertaining and instead becomes transformative. This is how the seeds of wisdom held in myths are transferred from the cauldron that holds them to the heart, mind, and spirit of those who are immersed within them.

When you examine your Pwyll qualities, the archetype that is Pwyll is no longer other but rather an inexorable aspect of who you are. Immediately your relationship with the myths that form the cornerstones of Druid practise is transformed. In an ordinary sense, the form or shape of a myth is usually a book or other multimedia technology that relays its contents as information in the guise of a story. But that shape is altered when our relationship with it changes, and this is what happens in the process of applied mythology, where the hero is you. The shape and form shift across the chasm of perception to become something that is real. How we do this is to shift our form from being the observer to being the participant. This is the true nature of transformation, and in Druidry there are ample opportunities for continuous transformation as we move deeper into the forest of our inner wisdom.

For now, let's turn our attention to the initial stages of Pwyll's wild awakening, which of course is yours, and consider how your Pwyll qualities manifest in your life.

Look at the following seven qualities, and before you read any further, give each one a brief description of how you understand each term. What does it mean to you?

* * * * * *

☞ *Caution*

....

....

....

☞ *Consideration*

....

....

....

☞ *Deliberation*

....

....

....

☞ *Understanding*

....

....

....

☞ *Intelligence*

....

....

....

☞ *Patience*

....

....

....

☞ *Wisdom*

....

....

....

* * * * * *

These attributes reflect your Pwyll qualities and may well be facets of your persona that you have rarely or never had cause to examine. However, each one is an essential quality required for the journey ahead and will assist you in your own journey through the grove of the Druids. They will be the measure that will record the procession of your journey and the depth of connection you will achieve in becoming a Druid.

Begin by examining each one in turn before considering how it is expressed in your own life.

To be cautious is to employ care and attention in your tasks; it is a defence mechanism whereby we take care of self and, by proxy, others. Caution requires judgement and the use of one's skills of discernment to assess a situation or a new group or person we may come into relationship or connection with. There are times when we may behave with little caution and are willing to take immense risks, some of which may be calculated while others are employed with gay abandon. Consider this Pwyll quality and how it manifests in your life, and use the space below to explore how each one is expressed in your life.

☞ *How do I employ caution in my life?*

....

....

....

* * * * * *

Consideration is the act of utilising careful thought and the impact of thoughtfulness; it is taking time to consider what you do and even what you say. It is how we analyse and assess our thoughts before they move into action or consider the value and integrity of an extrinsic influence on our own thoughts and internalised plans of action. This is the organisation of the inner world and the deepest recesses of the mind into articulate thought. There are times where our sense of consideration may knee-jerk out of control, where the mouth speaks before the mind is fully engaged. The path of consideration is to evaluate the impact of thoughts on one's own inner world. Consider here *how* you consider; this will require you to analyse the process of thoughts and thoughtfulness as they are initiated and consolidated by your brain and mind. We are human, and there are times when even the best of us has moments of being thoughtless, where our actions may betray our usual decorum and common sense. Exploring this aspect of your Pwyll quality is not about beating yourself up when you do act thoughtlessly, but rather attempting to understand what caused you to be thoughtless in the first place.

☞ *How do my skills of consideration manifest in my everyday thoughts and decisions?*

....

....

....

· · · · · ·

Deliberation implies that careful caution and deliberation are internalised into gentle thoughts that allow you to weigh your options. It intrinsically arises from consideration and careful and thoughtful discussion with oneself. If the path of consideration is to evaluate the impact of thoughts on one's own internal landscape, the function of deliberation is to analyse and make sense of how the world outside of oneself will be impacted by the action of thoughts. If you are prone to knee-jerk reactions, your skills of deliberation may be the poorer for it. This is the process of internal dialogue where options are weighed and the weight of words measured by their potential impact, which may inspire, empower, destroy, or crush that which finds itself in the path of its expression. Honesty is required for effective deliberation, but often we may not be honest with ourselves and hide aspects of ourselves from internal deliberation for fear of triggering thoughts and responses that we may be uncomfortable with. An individual who has strong internal deliberation skills is most effective at facilitating deliberation in the external world. Deliberation leads to negotiation and mediation, meaning that those who can bring about peace do so by their powers of intentional deliberation.

Are you an individual who thinks carefully and with good intention? Are you able to cause others to find peace and harmony within arguments and disagreements?

☞ *How do my qualities of deliberation manifest in my life?*

....

....

....

• • • • • •

Understanding is a result of direct relationship with an object, concept, or other extrinsic force. To understand is to forgive; to understand is to be empathic. The opposite of understanding is ignorance and indifference. By exploring our Pwyll qualities, we move into a profound relationship of understanding our idiosyncrasies. Often, we behave in certain detrimental manners simply because we do not understand what is happening to us on a deep internal level. When we examine the various Pwyll attributes, we initiate a process of deep understanding that forever alters the way we perceive ourselves. When we strive to understand ourselves, we glean a better understanding of the world around us and those who inhabit it. We often fail to understand the position of others or the choices of others, for we are unable to perceive ourselves in their situation. The path to understanding can be uncomfortable and cause one to look at oneself from an entirely alien perspective. There are many folks who make no moves towards understanding; safe and secure in their own insecurities, anything beyond their reach of acceptability is unworthy of understanding, and yet how we strive to understand reflects the quality of our humanity.

☞ *What does understanding mean to me?*

....

....

....

* * * * * *

Your intelligence is the acquisition and application of your amassed knowledge and skills; it is your ability to be logical, rational, and simultaneously self-aware. This is your centre of critical thinking and your ability to solve problems and springboard your creativity into actuality. Your intelligence is not a measure of how clever you are; intelligence is amassed, whereas cleverness is instinctive and generally associated with your inherent creativity. Our intelligence enables us to make sense of the world by means of verbal, spatial, mechanical, and numerical methodologies. It is a taught skill. While some may have a greater genetic aptitude for one or several of the aforementioned methodologies, we generally increase our intellectual abilities through study and the assimilation of information and knowledge. However, it would be foolhardy to consider that intelligence equals sagacity, for they are not mutually comparable. A highly intelligent individual may not necessarily be equally gifted with wisdom. Druidry requires one's intellect to learn; wisdom is gleaned from putting that learning into practise.

☞ *What is the nature and expression of my intelligence?*

....

....

....

* * * * * *

Patience is the most enduring quality of Pwyll, for it expresses your propensity to be accepting and tolerant. The depth of your patience will dictate your ability to endure challenges and the difficult periods in your life and that of others. Being patient requires one to be calm and cautious. All the previously explored qualities go into the making of patience. We inhabit a world where the virtues of patience have been abandoned for a "I want it now!" culture. In a world of smartphones and quick delivery of goods, our levels of patience may have somewhat diminished, and the idea of having to wait for something is anathema. Patience reflects our ability to employ self-control, humility, and generosity in equal measure.

☞ *How patient am I? How do I express my patience?*

....

....

....

· · · · · ·

Combined, these qualities lead to wisdom and your ability to be sagacious and utilise the previous six qualities in a manner that leads to conclusions that are peppered with good sense and sophistication. In Druidry, the Druid is perceived as inherently wise, but wisdom is not something one is born with; rather, it is something that one develops from examining the internal and external world and forging enduring and sacred relationships. Wisdom is something that is expressed out of experience. A popular social media meme perfectly captures the essence of wisdom in a lighthearted sense: knowledge is knowing a tomato is a fruit; wisdom is not putting a tomato in a fruit salad.

☞ *Am I wise? How do I express my wisdom?*

....

....

....

· · · · · ·

These aspects demonstrate the depth of self-awareness an individual possesses and expresses, and while they are predominantly intrinsic qualities, their impact on the world at large is significant. They reflect the inner constitution of the individual and act as our first gauge for the assessment of self that has been a requirement of spiritual exploration since ancient times. The famed inscription above the Temple of Apollo at Delphi reads *Know thyself*, a testament that the ancient cousins of the Celts, the Greeks, took the exploration of self as fundamental to the development of wisdom.

Your task is to meditate on each one and consider how they express themselves in your life. This is not a time to be lenient with yourself; be honest and express your Pwyll qualities to the best of your ability. In doing this simple exercise of self-examination, you will have simultaneously broken down one of the main stumbling blocks of Druidry and myth: the inability to place oneself within myth. Your familiarity with these myths may just be beginning, but your relationship with them can never be the same after this exercise. More of these will follow through the course of this book.

Held within the innocent appearance of a myth are the facets of wild awakening that sing of the hero's quest to discover truth. Yet truth is a fickle mistress; it is often a treasure of darkness and can mean a myriad of different things to different people. Yet the hero's task does not imply a destination per se but rather the wonder of the journey. As a beginner on the path of Druidry, the moments of your wild awakening are important, for they express something of the nature of you. They are important to capture and journal and explore, for in them are the pearls of wisdom and truth that will lead to the blossoming of your unique expression of Druidry. While many Druids belong or have trained with the various Druid schools and orders that thrive today, the individual actions and practises of the Druid are beautifully personal and have their foundation in relationship with the sacred.

Touching the Sacred

The moment of wild awakening often arises from an experience of the sacred. But what is sacred, and what do you classify and identify as sacred, and what function does the sacred have in your life? Human beings have an inherent propensity for the sacred, which can be perceived, observed, or sensed even in the most mundane of activities or places. Often when we touch the sacred, we encounter a moment that inspires awe—where a feeling or emotion that we cannot wholly articulate fills the heart, body, and mind. In our daily lives we mostly deal with the profane aspects of daily living, or that which is not related to the sacred or religious. When something is profane, we use it on a superficial level; we may value it, but it does not necessarily bring to our lives any deep meaning. However, when something is sacred in origin, it speaks to us on a different level and moderates our behaviour and connection to it; we will generally act and feel differently when faced with the sacred.

Much of what is sacred in our world is often so obvious that we may not immediately notice it—that is, until it is threatened in some manner. Trees that are to be felled for a new highway instil a profound response in otherwise ordinary people, who suddenly feel compelled to tie themselves to them. Examples of protestation and action can often arise from when we suddenly sense the sacred in something and are compelled to act to defend it. The obviously outward expression of sacred space in the guise of churches or mosques or stone circles are merely the tip of the iceberg of sacredness. That which is sacred can be sensed in the most ordinary of moments or with an encounter as simple as a wave crashing to shore or a single tree on a rocky outcrop. To find the sacred in your moment of wild awakening is to move into relationship with the nature of that which called to you. Therefore, it is beneficial to analyse those pivotal moments in your life. The moment of wild awakening has within it the pearl of sacredness; it is wild and awakening because it contains within its very experience the breath of the sacred.

It may be something beyond ordinary articulation at the time it happens, but what makes it exquisitely different from any other experience you have had is the awe and wonder that is instilled in you when you touched and felt the sacred. These precious moments are filled with a magic that causes us to see the world and perhaps our place within it from a slightly different angle. They are the moments that awaken the spirit within and open the eyes to a landscape that appears more vibrant and more energetic than the one we perceived only moments before. And as previously described in my own moment of wild awakening, they are often simple, without drama or pomp and circumstance; they are moments that hold within them the jewel of the spirit as the world and the universe sing your soul back home.

With this in mind, let's stop and give pause and thought to your moment of wild awakening.

EXERCISE

Cast your mind to a moment where you sensed something stir within you. Did your experience—however subtle—mirror some of mine or of other people around you? What compelled you to see the world through different eyes? Now write that experience down so you may refer to it in the future. Worry not if what you experienced did not come with bangs and whistles, for quite often a moment of wild awakening is subtle and unassuming yet profoundly moving.

☞ *My moment of wild awakening was...*

....

....

....

You may have experienced several moments of wild awakening; if so, jot them down. Now consider other patterns of influence such as the seasons, time of day, and location. Then consider the other details in your life at the time such as situations, challenges, and joys. Now consider the impact that experience had upon you and the actions you have subsequently taken.

An exercise of this manner is simple, yet its ability to inspire is limitless.

3

TOWARDS A DRUID CONSTITUTION

To HAVE A moment of wild awakening is one thing, but to suddenly adopt a title and become a Druid is quite another. The descriptions of inspired awakening given above could result in the receiver exploring any number of spiritual traditions, so why would one suddenly be drawn towards Druidry in particular?

Right now you are holding a book that focuses on the Druid path of spiritual expression. There will be several reasons why this book found its way into your hands. The trick here is to consider that your impulse alone may not have been the only reason you are drawn to exploring the nature of Druidry; other forces may well be at play to inspire you. Your experience of what might be classified as "other forces" might be ideas and concepts that you are already familiar with or it may be a totally alien concept to you. At this point I would like for you to consider the nature and even the reality of such forces as we delve into the influences that attract people to one tradition over another.

We all possess an internal constitution that is attracted to some things more so than others, and this constitution applies to all the accoutrements of life—from our taste in music and movies to style and décor to writing styles and artwork and matters of spirituality and religion. This constitution is difficult to articulate and quantify, but it is there nonetheless; our lives are directed and expressed by that which we are compelled to experience and enjoy. Human beings possess three forms of internal constitution that profoundly affect their lives: cultural constitution, worldly constitution, and psychic constitution. If we explore each of these in turn, we can glean insight into the possible reasons why you are drawn to this path at this point in your life.

Cultural Constitution

This is informed and expressed by the programming of our upbringing and the society into which we are born, raised, and live within. It has a local component that is informed by the values, ethics, and morality of our familial circles and localised communities. These can often be governed and inspired by religious affiliations and ideals, but primarily they express the fundamental principles of the culture in which one is nurtured. Formal education through schooling systems further enforces the principles of culture. Our interactions with the wider world are primarily viewed through the lens of our cultural constitution. This is programming in the true sense of the term, and it is the part of our constitution that gives us the greatest stability and sense of collective identity while simultaneously causing us at times to be at odds with it.

Our cultural constitution can often be a double-edged sword. For millions of individuals, it allows the freedom to express the other two categories of our constitution without fear of negative consequences, while for millions more it may oppress and even condemn elements of worldly and psychic expression. To offer you a personal example, I am a gay nonbinary person living in the country of Wales within the United Kingdom of Great Britain. My familial, professional, and localised community cultural influences are almost exclusively Welsh. Wider influences come from the English-speaking nations of the United Kingdom and its governing bodies and laws. The freedom I have to express my individuality is embraced and protected by the culture in which I reside. However, in seventy-one countries my homosexuality is criminalised and in eleven of those is punishable by death. The experience of a similar individual within those countries will be vastly different to my own. The lens through which I view and interact with the world is given expression or limited by my cultural constitution.

The likely audience for this book will be those occupying affluent Western societies, with a relative freedom to explore the nature of spirituality and religion. Religious expression is often tied into the complex nature of our cultural constitution. Here in my native Wales, Christianity was the predominant expression of religion for centuries, but this has significantly waned in recent decades. The Druids have always held a romantic and culturally significant position in the heart of the nation. The spirit of the Druids has always been a vital and dynamic aspect of my cultural constitution. For you, your cultural constitution may not be one that is immersed in Celticism, but for reasons that may be beyond ordinary articulation you are drawn to these accoutrements of culture. The reasoning for this is threefold and weaves together your cultural, worldly, and psychic constitutions into a wondrous fusion of expression. With that, proceed to answer the following question.

* * * * * *

☞ *I understand my cultural constitution to be...*

....

....

....

Worldly Constitution

This category articulates the variety of colour that is expressed in the world and moves the individual to be drawn to some things over others. It expresses mundanity, secularity, and sacredness all at the same time. There are elements of the human condition and experience that transcend locale and culture and may draw people from every corner of the globe. Our worldly constitution is inexorably linked to our function as a species; it is the nature of being human that is expressed here. Superficially these include the types of music that we enjoy listening to, and often these individual tastes are not limited to our cultural constitution. On a mundane level it dictates if one prefers soccer over rugby, Monet over Dalí, Shakespeare over James Herriot, and reality TV over documentaries. On a sacred level one may be attracted to the mystical hieroglyphs of ancient Egypt or the temples of the Far East or the wanderings of the Sámi people. What we sense through our worldly constitution is the family of humanity.

One may be drawn to the accoutrements of other cultures while firmly being ensconced in one's own. This is the crayon box of human existence, where we can play with all the colours or limit our experience to certain shades and hues that appeal more than others. Quite often we are unable to articulate why we are drawn to something that another person may find utterly unattractive or quite abhorrent. Our worldly constitution fills our world with diversity and variety. Consider how you comprehend your worldly constitution and how it manifests in your life.

· · · · · ·

☞ *My worldly constitution expresses itself as...*

....

....

....

Psychic Constitution

The early twentieth-century occultist and writer Dion Fortune coined the term "psychic constitution" in her seminal work *The Mystical Qabalah*. It refers to the quality of attraction that draws an individual towards some systems, practices, and traditions over others. At times these can be countercultural, where one has absolutely no first-hand experience with what they are being drawn towards. In my conversations with Druids across the globe, I have heard many refer to it as a calling that they can neither ignore nor suppress but are unexplainably attracted to. This is often the case with the Druid traditions. Druidry has its origins not only in the ancient Celtic cultural continuum, but also in modern Celtic identity and expression. Often those drawn to Druidry have no direct connection to the modern Celtic world but are inexorably attracted to it. Many live in far-flung countries and may have never visited a Celtic nation. Others have ancestors that lived here in ages past and feel as if something from their heritage is calling them.

There may be no rhyme or reason as to why one's psychic constitution is drawn to one expression over another. The issue is highly speculative, subjective, and beyond the scope of this book to explore. However, it can be described as a profound longing for something that is not necessarily one's own birth culture. This differs from one's worldly constitution in that this category focuses on the numinous and spiritual; its impact is felt deeply. If worldly constitution is superficial, this aspect runs deep within the unfathomable currents of the spirit itself. This raises some questions and issues of appropriation, a subject I will deal with more fully a little later.

Many cannot identify any real-world connection to their love or passion for the qualities of another culturally specific spirituality or set of symbols and myths. For a myriad of people attracted to Druidry, they cannot suppress their attraction to it.

Subjectively, one could explore the nature of the psychic constitution from several different and interesting angles. It may arise from early influences in infancy and childhood such as storytelling, TV, and movies; it may be from a distant ancestor or a sense of one's familial origination. Within the modern New Age movements there is often a belief in past lives and the filtering of influences from other incarnations into the present. For some, they simply cannot explain the draw, and neither can they ignore it. Exploring one's psychic constitution is an interesting sojourn into the realms of the numinous, a rabbit warren of potential new discoveries and illuminations.

The term *psychic* is an adjective that describes an individual that claims to possess extrasensory perceptive abilities beyond the scope of modern science to measure or quantify. Etymologically it is derived from the Greek word *psychikos,* meaning "of the mind," or mental; it is related to the term *psyche,* which simultaneously refers to the human mind and literally as "breath," or to blow upon. There is insufficient scientific evidence to substantiate human psychic abilities as fact. Since the inception of the term psychic in the late nineteenth century to describe unquantifiable supernatural skills, its use in language is commonplace. A glance at any online or physical bookstore will result in a baffling array of popular material that demonstrates the continuous popularity and intrigue of the psychic.

Are Druids psychic? Many practitioners will utilise what is commonly perceived as psychic tools, from tarot cards or runes or ogham staves used in divination to the art of deep listening to the powers of nature. The reasons for using these abilities range from the gleaning of clarity or direction to prophesy and prognostication. In Welsh mythology a beautiful example of psychic ability is demonstrated in the fourth branch of the Mabinogi, where Math, a magician and high king of Gwynedd, can hear any words uttered anywhere in his kingdom if they are caught by the wind. It captures the essence of psychic or extrasensory perception and its deeper meaning of that which is related to breath or to be blown upon. In my own musings I consider my psychic skills to be something that relate to the mind as a receiver that can catch numinous information or impressions and bring them into my consciousness.

While we may all possess a psychic constitution, the depth of interaction that we may have or wish to have with our psychic abilities is not a necessity or requirement of Druidry. In this discourse it is enough at this juncture to consider that something unknowable may call one into cultural patterns that may not be entirely of one's genetic or cultural history.

How do you make sense of the term *psychic*, and what relevance does that have? In relation to Druidry, have you an awareness of a deep current that draws you to this tradition? Consider these questions and answer the following:

· · · · · ·

☞ *My understanding of my psychic constitution is expressed as...*

....

....

....

· · · · · ·

By exploring the facets of your own constitution with the previous discourse and exercises, you will have initiated a subtle transformative process. Any spiritual exploration does not exist in a vacuum and is not a one-way street; there is the tradition of a system that one is attracted to on one hand and the engagement of the human being on the other. This attraction causes a tension between the individual and the ethereal system that they are drawn to. The danger is that it simply becomes something that one uses for the sake of appearance, trend, or a sense of belonging to something different. The function of any spiritual path is to transform the individual, which simultaneously transforms the tradition.

Druidry cannot be a one-way street. It is not something that is used, for it contains within it the pearls of sacredness. It is something that one is in relationship with, and any relationship worth merit is profoundly transformative on all sides. Your transformation ultimately transforms the expression of Druidry for you become a vital aspect of its nature. As with many occultists and magical practitioners, Druids spend time understanding their own inner currents; this involves some introspection and the exploration of the self to better understand the ebb and flow of one's inner tides. This requires a profound sense of self-honesty and integrity, for to explore the nature of self is often a difficult and fickle task, but small exercises such as the ones you have just engaged with move the individual deeper in the flowing currents of the self, and it is there that transformation ultimately occurs. The psychological exercises utilised in this book may on the surface appear to have little to do with Druidry, but on the contrary, they enable you to know thyself. To be oak-wise implies a relationship with something other, and for any relationship to be successful, we must learn to know ourselves to better serve the reciprocity of relationship.

4

DRUIDRY AND CELTIC SPIRITUALITY

THE ORIGINAL DRUIDS were the spiritual elite of the European Celtic cultures of continental Europe and the islands of Britain and Ireland. They existed within a cultural continuum that archaeology and anthropology identify as Celtic. This requires some further exploration by examining a little of what Celtic spirituality is and how a Druid differs from any other spiritual practitioner.

Celtic spirituality can be defined as any spiritual expression or set of systems that utilises the language, art, mythology, and folk traditions of the people and regions commonly referred to as being Celtic in origin or expression. This is not limited to a Pagan expression but can be utilised in any religious identification. The Christian Celtic church continues to be active today, with many adherents connecting to themes that are influenced by the Celtic cultures, and they do so within a monotheistic Christian identity. In the twenty-first century there are many Christians who also identify as Druids. Celtic spirituality is not rigid and immovable; it can easily adapt itself to the needs and requirements of the people. However, it is important to understand that this book, like its author, focuses on the Pagan expression of Celtic spirituality. As a Pagan Druid there will be little, if any, focus on the Christian element of Celtic spirituality in this book. To make that statement is not to denigrate the validity of Christian Druids; it is simply not in my frame of reference nor experience to adequately explore.

Celtic spirituality is not limited solely to Druidry. There are witches, magicians, and Pagans the world over who work with modern Celtic deities, themes, and myths without ever feeling the need to call themselves Druids. With that in mind, there must be something that defines what a Druid is and why the differentiation exists. With its etymological association with trees and the classical accounts of Druids worshipping in forest groves, the term Druid may be highly attractive to those who might identify as nature lovers. However, to have a love of nature is not enough to be a Druid; there must be something more definitive that cements that concept as something that is tangible. A Druid today is more than simply a person who is in love with nature. Anyone can be in love with nature and perceive an element of the sacred within it, but that does not automatically make one a Druid.

The Pagan traditions of the twenty-first century express the same love-of-nature principles, but not all identify with Celtic spirituality or Druidry as a label or identity for their expression of Paganism. In essence, Paganism in general is a clotheshorse that is clothed by the various traditions that pertain to a Pagan worldview; Druidry is one of them, and it does so through the lens of Celtic spirituality. The author John Beckett refers to this as the "big tent" of Paganism, and sheltering beneath its canvases are expressions of Paganism from all over the world. Each tradition carries the magic of heritage and ancestry; each brings a different gift to the feast table within the big tent of Paganism. Those items are flavoured with the lives, struggles, and achievements of the people who were responsible for their ancestral origins.

When we consider this wisdom, we can glean an understanding of why the term *Druid* and its practise of Druidry is relevant and appealing to the plethora of individuals who choose to call themselves Druids. It sings of a connection to something greater than the individual and offers a sense of permanence through the rivers of our cultural, worldly, and psychic constitutions.

Celtic spirituality is not limited to the past, for the Celts exist today; it is a spiritual expression that has at its heart the vitality of the Celtic cultures past and present. If we look to our northern European cousins, the Nordic peoples, we find a beautiful tapestry of spiritual expression based upon the Nordic myths and sagas and the folk traditions of those people. These have given rise to the modern practises of Heathenism and Asatru and other Northern traditions; they have at their heart the concept of culture that sings of their origin and inspiration. In a similar fashion, the Celts are the primary influencers of not only Celtic-inspired spirituality and spiritual practises, but also of the Druids. It was that cultural continuum that birthed, nurtured, and preserved them.

While most ancient cultures had the equivalent of a Druid, be it the noaidi of the Sámi people to the shamans of the Siberian tundra, their functions were similar. It was their cultures that differentiated them. To say that a shaman or a noaidi is just a type of Druid would be to do a cultural disservice to all those involved and immersed in those traditions. They are all expressions of culture and relationship and must be celebrated and honoured as such.

The Celts

The Celtic people of northern Europe and the British Isles had their origin in the Hallstatt region of modern-day Austria at the beginning of the Iron Age. Yet their influences, evident in the archaeological record, lie as far afield as the Xinjiang province of China and the discovery of the European Cherchen Man and his community. The term *Celtic* was first used by the classical authors in the sixth century before the Common Era to refer to communities in central and northern Europe who shared a commonality of language and art. According to Celtic scholars Miranda Aldhouse-Green and Ray Howell, "the term Celtic has the same sort of validity as today's use of 'European', encompassing linkages between groups of people while recognising regional diversity."[25] This commonality of the Celtic people's expression through art, poetry, and mythmaking is evident throughout the regions of northern France, the British Isles, and Ireland, and demonstrates a quality that transcends the locality-specific nature of the tribal Celts. The terms *Celt* and *Celtic* have their opponents who consider them to be unhelpful when attempting to designate a group of disparate people at times hundreds of miles apart. However, modern academia and anthropology find the terms useful as a designation for not only an ancient people but also a modern one.

The Celtic continuum is cultural and not to be confused with genetics. The culture of the Celts arrived in waves of succession that brought art, ideas, and spirituality to the various regions of northwest Europe and the island of Britain. It overlaid the population, not necessarily affecting its genetics but profoundly affecting its culture. While the term *Celtic* can be problematic from an academic point of view, it is necessary to

25 Aldhouse-Green and Howell, *Celtic Wales*, 1.

acknowledge that in the modern world the term *Celtic* can be categorised in two specific manners. The first category is the use of the term in antiquity, where groups of literate Europeans used it to describe and give meaning to their contemporary neighbours. It is a useful term for describing a common shared trait in the archaeological record of the Iron Age peoples of northern Europe and its islands. On the other hand, the term Celtic is a linguistic term that describes the cognate languages of modern-day Wales, Scotland, Ireland, the Isle of Man, Cornwall, and Brittany and their respective cultures.

The Celts, ancient and modern, share a commonality; it is the regional diversity of the Celts that breathes life and colour into the modern Druid traditions. It may be apparent to you that this book focuses on the Welsh/Celtic regionality of Druidry, but to make this statement is not to purposefully exclude the other regions and their cultures and languages. Brittany, Cornwall, Scotland, the Isle of Man, and Ireland all offer their own regional variations that add to the cauldron of Druidry. They each offer a slightly different lens through which one can perceive the various expressions of Druidry and Celtic spirituality. Druidry is a cauldron, and the cultures that retain Druidic lore, myth, and practise are the ingredients that, when cast into the cauldron, each add something unique to the magical brew that is Druidry. This book looks at Druidry through a Welsh lens simply because it is the path of the author. I encourage you to explore the regional diversity of the Druid landscape, but also ask that you do so respectfully, being mindful of the cultures that serve to preserve and guard the traditions, myths, and legends that colour their cultural landscape.

Our literal knowledge of the Druids comes primarily from the authors of the classical era who encountered the Druids as they moved and conquered the various countries and states of Europe. The Druids represented the spiritual and religious element of the Celtic people. Other cultures may well have had their spiritual elders and leaders, but they were not called Druids. To honour the term *Druid* in memory and in practise, it is important to acknowledge the culture that held them—the Celts. The ancient Druids were what we would today identify as Celts; it is not entirely clear if the term *Celtic* was one that they used for themselves as an identity. However, not all Celts were Druids, in the same manner that not all Christians are clergy. Something differentiated the Druids from the ordinary people. While the archaeological and folk record of Celtic nations demonstrate a spiritual practise among the ordinary people, they would not have identified themselves as Druids or followers of Druidry. The same is true today; a witch who incorporates Celtic deities or Celtic folk magic in their practise does not necessarily identify as a Druid. Druids practise expressions of Celtic spirituality, but not all practitioners of Celtic spirituality are Druids.

From the classical authors, it is apparent that the doctrine of Druidry had its origin in the island of Britain and moved from there into Gaul (northern France). If the classical authors and in particular Caesar are to be trusted, the Druids represented a singular priesthood within Celtic culture who wielded enormous political and religious sway over the people and their leaders. There are issues with the testimony of the classical authors, and they may well contain swathes of propaganda and ulterior motives lost to us, but they also represent the only direct information that has survived the ages.

The Celts Today

It is important at this juncture to pause a while and consider the nature of that which is Celtic in the modern world and its relevance to spiritual practise. When the term is used, there is a tendency for the individual to immediately think of a people long since passed from the face of the earth. The use of language when referring to that which is Celtic is invariably done in the past tense, which as a Celt is somewhat disparaging and just a tad offensive, for it dismisses the fact that we are indeed quite current and apparent in the here and now. The Celts did exist all the way back in the distant past during the European Iron Age and well into the first century of the Common Era, but it is equally as important to acknowledge that the Celts are alive and well today and continue to express their culture throughout the six great Celtic nations and beyond.

Today the Celts of the twenty-first century are identified as those who inhabit the Celtic-speaking regions of Europe; namely, Brittany, Cornwall, Wales, the Isle of Man, the island of Ireland, and Scotland. In turn, the language structure of these nations is shared between that which is referred to as P-Celtic, or Brythonic, which consists of Brittany, Cornwall, and Wales, and the Q-Celts, or Goidelic, from Ireland, the Isle of Man, and Scotland. A commonality is expressed through the use of these languages, and while on the surface they do appear quite different, there are cognates that reveal the commonality of culture. The locally diverse nature of the Celts both ancient and modern is demonstrated in the differences between them. These differences are celebrated rather than berated, for we can sense a communal spirit that unites us. That the Celts thrive to this day is not to say that we have not struggled to maintain our identity. From the invasion by Rome two thousand years ago to the Normans, Vikings, Saxons, and the colonisation by the imperialism of England, the British Celts—the Welsh, the Cornish, the Irish, and the Scots—have faced continuous threats to their identity, a struggle that has real-life impact today.

As a Celt, my cultural identity is important for several reasons. It connects me to my ancestors and the land which nurtures me. It serves to identify the family of languages that I belong to, and it stands up in defence of a cultural identity that has been constantly attacked and denigrated by the ruling powers and politics of the British Empire. There are subversive powers that continue to strive to dismiss a Celtic identity, for ultimately nations like Wales continue to be a colony of England. The atrocities of the British ruling elite against indigenous peoples worldwide are well attested, and many moves have been made in recent years to correct the prejudices and wrongdoings of the past. The relationship between Wales and England is complex and fickle, as it is between the ruling seat of Westminster and Scotland. It has at its heart the historical attempt by the ruling classes of the British Empire to neutralise an identity in the western fringes of the island that is predominantly non-English. To this day we are continuously told that Celtic is something that does not exist, for the most effective way to devalue a populace is to render them as irrelevant and without identity. Colonial prejudice persists to this day and is intimately tied to a Celtic identity that the empire has spent centuries of time and masses of money to quell its influence.

To identify as a Celt is to make a cultural and political statement. We choose to exist. We choose to celebrate and hold our culture and language as important aspects of our identity. Our greatest heroes are those who strive to learn our languages and immerse themselves in a culture that is three thousand years in the making and has stood up and fought against tide after tide of hostile attempts to annihilate us. Modern Celtic spirituality serves to perpetuate a threatened culture and makes enormous bounds to help it survive and thrive. Can you be a Celt today? Yes, you can, for it is entirely cultural. Make an effort to learn the language and immerse yourself as much as you can in the issues that are important to modern Celts and the struggles that they have endured over countless generations.

The above statement is not intended to be anti-English, but to point out the very real consequence of colonisation and its influence. Ironically, it is the English-speaking New Age and spiritual traditions that are currently making significant impact on the validity and magic of Celtic spirituality worldwide. In doing so it serves as a component amongst many to heal the damage of colonisation and the denigration of indigenous culture. There is genuine interest in Celticism today, with many spiritual traditions incorporating elements of Celtic culture into their practise. The largest Druid order in the world, the Order of Bards, Ovates and Druids, is an English language-based order headquartered in southeast England. Their work over the last half a century has done much to promote the validity of Celtic spirituality and mythology to a global audience. This has resulted in a profound appreciation for the Celts and the wisdom of a culture that has, against all odds, endured to this day. These are heroic acts by people who strive to imbue the wisdom of the Celts into modern, applicable practise.

Cultural Appropriation vs. Cultural Appreciation

There is a danger in any exploration of a culture that is not one's birth culture that an individual may inappropriately utilise symbols, art, language, or traditions in a manner that denigrates or exploits. Cultural appropriation is a form of social plagiarism where elements from a minority culture are exploited by members of a dominant culture. Prime examples of this were rife in the 1980s and '90s where Western white people took it upon themselves to teach elements of indigenous Native American spirituality without acknowledging the suffering and atrocities that the indigenous culture had endured. Many had had no formal training or connection with any indigenous peoples and strived to monetise the traditions to their own ends. This demonstrated a complete lack of empathy and understanding for a culture that had suffered centuries of denigration and attempts at their eradication. Other forms of appropriation are subtler than the previous example and may not have any monetary return; an example would be wearing an indigenous American headdress and sacred attire and using it as a Halloween costume. This is also cultural appropriation, for it is demonstrative of ignorance and a lack of understanding that the dress is something deeply sacred.

At the heart of cultural appropriation is exploitation, where the dominant culture benefits by the denigration of the minority. Often such actions can be deemed highly offensive; one example is the practise of blackface, which had its origin in prejudiced attitudes towards people of colour, mocking those of different skin to the dominant culture. The appropriation of Celtic culture has been an issue in the New Age movements since its inception, with many groups and teachers professing to being the sole guardians of ancient Celtic magical traditions. For a large sum of money, these traditions can be revealed to you, but usually result in nothing of any cultural value being shared other than exploitation of the term *Celtic*. I continue to see videos of people attempting to speak in what may appear as mystical arcane Welsh incantations but are essentially poorly constructed translations that do not take into consideration the intricacies of language and its structure and rules. This is appropriation, for it serves only to promote kudos for the individual and does nothing to preserve culture.

One can appreciate a culture without appropriating it and take action to modify one's connection to that culture in a manner that honours rather than dishonours. There are many ways of achieving this, from learning some of the Celtic languages and enquiring as to what matters to those who inhabit the Celtic lands, finding out what is important to them and what, if anything, you can do for them. This can be as simple as becoming a member of a heritage group or a language preservation society or contributing to charities that make a difference in the Celtic heartlands. It is important to consider that the primary difference between cultural appropriation and appreciation is education. If in doubt, seek out a native person of that culture and ask for their advice or input.

5

THE DRUIDS THROUGH TIME

BEFORE ANY FURTHER elaboration can continue, we need to pause and consider the tripartite structure of Druidry history. To do this is to place the Druids, past and present, into the context of time to see where they came from, how they evolved, and who they are today. It is a history that is almost three thousand years in the making, and much of it is subjective and possibly the result of propaganda by the classical authors. It is, however, important to capture a glimpse of the timeframe of Druidry and the continuous influence and inspiration that this enigmatic priesthood has instilled into the popular imagination since the dawn of the Common Era.

The history of the Druids can be categorised as follows, and I shall describe the nature of each in turn:

- historical: Iron Age or early Druidry
- cultural Druidry
- inspired spiritual Druidry

Historical: Iron Age or Early Druidry

This era is mostly composed of the accounts of Druidry as given by the classical authors of the first centuries before the Common Era and several centuries of the Common Era. It runs adjacent to the archaeological record. Riddled with misconceptions and diluted by time, we may never know the truth of what the classical authors witnessed or the depth of honest representation that is included in their writings. It is not the intent of this book to articulate a comprehensive history of the Druids. Our time is best served focusing on the practical aspects of being a Druid today and the paths that we have weaved through time to arrive at this point. However, to dismiss the past entirely would do a disservice to the Druids and their colourful history. This short discourse will strive to offer a snapshot of the ancient Druids and our understanding of their place in history—essentially where modern Druids have come from. We begin this journey by looking to the historical or ancient Druids of the Celtic Iron Age through to the invasion of Britain and Gaul by the Romans.

The image of priests clad in white robes with long beards and sickles of golden metal cutting mistletoe from the treetops under a full and gleaming moon is entrenched in the public imagination. It is romantic, powerful, and hints at an ancient populace of priests that had something about them that we long for in the current era. The image is enigmatic and pulls at the human imagination; poets have written about them, imaginative antiquarians have invented a past to accommodate them, and archaeologists have despaired at the sheer lack of anything that directly relates or pertains to the Druids per se.

Each era of human civilisation has its own set of traumas and challenges, and in effect we all long for the good old days, a time that was simpler and perhaps more accustomed and attuned to the tides of magic. The ancient Druids certainly invoke this sense and feeling. So many people throughout the modern Pagan revival of the last 120 years have sought the wisdom of the Druids and compared their practises to them and held them as their magical inspiration. It is from the memory of the ancient Druids that Druids exist today, not as an unbroken apostolic line of succession, but as people who sense a continuation of magic that is linked to the land, to language and culture and art, and to an ancient worldview that may well save our current human world and the biosphere that we inhabit. It is the longing for an old magic that created a new magic in a new world, one that is applicable and relevant to the modern era.

The echoes of the old Druids pull at a memory within us, causing us to seek them out, perhaps in the hope that some of that romanticised power and wisdom will seep into us by magical osmosis. The Druids have intrigued, mystified, terrified, and puzzled historian and layperson alike. Throughout modern-day Brittany, northern France, and the islands of Britain and Ireland, one cannot go too far without happening across a Druidic association of one form or another. The Druids have coloured these lands for millennia, and they continue to cause intrigue and invoke curiosity and controversy to this day. There are treasures aplenty and clues to the religious activities of an ancient priesthood scattered throughout the ancient Celtic world, but do they tell us anything concrete about the Druids themselves? Do we have any evidence that they existed at all? And if they did, why is it that we know so very little about what they did and how they did it? What did they believe, and how did they practise their Druidry? Who were they, and why are so many intrigued by them to the extent that they would take the name and title of an ancient northern European priest-caste and adopt it? These are questions that we must explore on our journey through the dappled groves of historical Druidry.

The historian Ronald Hutton in *Blood and Mistletoe,* his important work on the Druids, says that "the Druids may well have been the most prominent magico-religious specialists of some of the peoples of north-western Europe."[26] If the most prominent historian on Paganism and Druidry in the twenty-first century can make such a claim, where does his information come from? Our primary source of literal information regarding the ancient Druids is to be found within the various written accounts of the classical authors of Rome. One may assume that anything the Romans may have expressed about the Druids is riddled with misconceptions and propaganda, but this is not entirely true. The might of Rome may well have subjected the British Isles to their conquering efforts, but their writings also reveal a wealth of information about the Druids as the priestly case of the British and Gaulish peoples. Much wisdom can be gleaned from their writings, but in doing so, we must be mindful of the Roman agenda; they came here to conquer, not to weave seamlessly into Celtic society. Britain would be a different place after the exit of the Romans, but our view of the Druids would forever be altered by their accounts.

If we cast our attention to some of the accounts of the classical authors, we can glean further inspiration about the relationship the Roman culture had with the Druids. You

---

26 Hutton, *Blood and Mistletoe,* 1.

will note that these span a vast period from just before the Common Era to approximately the third century of the current era. Much of the barbarous nature of the Druids come from the earlier period of classical writing, and I cannot honestly offer an account of the early Druids without touching briefly on the contentious subject of human sacrifice.

Diodorus Siculus, speaking of the Gaulish people and their Druids between 60 BCE and 30 BCE, offers a bloodthirsty account in which he praises the intelligence of the Druids and the Bards and their skills in philosophy and theology and seership while simultaneously berating them for their use of human sacrifice and ritualised murder.[27]

Diodorus continues to remark about the brutal nature of the Druids, yet he speaks of them as having the profound ability to bring about peace. Elements of his writing are often contradictory and riddled with praise and denigration in equal measure. His language may seem harsh to us in the twenty-first century, but it is not clear if his comments of human sacrifice are disparaging or simply stating the obvious. He, after all, inhabited a culture that frequently put people to death for not only religious purposes but for entertainment. It is from this classical era that we happen across the popular image of the grim yet enigmatic image of the Wicker Man: an enormous wooden lattice in the shape and form of a human man filled with straw, animals, and humans and then set alight as a sacrifice to the gods.

It is from this and other passages that the image of the Wicker Man prevailed into modern imagination, albeit there is little to no evidence of such a structure used to dispatch its prisoners. However, later writers were to reiterate these concepts. Strabo, who lived between 63 BCE to 24 CE, wrote "They [the Druids] would make a large statue of straw and wood and throw into it cattle and all sorts of wild animals and human beings, and thus make a burnt offering."[28]

What may not at once be obviously apparent is whether the authors themselves were witness to the atrocities that they describe. On closer examination it transpires that Strabo and Caesar were writing from much earlier accounts. The question of human sacrifice is contentious, and there is no doubt that some archaeological evidence from finds such as the Lindow Man do imply a culture of sacrifice, but they do so without context. We are not privy to the details of these deaths, ritualised or otherwise, and

27 Philip Freeman (trans.) in Koch, *The Celtic Heroic Age*, 13–14.
28 Forston, Benjamin (trans.) in Koch, *The Celtic Heroic Age*, 19.

it is impossible to know if the Druids were even involved. Often the sentiments expressed are akin to sensationalistic journalism, with Strabo also accusing the Irish and the Britons as having cannibalistic tendencies and labelling them as man-eaters and, oddly, as herb-eaters. No liturgical, religious, or ritualistic explanation or intention has been discovered. Modern day scholars and experts on the ancient Druids conclude that the evidence of Druid-led sacrifice is sketchy and unreliable. The Romans, after all, had good reason to paint their adversaries in bad light.

It is likely that these dramatic accounts of mass human sacrifice were a form of classical "fake news" to identify the Celts and their Druids as barbarians whose practices were unsavoury and cruel. It enabled Rome to paint the Druids as their arch-perpetrators. However, we cannot discount the possibility that the Druids did, in fact, perform human sacrifice. In the small lake of Llyn Cerrig Bach, human bones were discovered among the metalwork that contained chain gangs. We will never know the truth, but the issue of human sacrifice is sensationalistic enough to cause eyebrows to raise. The subject of sacrifice is contentious and yet it has been a part of human history from prehistoric times until the modern day, from the sacrifice of Christ to the sacrifice of human beings in times of war. The sanctity of past rituals eludes us, as do their justifications.

The association of Druids with grim rites continued for centuries; indeed, it continues to this day. What is apparent is that the classical authors attributed an extraordinary and often supernatural quality to the Druids, and it is often unclear if these comments are admirable or derogatory. However, in the Common Era many classical authors did not hold back in their description of the Druids. What is unclear is the origin of their opinions, as the later authors were almost always reliant on past accounts.

The classical author Lucan (39–65 CE) writes in his *Pharsalia* a compelling passage that seems to attribute supernatural qualities to the Druids and how they possessed a profound knowledge of what lies beyond the edges of life:

> While you, ye Druids, when the war was done,
> To mysteries strange and hateful rites returned:
> To you alone 'tis given the heavenly gods
> To know or not to know; secluded groves
> Your dwelling-place, and forests far remote.
> If what ye sing be true, the shades of men
> Seek not the dismal homes of Erebus
> Or death's pale kingdoms; but the breath of life

> Still rules these bodies in another age—
> Life on this hand and that, and death between.[29]

Erebus is a god of shadows and darkness, while Dis is akin to a place of torment; however, these are references from Lucan's own culture and that of the Greeks superimposed onto the Druids. His account further reiterates that the Druids were privy to certain wisdom and knowledge that appears occult or from supernatural origins. The romance and idealised images of Druids that exist today were seemingly prevalent in antiquity.

Aside from the grim accounts and propaganda literature of the classical authors, what can we learn, if anything, about the spiritual significance and function of the Druids? Writing in the third century of the Common Era, Diogenes Laertius captures a glimpse of the enigmatic nature of the Druids and their skills and abilities by describing how they transmit their teachings and instructions in riddles, and that they actively urged the worship of the gods, the abstinence of evil, and the preservation of manly virtue.

The first quality, that of speaking in riddles, has continued into modern times; the Bards of Wales and Ireland certainly maintain this spirit in their prose and rhymes. Another tool, called a colloquy, is a system of formal conversation that often answers a question with a question. This seemingly infuriating technique caused the student to think on their feet and delve deep for clarity. Of interest is that Laertius remarks on the practise of manly virtue, a contentious and paradoxical statement when one considers the meaning of the term *virtue* as a behaviour showing high moral standards. Morals are highly subjective and personal and are often guided by the sensibilities of society, and it is apparent from the classical authors that the ancient Celts' sense of sexuality was rather liberated, much to the dismay of some authors. We can capture a glimpse of this in the works of Diodorus Siculus, writing in the decades between 60 and 30 BCE, in which he describes that the Gauls in particular paid little attention to their women and preferred instead to have intercourse and sexual relations with other men.

It is difficult to deduce if Siculus agreed with the acceptance of homosexuality in Celtic culture or not, and while he does not specifically state that the Druids themselves engaged in same-sex relations, it is an interesting comment on the attitudes of sexuality within Celtica.

---

29 From https://www.perseus.tufts.edu/hopper/text?doc=Perseus%3Atext%3A1999.02
.0134%3Abook%3D1%3Acard%3D396.

Returning to the subject of the magical arts and matters of spirituality to see what we can glean from the classical authors, a general internet search with the topic Druid or Druidry will invariably result in the associated terms Bard and Ovate. It implies a system of ranking that has its inspiration in the classical texts. In his *Geography*, Strabo claims that the Druids had three ranks within their priest caste:

> Three sets of men are honoured above all others: The Bards, the Vātes and the Druids. The Bards are singers and poets, the Vātes oversee sacred rites and are philosophers of nature and the Druids, besides being natural philosophers, they practice moral philosophy as well.[30]

This account, in addition with several other observations, are primary sources for the designation of the three grades of the Druidic religion—Bard, Ovate, and Druid—that are mirrored today in some Druid orders and groups. Very little exists in the vernacular or in the mythos of Britain to suggest that this was a universal construct; in the Welsh tradition, little if anything is mentioned of the Ovates. In contrast, the terms *Druid* and *Bard* are prevalent throughout the Welsh tradition. The designations are, however, terms that have proved useful for the modern practise of Druidry and are generally accepted. Some of the largest groups of organised Druidry such as the Order of Bards, Ovates and Druids and the British Druid Order structure their teachings to conform to this ancient designation. I shall explore this in depth a little later.

In addition to the ranks, it is evident that the classical authors and later Celtic Bardic traditions maintained that the Druids were capable of using supernatural or magical abilities including prophecy. In addition to the practise of magic, albeit no actual detail of magical practise is offered in these accounts, Cicero (106–43 BCE) stipulates that the Druids certainly practised forms of divination.[31]

The archaeological record provides another snapshot of the Iron Age, the era in which the Druids occupied. Many have speculated whether the Druids existed in Britain prior to this age; alas, we have no concrete evidence to suggest that they did. However, with the plethora of ancient monuments that can be found scattered about the British Isles, it is evident that a prior culture of people was invested in activities that appear to have had a socio-religious element. While the liturgical components of these structures are unclear to us, their alignment to certain stations of the year is indisputable at numerous sites.

30 Koch, *The Celtic Heroic Age*, 18.
31 Koch, *The Celtic Heroic Age*, 14–15.

We may speculate on the possibility that the Druids were an extension of the earlier people of the stones, and yet we have no evidence to suggest the Druids used the monuments for themselves.

It may well be that the people of the stones, who have often been described as proto Druids, were the ancestors of the Iron Age Druids, and no doubt by blood they likely were their descendants. We will never know whether the Druids themselves were privy to the liturgical, ritualistic, and philosophical views of those who went before them. But, by the curious nature of the human condition, one can imagine that they may have been intrigued by their mysterious ancestors just as we are intrigued by the old Druids.

It appears from the classical records and the vernacular that the Druids chose groves—clearings in woodlands and forests, lakes, and other liminal spaces—as focus points for their ritual activities. No stone monuments from the Iron Age exist to express a Druidic connection. On the other hand, there are a mass of iron and metal objects found throughout Britain and Gaul, all bearing predepositional damage, which archaeologists believe imply a ritualised deposition of goods that were not previously used but created and deposited as new items.

Our knowledge of the ancient Druids is scant at best, and often the accounts of the classical authors are dismissed, yet to do so would be foolhardy. There is enough material over a vast span of time to demonstrate that the Druids were not only a real threat to the might of Rome, but also figures of distant admiration. Modern archaeology continuously unearths new evidence of life during the Celtic Iron Age, and it is likely that the story of the ancient Druids is far from over or complete.

Cultural Druidry

In Wales cultural Druidry can be seen expressed in the national and regional Eisteddfodau of Wales and the Gorsedd of Bards of the Isle of Britain. The term *Eisteddfod* (*Eisteddfodau* in the plural) is derived from the Welsh verb *eistedd,* meaning "to sit"; the *fod* suffix implies a sitting together of Bards and Minstrels, usually in a competitive sense. The term *Eisteddfod* is also widely used in modern Druidry to describe a period in any proceeding where an individual shares their creative talents. The Eisteddfod is intimately connected to the Welsh Bardic tradition (*Y Traddodiad Barddol Cymraeg*), which is woven into the very fabric of the movement. This tradition is truly ancient and has consistently existed in literature since the sixth century, with its oral aspect being significantly older. The Bardic tradition preserved ancient wisdoms and worldviews and recorded the attributes of ancient Celtic archetypes in the guise of praise songs and eulogies. In turn, the Bards were guardians of culture—a spirit that they continue to embody today. With Bardism being a fundamental principle not only of ancient Druidry (according to the classical authors), but also of modern Druidry in all its expressions, it demonstrates the tenacity of the Bardic spirit to survive the ages. It has remained a constant reminder of the ability of Bards to entertain, teach, preserve, and maintain a culture that continues to be celebrated and admired to this day.

Regional Eisteddfodau encourage the Bardic arts through competition and demonstration, leading eventually to the National Eisteddfod of Wales that happens during the first week of August. This moveable feast takes place at a different location each year, reiterating that the event is an integral aspect of every community in Wales regardless of size or location. It provides the people with the opportunity to gather and celebrate their language and culture, and at its heart is the prowess of the Bards. Over 6,000 competitors participate in nearly 180 competitions during the National Eisteddfod, with an excess of 150,000 people attending; it is simultaneously broadcast on national television. The primary ceremonies of the event are the chairing and crowning of the Bard, and the prose medal award, where the most proficient bards of Wales are selected. This is a moment of great national pride.

During these three ceremonies, the winning Bard is attired in elegant robes and led to the main stage in front of thousands of witnesses to be met by a company of hundreds of Druids in gowns of blue, green, or white. The Druids consist of past crowned or chaired Bards, previous Archdruids, and those honoured into the Gorsedd (meaning a throne or mound) for services to Welsh culture. The Druids provide a powerful symbol of the continuation of tradition and their association with the Bardic arts, and they do so by symbolically connecting the modern Druids to the enigmatic image of the Iron Age Druids. In turn, Bardism is perceived as the craft that gives outward expression to the mysteries beheld by the Druids. The Archdruid of the Gorsedd of Bards of the Isle of Britain presides over the crowning or chairing of the Bard. Non-Welsh people watching this spectacle in person or on television might be utterly convinced that what they are witnessing is a blatant Pagan ritual, full of rich symbolism and secrets. They would, however, be incorrect in their assumption.

The rituals of the Gorsedd of Bards, presided over by the Druids at the National Eisteddfod, are inspired by the works of poetic genius Iolo Morganwg, who in 1792 on the summit of Primrose Hill in London on the day of the midsummer solstice proclaimed, "I am giving you the patriarchal religion and theology, the divine revelation given to mankind, and these have been retained in Wales until our own day!"[32]

In that moment he announced to the Welsh the rediscovery of their ancient Druidic tradition. He offered the Welsh a cohesive history that they could be proud of, and one that rooted them back into the land that they loved and reached back into prehistory. None of this was entirely true, of course; Iolo was a visionary and a man who was determined to give the Cymry back their rightful identities as original inhabitants of the Island of Britain and inheritors of Druidic wisdom. His fabrications were quickly adopted by the people who saw within them a sliver of hope for the future. But his imaginings were not wholly without kernels of truth, for he blended truth with fiction in a manner that caused his fabrications to become almost inseparable from truth. Recognised today as a Bardic genius, he is the father of cultural and inspired Druid ritual.

While invoking an ancient priesthood and using symbols and iconography that may appear Pagan in origin, the rituals of the Gorsedd of Bards at the Eisteddfod are, in fact, theatre. But to make that statement is not to denigrate the power of theatre; after all, ritual is the original form of theatre. The Eisteddfod rituals are cultural treasures of the people of Cymru. They appease our cultural needs with elements that are tied into our indigenous identities, therefore they are very powerful and emotive things, for they alter the way we place value on who we are as a people and a nation. They bring meaning to our sense of place, where we come from, and satisfy our need as a consistently conquered and colonised people to feel that this is our home and we belong here, regardless of how many times we were invaded in the past. In Wales this desire for cultural richness cannot be separated from an ancient ritualistic and spiritual component—the Druids. In the Welsh imagination—and thanks to the likes of Iolo Morganwg and the Welsh Bardic tradition—the Druids embody the quintessence of what it means to be Celtic.

---

32 Miles, *Secrets of the Bards of the Isle of Britain*, 56.

Inspired Spiritual Druidry

Neopagan Druidry is an expansion on the previous categories, and its evolution has quenched the thirst not simply for cultural meaning, but for spiritual meaning. In the last century there has been a defined growth in people seeking spiritual meaning in their own landscape and culture, and this gave rise to the modern Pagan movements. Their evolution is a reaction to the need in humankind to have a sense of place, of rootedness, and to feel that intensely and on a profoundly spiritual level. As previously explored, the various constitutions that instigate an attraction in an individual can pull one towards the sphere of Druidry in ways that one may not be able to fully articulate. But this attraction is not new; it has existed and drawn people towards identifying with an ancient priesthood for centuries.

Modern Druidry cannot be pinpointed to a single moment; it is a distillation generations in the making. Iolo Morganwg did not exist in a vacuum but was a product of an era that had a profound interest in the idea of Druidry. Iolo's particular lens was Welsh, but the English were also interested. The early decades of the eighteenth century saw influential figures like the physician and antiquarian William Stuckley and his adamance that Stonehenge was, in fact, an ancient Druid temple, to John Toland's founding of what would eventually be called the Druid Order in 1717. When Iolo Morganwg came on the scene in 1792, he himself was a product of this earlier distillation of ideas that saw the Druid as an enigmatic and quintessentially British figure that could reconcile the austere Anglicisation of Britain and temper it with an ancient philosophy that quenched the thirst for a national identity that was somewhat lacking. For many this reconciliation perceived similarities between Old Testament teachings and those of the ancient Druids; others took a stronger anti-Christian stance that strived to move away from the overreaching powers of the church. By the early twentieth century, with over a hundred and fifty years of modern Druidic history under its belt, Druidry was prime for a revival in a new and illuminated age.

The British Circle of the Universal Bond allegedly formed at Stonehenge on Midsummer's eve in 1912; known today as the Druid Order, it evolved to become an influential melting pot of Druidic ideas and practises that were paramount in inspiring current Druid orders. It is famed for its images of Druids in pristine white robes at Stonehenge during the summer solstice. An early member of the Druid Order was an Englishman by the name of Gerald Gardner, who would eventually become the father of modern Wicca. It is likely that it was at the order where he met Ross Nichols, who would go on to form the Order of Bards, Ovates and Druids, which is presently the largest Druid order in existence.

This potted history serves to demonstrate that the history of modern Druidry, while evocative of the ancient Druids, is an intricate knotwork of individuals and ideas that germinated during the eighteenth century, often referred to as the century of lights. This period of enlightenment saw the seeds of modern Druidry be planted in the fertile soils of new thoughts and new ideas. It would take over a century for these seeds to flourish into the trees that now surround the modern grove of Druidry, but the leaves and fruits of the modern grove are the product of countless individuals who served to water and feed them. Punctuated by various figures often enigmatic, often contentious, history highlights certain figures to have had significant impact on the development of modern Druidry, with William Stuckley, Iolo Morganwg, William Price, and Ross Nichols being some of the prominent names.

Modern Druidry is intimately connected to Wicca, the religion created by Gerald Gardner, which is a form of Western esotericism that embraces and practises Witchcraft. Nichols and Gardner spent significant time together sharing ideas about their various interests; they are the fathers of modern Wicca and Druidry respectively. This shared history can be seen emulated in the membership of both traditions, which often overlaps. Today there are as many Wiccans and witches who are also Druids as there are Druids who are Wiccans or witches. If a definition can be cemented between the two traditions, it is that Druidry tends to follow a path that is predominantly, although not exclusively, Celtic. Wicca, on the other hand, is more eclectic in its cultural qualities and practises. Can you be a Wiccan or a witch and a Druid? Yes, you certainly can.

Eventually Druidry was to spread its wings and fly beyond the shores of the Celtic homelands and settle in places as far flung as the United States of America and Oceania. Today Druidry is a vibrant tradition in many countries, from South America to Australasia. In a modern sense, it is a tradition that is approximately 300 years or so in the making, give or take a few decades, but its roots reach back much further. If we consider the image of the oak tree so loved by the Druids, we can assign its various parts to the history of Druidry. The tap root reaches down deep into the soil; it points to the darkness of the past and the inspiration of the ancient Druids. The shallower lateral roots are nearer the surface and connect the tree to the traditions of Bardism, medieval mythologies and legends, and the Celtomania of the seventeenth, eighteenth, and nine-teenth centuries. The trunk of the oak is the expression of modern Druidry since the early twentieth century; it has grown wide and is filled with wisdom that rises from its roots. The branches of the oak carry the leaves and acorns of Druidry that reach into the future, with each falling acorn inspiring a new generation of Druids. Its autumn leaves, rich with expression and experience, dissolve back to nourish the ground upon which the great oak stands. There were times when the oak was cut down, sawn in her prime, yet her acorns were strong and sprouted new trees that emulated the parent while car-rying unique expressions of their own. This is the tree of tradition; she is not one single tree but a family of oaks that continually grow in the metaphorical grove of the Druids.

6

BARDS, OVATES, AND DRUIDS

SEVERAL MODERN DRUID orders, inspired by the past, continue to delineate their Druidic expression akin to the classical divisions of Bard, Ovate, and Druid. This is not an exclusive practise, but it is worthy of a gentle unpacking.

The Bard can be described as the disseminator of indigenous wisdom, the keeper of culture, and the mouthpiece of history, satire, tradition, and inspiration. The job of the Bard is to share the breath of Awen and allow its wind to blow through them. They are the record keepers and the guardians of story and myth.

The Ovate is the walker between the worlds, the magician, prophet, and healer. They are the skilled crafters of magic. The Ovate can at times appear almost indistinguishable from that of a witch, for so much of their practise is steeped in folk magic. An Ovate can peel back the veils that hide the seen from the unseen. They often possess excellent skills of divination and oracular abilities.

The Druid is the spiritual elder, the ritualist, the teacher, and philosopher. Popularly adorned in white robes, they invoke the quintessential image of the ancient Druid. They are enigmatic and mysterious and exude a sagacity that is intimately connected to the meaning of the word itself, those who are oak-wise.

These can be expressed as unique disciplines, and that quality can be seen in the training programmes of some modern Druid orders. The same system is also utilised in the Eisteddfod's Gorsedd of Bards, albeit with the Ovates designated as those who have excelled in science, literature, and music. In modern Druidry the designations do not necessarily imply a rank or a hierarchy; it is common for some practitioners on completing all three expressions to revert to being identified as a Bard or an Ovate as per their choosing and calling. In essence, the Druid contains the experience of the Bard and Ovate and may flit between one or the other at will. Rather than elevations or steps on a ladder, the three expressions of Druidry are best seen as groves that appear as interconnected circles. We can visualise this by drawing three circles thus:

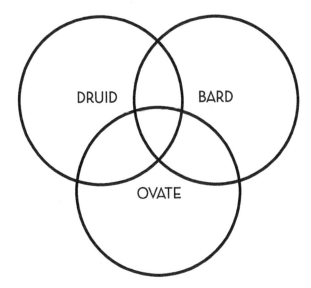

Where the circles overlap, they form a triquetra, three interlinked arches so common in Celtic art past and present. When the outer edges of the circles are erased, the triquetra is revealed. In turn, the triquetra symbol, like the triskele, is often employed by Druids and Pagans to demonstrate the tripartite nature of their worldview and wisdom. It is sometimes worn as a piece of jewellery or used to adorn journals and decorative items.

Akin to Celtic knotwork, the expressions of Druidry are not separate and neither is one better than another, as demonstrated by the triquetra; they are interdependent. One cannot exist without the other. While the system of Bard, Ovate, and Druid is beautiful and evokes a memory of the past, it is not exclusively used in all Druid traditions. It may be something you are attracted to, and if so, there are various orders (a list of which can be found in the resources section) that will guide you to a deeper understanding of the three expressions. For many solitary Druids, the gifts of the Bard, Ovate, and Druid are embodied within their own personal experience and expression of Druidry. The aim is not to reach the title of Druid; rather, it is the journey itself that matters. Druidry is a path, not a destination. The qualities of the Bard, Ovate, and Druid swim within you as a tripartite expression. Finding what those are enables you to discover your own Druid identity as well as offer you keys to focus on your strengths and abilities.

Meditating on the triquetra provides a reflective opportunity to consider how the three disciplines of Druidry move within you.

EXERCISE

We have a propensity to be attracted to certain interests and disciplines within a spectrum, so to discover the expression of your own unique Druidry, perform this simple but enlightening exercise. Consider this circle, which holds within it the experience of the Bard:

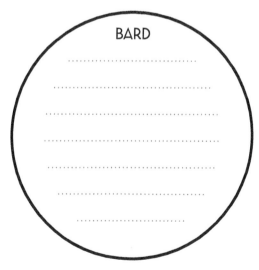

Now contemplate what that means; you may have preconceived ideas of what a Bard might be or you may have very little understanding of it and may need to research it online or in books. With your finest pencil, begin to insert words that describe your understanding of a Bard into the circle. Write as many as you can to fill the space. As you do, consider the function of the Bard, not only as an individual who serves as a guardian of culture and tradition, but as someone who creatively expresses their Druidry; this may be through voicework, music, poetry, writing, art, dancing, sculpture, cooking, the crafting of tools...the list is limited only by your imagination. When you have exhausted your list, stop; consider which ones apply to you. You may have an interest in several of them or as few as one, but consider how the qualities of the Bard are present in your constitution, and as you do, circle those words with your pencil or use a different coloured pencil to highlight them.

Now consider the circle of the Ovate and what your understanding of that is:

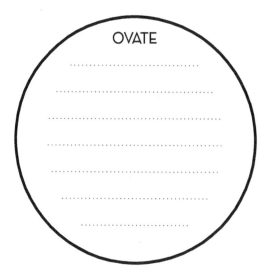

Fill the circle with as many words as you can imagine that will apply to the meaning of Ovate. As you do, keep in mind that the Ovate is essentially a walker between the worlds. In their practise, some of their crafts may be like the practise of Witchcraft. The herbalist, the healer, diviner—all these things and more swim within the Ovate's experience. When you have exhausted your list, consider which ones you are particularly drawn to and highlight them.

Now move onto to considering the final circle:

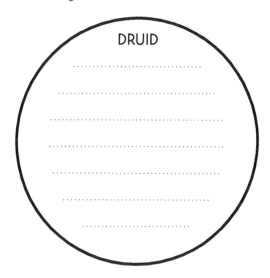

What do you think the gifts of the Druid are? This might be a little trickier, for so often much of the Druid's gifts belong to the mental and the philosophical, and at times they may appear limited to administrative and organisational skills. Fill the circle with as many words as you can think of, and then consider the ones you feel a tendency to identify with or are drawn to. As an example, in my own practise, I am very much pulled towards being a ritualist; writing, organising, and conducting rituals is something I very much love doing. I identified this quality early in my path and was then guided by various means and encouraged to pursue this skill. Another love of mine is celebrancy and the creating of bespoke rituals for rites of passage. What are you drawn to?

Ponder on the circle for a while, considering also which expressions you might also consider worthy of pursuit. Highlight them.

Now visualise all three circles moving together; as they do, they create the symbol of the triquetra. The energies of the circles are now intertwined within the triquetra shape. Using the new clean symbol on the next page, and within the triquetra pattern, draw a spiral to represent each quality that you currently express or are attracted to. This is not an exact art but rather symbolic of the gifts that you bring to Druidry. Fill the triquetra shape in any order with spirals until it is full. As you draw each little spiral, speak out its qualities; for instance, you might say: "I draw this spiral—it represents my love of listening deeply to others (Ovate); I draw this spiral to reflect my love of singing (Bard);

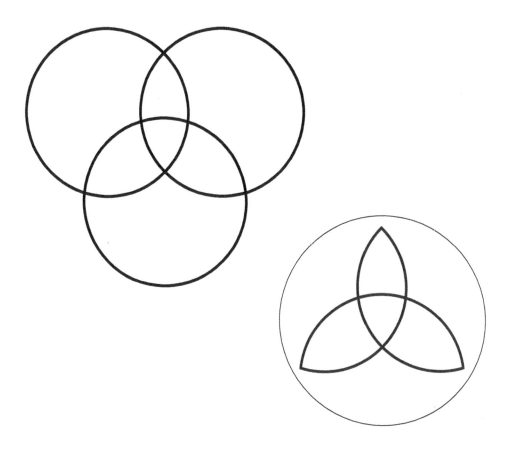

I draw this spiral to represent my love of philosophy (Druid)." Keep in mind this is not a competition; do not compare yourself to another Druid. It is not a numbers game but rather a way to explore what gifts you bring to the grove of the Druids. Quality over quantity is tantamount.

Finally consider the triquetra without the circles that went into its making. This time write the words of your skills and qualities to encircle the triquetra, using the image above. Each quality is a gift that energises the triquetra while simultaneously reaching from it to affect the external world; it is your personal Druidic expression. On the opposite page is an example of my personal Druid triquetra, give or take a few skills.

The triquetra is not a static thing. It is energetic and dynamic; its qualities ebb and flow, and sometimes new skills and interests are added to it. It is a living thing that reflects the individual Druid on a symbolic level. Symbols can often be abstract or pretty

but vague, but the point of a symbol is to bring meaning to something. By using ancient symbols in a way that makes them pertinent to our human experience, they take on another level of relevance. With that in mind, use the triquetra; it is no longer a mysterious symbol from the distant past but is your symbol that reflects your Druidry. Draw it, wear it, paint it, and adorn your things with it, knowing that as you do the triquetra is yours and yours alone. Now your task is to bring your triquetra into being—to exude the qualities therein and be the best that you can possibly be at achieving them. Bear in mind that in the same spirit as Druidry, these are journeys and not destinations. I have been studying the Welsh myths for over thirty years. I will never arrive at a place of complete knowledge; it is an ongoing affair with the mysterious. My personal triquetra is a daily reminder of what Druidry brings to my life and what gifts I offer it. A simple silver triquetra adorns my main altar, and it is here where I consider and contemplate those qualities.

There are times when some parts of the triquetra shine brighter than others, and sometimes their light may well dull considerably. But all in all, they shine as a reflection of the gifts you bring to the tradition. They are constantly evolving and held in the swirling patterns of the triquetra. Make it your own.

7

BEING A DRUID TODAY

It is wise to sometimes take a reality check and ask the obvious question: Can one realistically call oneself a Druid today? And if so, by whose authority? By striving to be oak-wise, a Druid is an individual who strives to embody the qualities of the mighty oak. For some, teaching and initiation into an order of Druids is the right way for them, but this is not the path that everyone chooses to take or feels comfortable in undertaking. By joining a Druid order or grove and undergoing their teaching programmes, you may be recognised within its structure as a Druid. Adopting the title for oneself is just as valid. In both cases it is important that one stops and thinks about what that means, not just to you but to the people around you. To know the oak—it's a rather bold statement to make, and to do so in a way that honours the dizzying history of Druids present and past, we must take on that mantle with sagacity, pride, and care.

To achieve this, we employ a category of mythological qualities that we explored earlier in this book, embodied in the noun and verb *pwyll* and utilising all those pwyll qualities in our connection to it. By taking pwyll of the title, we honour its meaning and significance not only as a word, but as a term that captures the sum totality of all things associated with it since its inception. When we take pwyll and consider the significance of the trees in our practise, we move into alignment with the spirit of Druidry itself, which is considerably more than simply a fancy of trees.

Just because someone loves trees does not make that person a Druid. My grandmother loved trees and my cousin is a tree surgeon and spends significantly more time with trees than I do; neither of them are Druids. In conversations with them, neither one would have the audacity to claim the title. Both individuals are Welsh and have an appreciation that the term carries some weight that is distinctly separate from simply a love of trees. Another friend has spent his entire adult life in service to trees as an arborist; he is a true dendrophile, yet he would be mortified if someone were to call him a Druid because he does not believe he is one. He has an appreciation of Druids or he would not be my friend, but first and foremost he is a dendrophile. That a Druid is just someone who likes trees does a disservice to the spirit of the Druid; it is not and should never be a vague term that is beyond definition. It exists for a reason, and that reason is over two thousand years in its making.

To be oak-wise is to strive to learn from the trees as spiritual teachers. It is to embody the qualities and attributions that are often associated with the oak: majesty, wisdom, strength, tenacity, and so forth. It is to perceive the wisdom of trees as metaphors for spiritual mysteries. The collective term for a gathering of Druids is a grove; in this sense, the grove itself represents the wisdom of oak, with its human members standing as representations of the trees themselves. We can learn from the grove as both a metaphor and a physical group of Druids.

The Druid carries the potential for the oak within them. An acorn doesn't have an oak tree held within it; rather, it has the *potential* for the oak within it. Many acorns simply return to the soil while a tiny percentage become the oaks of the future. Druids act in the same manner. We carry the potential of being oak-wise and yet sometimes that wisdom may elude us or we may misuse it. Wisdom is not something that is given; it is something that is incubated and nurtured. It comes from experience, observation, and learning. If we know anything of the Druids of the old world, it was that they were learned, a quality adopted by the Welsh Bardic tradition and emulated in myths and poetry. Druid orders and groves perpetuate this objective by offering programmes of learning aligned to their tradition or flavour of Druidry. The Druid embodies the tripartite qualities of intellect, instinct, and intuition in equal measure, striving to learn and be learned, for knowledge comes from the expansion of the mind. In turn, this expansion creates the fertile soil upon which wisdom can germinate and flourish. Aristotle said that "knowing yourself is the beginning of all wisdom," and by employing our pwyll qualities when we begin any exploration, we move into the currents of self and self-knowing, wherein the pearls of our own wisdom reside.

When we strive to know ourselves, we initiate a journey into wisdom, and this insight causes us to see ourselves as if from the outside, as an observer. Wisdom is all very well, but it is wrapped in the experience of a human person. Druids make mistakes, and some Druids are Druids for all the wrong reasons; we are fallible and flawed human beings. A Druid's function is not to transcend life or achieve a state of impossible perfection. Druids, just like the trees they venerate, are sometimes gnarly, stunted, or clinging for dear life on unstable ground. Others carry blights and disease that impinge on their ability to grow fully and healthily. Others were struck by lightning and carry the scars of trauma and distress with them, but still they reach for the clouds and shed their acorn jewels as they strive to be oak-wise.

The path of the Druid is not one that seeks a state of transcendent enlightenment; it is being in the here and now and actively participating in the awesome nature of the world around you. A Druid does not seek to be separate from the world, for we are of this world, and this experience is immensely magical. We have a finite amount of time by which we live life and strive for wisdom; that is a lot to balance. But Druids are not stuffy individuals who float through life on a liminal cloud of spiritual illumination. They are some of the most fun-loving, adventurous, and exciting people that I know. You can be whoever you choose to be in your life and still embody the virtues of being oak-wise. To embody and express the wisdom of the oak is to inspire as well as instill joy. Druidry allows you to celebrate who you are in this life while simultaneously embodying wisdom. It is an inclusive path that fosters and nurtures personal expression and serves to discover the wisdom of who you are. An oak tree strives to sing the song of their own being and wonder; an oak does not want or feel the necessity to sing like a rowan or a holly! To be oak-wise is to sing in praise of your own flawed and fabulous self and not compromise or change who you are to conform to the expectations of another.

All of these things and more go into the making of a Druid, so when we wake up one day and consider *I'm going to be a Druid!* we must pause, employ our pwyll qualities, and consider the meaning and implications of identifying as a Druid or a person who is on the path of the Druid.

If we return momentarily to the image of the oak and use it as a metaphor for the growth cycle of the Druid, we can glean further wisdom. Initially there is a moment of inspiration where the Awen blows through the individual; on a mature oak this process of inspiration is when an acorn falls or is plucked. It falls through the air to land upon the ground or is carried by other means to fertile soil. Therein the acorn lies; inspiration does not always lead to action—sometimes it can be smothered by the humdrum of life or dismissed altogether, at which point the kernel of Awen held in the acorn decays and returns to the earth. However, for some the breath of inspiration is too loud to ignore, and it drives the acorn down deeper into the soil, which is the consumed wisdom of all beings. It is here where that seed of Awen germinates and sends forth a single root to anchor itself in experience. The embryonic shoot rises from the acorn and breaks the surface of the soil, sprouting leaves for the very first time.

As seedlings, fledgling Druids are propelled towards the sky and yet find themselves in their most vulnerable position. Brand-new, the world is filled with excitement and potential, but this can often overwhelm the saplings—who, bombarded with information, must hold fast lest they be derailed or misdirected. The mature trees around them can appear intimidating or beyond their reach, but the seedlings are compelled to reach upwards.

As saplings, Druids learn to be flexible and adapt to their surroundings; they can use their powers of discernment to assess their environment and act accordingly. This is the time when Druids begin to find their feet and the first stirrings of what defines their Druidry will begin to express itself. It is the time when their identity as Druids becomes interwoven into their everyday lives and living. As saplings they absorb as much information and knowledge as they can, interacting with their environment; this is the first stirring of wisdom.

As Druids mature in experience and knowledge, just like our metaphorical oak, they begin to bear flower and fruit, and continue to do so as they age. That initial seed of inspiration is reciprocated as the Druids share their acorns of Awen with the world around them. It is at this stage that so many Druids become teachers and ritual leaders; they have found their home in their Druidry and have a good sense of who they are and what they can offer by means of their Awen. A good Druid grows a canopy under which other Druids might shelter and rest or seek sanctuary in their wisdom. A good Druid gives of themselves as much as they take from others. A good Druid recognises the potential of the saplings that are growing around them. As an elder, the Druid's duty is to continue to seed the ground around them with their wisdom and help germinate the oak-wise of the future.

Eventually the Druid reaches the end of their living, but the story does not end there. In forest ecology a dead tree is called a snag; in death the tree continues to nourish and feed. As Druids reach the snag of their own existence and become ancestors, their wisdom may continue to inspire and encourage the growth of new Druids long after they have left this world. In turn, the Druids are venerated as ancestors of the tradition by the trees they strived to nourish and nurture.

Druidry truly is the language of trees, but it is a shared language that has its roots in so many influences, some known and others lost to us. Language does not develop in a vacuum; it is a process that takes generations to achieve stability, but even then it is a living and vibrant thing, evolving and adapting to the people. The Druids may have their roots in the cauldron of the Celts, but they are significantly more than the total sum of their parts—they are a product of a melting pot of culture, art, language, and religion. The magic of Druidry is in its ability to continuously renew itself. In doing so it also honours and remembers its past but is not defined by it. Its definition is coloured by those who practise it. It was nearly lost to the world for centuries, but its resurgence is testament to the thought that the world needs Druids today more than ever. If this is correct, then the true question in all this is not *How can you be a Druid today?* but rather *What can you do as a Druid today?*

* * * * * *

The growth stages of the oak as a metaphor and teacher for the Druid can be peppered with challenges and dangers. Each growth stage carries a vulnerability, but those mighty oaks with their nourishing acorns have risen above those dangers to stand strong and wise. Having previously explored our wisdom, it is now pertinent that we examine the nature of things that might simultaneously diminish and contribute to it.

8

ANXIOUSLY ANXIOUS:
THE MYSTERIES OF PRYDERI

EARLIER IN THIS book and by proxy of the first branch of the Mabinogi, you were introduced to Pwyll not only as an extrinsic mythological concept but as an intrinsic aspect of you and your journey. This exploration helps to internalise the myths and brings them to life in a way that reading them alone does not. In this section we continue with that journey and consider the offspring of Pwyll and his consort Rhiannon, the stolen child Pryderi. Within the first branch, his birth is described thus:

> On the night he was born, women were brought to watch over the babe and his mother. But the women fell asleep as did Rhiannon. The women were six in number. They kept a watch for some of the night, but before midnight they had all fallen asleep and awoke near dawn. When they awoke, they looked to where they had placed the child, but there was no sight of him.
>
> "The boy has been lost!" said one of the women.
>
> "We shall be burnt alive or put to death for this!" cried another. "What on earth can we do about this?"
>
> "I have a plan," said one of the women. "There is a staghound bitch here, and she is with pup. We shall kill one of the pups and smear its blood upon Rhiannon's face and hands and scatter the bones beside her and swear that it was she who destroyed her son. The word of six shall be stronger than hers."

As the day broke, Rhiannon awoke and looked for her child. "Where is the boy?" she asked.

"Lady, do not ask of us for the boy—we are none but bruises and blows from the struggle with you! We have never seen a woman fight with such strength as you, and it was useless for us to struggle with you. You destroyed your son yourself; do not ask us for him!"[33]

The child's mysterious disappearance coincides with the appearance of a golden-haired child in the court of Teyrnon on May's Eve. He raises the child with his wife and names him Gwri of the Golden Hair. The child matures at a startling rate and bears a striking resemblance to Pwyll. Teyrnon realises that this child is the stolen son of Pwyll and Rhiannon and reunites him with his parents. Rhiannon, who has suffered punishment ever since, is suddenly relieved of her pryder and the child is renamed Pryderi. This noun shares a commonality with other names in the myths of Cymru, and we gleaned some of this wisdom in our exploration of Pwyll. Here we discover that the name Pryderi contains the root noun *pryder,* which means "the cause of anxiety, concern, distress, disquiet, and fear."[34] In the relieving of Rhiannon's pryder, the child is renamed, and a world of mystery and meaning is revealed to the seeker.

Pryderi is synonymous with one's own journey through birth and into the early stages of growth towards maturation. A lot happens to us during this time, much of which is fickle and contradictory in nature as individuation develops. The meaning of pryder in our own lives becomes tangible as we strive to find our place in the world. Pryderi is the human condition of becoming self-conscious, and it is riddled with dread and anxiety. From unity with the great queen Rhiannon who symbolises the powers of the great mother, the child is stolen and mysteriously appears in a distant location. This initiates the separation anxiety that all humans experience as we become increasingly aware of "I" and "other." The mother symbolises the infinite oneness of the universe; she is also the portal through which the eternal self experiences the apparent and finite self. As a metaphor for earth, the mother also acts as the grave portal of returning to the infinite.

Our internal Pryderi qualities programme how we seek and connect to the numinous. As we grow through infancy and into childhood, the innocence and sense of sim-

---

33 Translated by the author from *White Book Mabinogion*, edited by J. Gwenogfryn Evans, 1909.
34 Bevan and Donovan, *Geiriadur Prifysgol Cymru*, 2916.

ply being is slowly stripped away from us. By our late teens we are compelled to go on journeys to discover who and what we are. This is initiated by separation anxiety that is indicative of the pryder that we feel because of individuation. We can see the symptoms of this anxiety within the expressions of humanity, where so many will attempt to latch onto something that offers them a sense of fullness. We overeat, remain in bad relationships, feed habits and addiction—anything to provide a taste of the union and fullness that we felt upon arriving in this world and subsequently lost as we matured. Community and a sense of belonging buffers this anxiety and serves to develop a worldview in which we do not feel so isolated and alone. This pryder or anxiety is ingrained into our programming, and people deal with it in different ways, but primarily they deal with it by finding and maintaining meaning. When life has no meaning and value is stripped from our lives, our pryder increases to a cracking point where mental health issues arise and illness may follow.

For swathes of humanity, the antidote to this pryder is religion and spirituality, but this can bring its own set of anxieties. For many, religious values are programmed from infancy, and many are conditioned to follow a certain path of unity with the spirit. For others, this is not enough and does not quench the thirst of unity that they crave. For people like myself, Christianity was my only structured option, but it did nothing to quell the disquiet in me to feel connected to something bigger than myself, to be immersed in mystery and not undone by it. Finding a new spiritual expression can bring its own set of anxieties, and you may well be feeling them right now, where the mind can be plagued with questions—*Am I doing it right? Is this the right thing for me? What if I don't know what to do? People might ridicule me. I can never ever be oak-wise!*

The antidote to pryder is in becoming Pryderi. In doing so, we move into an understanding of the causes of our anxieties and distress, and this begins by developing a relationship with the self that serves to transform our pryder. This is not a new concept— the principle of "know thyself" is an ancient one that contains seeds of truth; the futile search for meaning beyond oneself is a journey plagued with distractions and paradoxes that can bewilder and steer one's course into disorientation. In Pryderi, Rhiannon's anxieties are ended and her distress eliminated, and in turn Pryderi himself is returned to the wholeness and unity that his mother represents. He is no longer enslaved to the not knowing, the uncertainty of who and what he is; meaning is returned to him. This is not to imply a state of perfection; instead, it is an understanding of the mechanisms that instill pryder. In spiritual traditions there are various names that describe this unity and the assimilation of pryder: self-realisation, enlightenment, illumination, unity consciousness, oneness. The implication here is that spirituality in whatever form can transcend pryder and transform it into the first steps towards joyous unity. In the Druid tradition we call that first step Pryderi, meaning to own one's anxiety and fears, to know them and not be enslaved by them. This is all well and good, but how does one do that?

The clues are held within the stories themselves. In Druidry we look to the natural world for a sense of unity and wholeness. When the child is taken mysteriously from Rhiannon, he is found in the abode of Teyrnon, whose full name is Teyrnon Twrf Liant, meaning Great King of the Roaring Flood, which is synonymous with the tidal bore of the nearby River Severn. His name is derived from the Celtic god Tigernonos. He is the Lord of Gwent is Coed (Gwent of the lower forest), a county in southeast Wales that was split into two forest realms. The child is nurtured and raised within a forest setting with his companion being a foal. Further mystery is subtly conveyed through the function of the animals that we may often ignore as just a detail in the story; the foal represents the developing sovereignty and instincts of the child. By assuming our internal Pryderi, we strive to discover our self-sovereignty and our true nature. The subtle teachers of this truth are held in the powers of the forest, its animals, and the combining of sea and fresh water in the guise of the Severn tidal bore. The sea symbolises wholeness and unity and the freshwater river the apparent identity. The entire sequence of stories surrounding Pryderi is separation and reunion with wholeness, to know that we are more than just a drop in the universe; we are vital parts of its entirety.

Pryderi represents the big questions in life that can spark anxieties, but working with our pryder can also assist us in spiritual direction and expression. Coming to Druidry fresh and new brings with it a host of anxieties; direction and clarity may be lacking in the tentative years of study and practise. These anxieties can be dispelled or assimilated neutrally when we set parameters and goals that maintain the flow of our newfound Druidry. Spiritual traditions the world over maintain practices that guide the trajectory of one's spiritual direction, and these are achieved by daily practise, meditation, ritual, study, prayer, and so forth. A lack of direction can spark anxieties, especially when transitioning from another path or no path to a new one. By working with the causes of our anxieties, our pryder, we are armed with understanding the flow of one's own currents and what we need to maintain that flow. In the study of Druidry you can offset any directional anxieties you have by setting goals that maintain your Druidic flow. Some suggestions are:

- Maintain a frequent questioning practise of contemplating and then journaling the reasons for you wanting to become a Druid; by doing so you are creating a flow dynamic that you can refer to and chart your development.

- Aim to study by reading three different books per season, one within the modern New Age genre, one that is historical or anthropological, and the other in the genre of story or mythology.

- Aim to learn a practise to at least intermediate level within the next three years. This can be anything from divination techniques to herblore and herbcraft. Stick to it and maintain good consistent practise.

- Take a course on Druidry, either online or by joining an order or grove.

- With the aim of perpetuating the principle of being oak-wise, for the next twenty years and by using the popular Ogham tree system, learn all you can about the trees by studying one tree per year.

- Assess how your Druidry is in service and what you can do to be in service to your community, human and non-human alike.

Setting goals and targets may appear clinical and almost corporate, but to do so is to alleviate the descent into unorganised and unruly pryder. The Druid grows in their ability to maintain their Pryderi state, but this is not to suggest that we do not fail—of course we do, we are flawed and fickle—but by knowing who we are and how we work, we are less likely to be undone by our anxieties and fears. The trick in all of this exploration is to remind yourself that Pryderi, just like Pwyll, is not simply a character in a myth; he represents you. Changing the mindset of how we connect to myths is paramount to working with them effectively. By internalising Pryderi as the champion of your own pryder, you are working with the myths in a deeply transformative way that will forever influence how you perceive the mystery they allude to.

With that, we will take a closer look at your pryder.

· · · · · ·

☞ *The things that make me most anxious are...*

....
....
....

☞ *The things that concern me most are...*

....
....
....

☞ *I am distressed by...*

....
....
....

☞ *The things I fear most are...*

....
....
....

☞ *I deal with my anxieties by...*

....
....
....

☞ *I deal with my concerns by...*

....

....

....

☞ *I deal with distress by...*

....

....

....

☞ *I deal with my fears by...*

....

....

....

The antidote to this is the joy that Rhiannon feels on being reunited with her child, and while the narrative is not explicit, the implication is that Pryderi is also returned to a state of joy. By evaluating that which brings us joy, we are more able to ameliorate our pryder.

• • • • • •

☞ *I define joy as...*

....

....

....

☞ *The things that bring me the most joy are...*

....

....

....

☞ *I express joy by...*

....

....

....

☞ *My anxieties are transformed into joy by...*

....

....

....

⁕ ⁕ ⁕ ⁕ ⁕ ⁕

By examining our pryder, we are not attempting to vanquish those emotions, for they are an inherent aspect of who an individual is. Pryder is not something we try to overcome; it is something that we strive to understand. By doing so, we lessen their ability to unhinge us and drive us off course. Akin to many spiritual practises and traditions, Druidry is a form of therapy where we learn as much about ourselves as we do about the world we inhabit. To me, Druidry and its practise is a source of tremendous joy that serves to offset some of the pryder. It is a constant work in progress. In its wisdom Druidry teaches us that, regardless of how much we want to, we cannot cure the world of all its sorrows, but we can choose to live joyously.

⁕ ⁕ ⁕ ⁕ ⁕ ⁕

Thus far we have incorporated two mythological functions as teaching tools that move us closer to the mysteries that swim at the heart of the Druid tradition; a third function will be presented to you a little later. Tripartite structures were and are important to Druidry, so with that we shall delve deeper into the significance of wisdom relayed in sequences of threes.

9

THE POWER OF THREE:
TRIADS AND TRISKELES

THE TRISKELE SYMBOL, sometimes also known as a triskelion, is a trilateral symbol that is constructed by three interlocked spirals that emanate from a central point. It is an ancient symbol that can be found on Neolithic monuments throughout Europe. It has been discovered on La Tène–style Celtic art from the Iron Age, the Celto-Romano period, and is still used to this day. Akin to the triquetra, it is a useful symbol upon which we can place an innumerable amount of Druidic wisdom in the form of triads. In turn, these are helpful in organising ideas, principles, and patterns into a cohesive manner that is easily assimilated into memory. Triads are intimately connected to the spirit of Druidry and are a long-established discipline within the Welsh Bardic tradition. According to Celtic scholar Rachel Bromwich, triads "evolved as a part of the teaching given by the poets [bards] to their juniors, pupil bards being required to learn the triad by heart."[35]

In addition to Bardism, the triad system was utilised in secular society as a method for cataloguing technical information, medical treatises, legal codes, and the use of grammar and language.[36] The versatility of triads is exemplified in their longevity and can be found in Welsh mythology, in the works of Iolo Morganwg, and in modern Druid

35 Bromwich, *Trioedd Ynys Prydein*, lviii.
36 Bromwich, *Trioedd Ynys Prydein*, liii.

orders and groves. They can record historical and legendary events as well as wisdoms and inspirational quotations; they can be used to categorise and structure ideas and philosophies and act as a trigger to memory. These can appear as single words or as long sentences; they can condense information into bite-size pieces that enable the Druid to recall and remember. By placing the triads on a triskele, we create an effective system constructed of a symbol (triskele), a system (the triads), and connection (memory).

By creating triskeles and triads, we are more easily able to work with the various principles of Druidry in a manner that is cohesive and prevents one from going off track quite so easily; they encourage focus and structure. The triskele evokes the triads and causes them to spiral into meaning and significance. On a simplistic level, we can see the triskele as reflecting the existence of the three sacred realms of land, sea, and sky, which I shall explore in greater depth later. It can also be taken to represent the three worlds: physical, mental, and celestial, or body, mind, and spirit. The correspondences are endless, but it is pertinent that some examples are offered here to demonstrate their potential usefulness. What follows are three examples of triads that are cornerstones of the Druid tradition.

The first triad that we will explore are the foundations upon which modern Druidry stand. These are expressed here in both Cymraeg and English; combined, they form the Triad of Foundation.

The first foundation is that of science and magic, and while these may appear to be in diametrical opposition, in the Welsh tradition of Druidry they are perceived as sibling energies. Magic has its own unique chapter later in this book where I explore it in some depth. In the Welsh language, the term for science (*gwyddoniaeth*) and magic (*hudoliaeth*) are intimately connected, and each reflects mystery and wonder in their own unique way. A Druid should strive to have knowledge of both. As a spirituality that is inspired by the natural world, it is important that we understand how the world around us actually works. In doing so, we open our minds and intellect to the wonders of the world and our position in it. Some of our modern technologies would be indistinguishable from magic if witnessed by our ancestors. In studying various sciences, we discover the interconnectedness of things. It is important that when we celebrate the height of the sun's power at the Summer Solstice we actually have an understanding of what the sun is and how it works. Studying the sciences not only opens our minds to knowledge, it also transforms us from passive observers to active participants in the wonder of the universe.

Magic allows for us to move into the currents of nature and affect the course of the energies that surround us. Science and magic work hand in hand to lead us to being oakwise on a mental and practical level. Knowing how something works does not remove the magic from it. I was fortunate to witness the aurora borealis during a visit to the Arctic Circle. The scientific Druid in me understood what was happening: solar winds and charged particles striking the earth's atmosphere and releasing energy. The magical Druid in me appreciated the sheer drama and awe of it; it was nature putting on a show of wonder simply because she can. Science does not negate magic; they work hand in hand to initiate a state of Druidic wonder.

The second foundation of Druidry spins out and finds expression in the spiral of practise and community (*ymarfer* and *cymuned*). Druids are individuals who are engaged in a practical spirituality that has both esoteric and exoteric components. To wander the forests and contemplate the mysteries is glorious and profound, but Druids are also practical people that craft their spirituality in a way that has real-world influence. This is intimately tied into the concept of community. To say that word is to no doubt spark the vision of a community of humans in your mind, but this would be quite erroneous, for often the communities that Druids engage with are not necessarily of the human variety. We can do much for our human community in innumerable ways, but Druids also serve non-human communities by working with trees; volunteering in national, regional, or local parks; engaging in beach cleaning; or nurturing and growing plants from seed. Many are drawn to animal- and nature-based charities to align their virtues with the animal kingdom. Others are driven by politics and activism. This is the practical face of Druidry, where the qualities of the personal triquetra are expressed in a manner that benefits the world around us. In the entire universe, from the smallest colony of cellular structures to the largest galaxies, all things work together to maintain equilibrium and momentum, and they do so by maintaining community. Druids are drawn naturally towards the communities that align with their virtues and are often compelled to assist in perpetuating, safeguarding, or protecting them.

On a human level, we are members of a number of communities, some of which are secular and others sublime. Often Druids feel the need to share their Druidry and will seek out communities of like-minded people to celebrate and learn with. In the twenty-first century we have virtual communities that offer us the opportunity to meet fellow Druids in the digital world, yet another concept that our ancestors would not be able to distinguish from magic. We are surrounded by communities, some of which we may not notice until we reach out and find them. Communities offer Druids a platform to practise their craft with others in meaningful ways that can create lasting ties of fellowship and kinship.

The third spiral in our foundation triad is that of history and tradition (*hanes* and *traddodiad*). These are the fertile grounds that form the foundations of modern Druidry. The past is not a clear path—it is often muddied by agendas and ulterior motives and written from the dominant force's perspective. The past can also be populated by problematic individuals that we may struggle to comprehend and reconcile with; the chapter on working with the ancestors provides further exploration of this. We are products of the past, and in some cases we are conditioned by it. It is the responsibility of the individual Druid to be informed of the past and the succession of individuals, from authors to groups that brought Druidry into the twenty-first century. It is a complex and varied history that covers nearly three thousand years across vast distances and cultures. It covers conquests and invasions, but it also reflects the tenacity of cultures that withstood the test of time.

Druidry is coloured by our history, and a spectrum of that is tradition, which is defined as a set of beliefs or customs that are passed down from generation to generation or within the parameters of culture. Traditions can be secular and pervasive; examples would be the consuming of a turkey at Thanksgiving or the erecting of a tree at Christmastide. In religious and spiritual practises, traditions provide momentum that propels them forward into the future. At their heart traditional practises have meaning and value, and their repetition cements them in the minds of the adherents. They become something that we do; we perpetuate them because they hold meaning. Tradition connects us to the recent and distant past. If something is repeated annually or monthly, it can very quickly become a tradition. They are methodologies by which we connect to the silver cord of history and the past.

However, to suggest that tradition is a gift from the past is not to imply that it is static. A tradition of any value is not a relic but a living thing; it is a creative force that works in unison with its participants. In turn, when the participants work the tradition with awareness of its origin and power, they are working with it, not simply repeating it for the sake of conformity alone. When an individual or group works a tradition for the sake of repetition or with the attitude of "This is just how it is done," then the tradition is in danger of dying, for it is no longer a living thing. In exploring tradition, we can glean an understanding of how all principles on the triskele are intimately if subtly connected. Tradition is the cord to the past, which in turn connects us to the practises of distant communities, and each practise is imbibed with a natural and supernatural science.

The second triad that we shall explore is the Triad of Truth.

89

Truth is a fickle mistress, and one person's truth may not be that of another. Humans have the uncanny ability to cause themselves to believe untruths, even when they know that deception is underfoot. Truth is a treasure of darkness; it knows not its nature unless light is cast upon it, and that light may come with ulterior motives. The truth can be manipulated and skewed to the agenda of a single individual or group. When truths become untruths, they may continue to be justifiably perpetuated. Truth is in opposition to untruth; it strives to reveal deception and lies and seeks to bring unified harmony, justice, and righteousness. The truth is often difficult to speak, especially when it is our own personal truth, which may be diametrically opposed to the truths of others. For the pursuit of justice and righteousness to prevail, telling the truth is essential. Deception, outwitting, and competitive strategies often go hand in hand with concealing the truth, or not being truthful. Backstabbing, idle gossip, and one-upmanship are all reflections of the power of untruth and its ability to incapacitate or stir troubling emotions. Discovering the truth can often cripple our emotional well-being, but knowing the truth allows for transformation to occur and healing to begin. Even when the truth is harrowing, it is easier to maintain than deception. Truth takes courage and inner strength, virtues that are in alignment with the aspirations of the oak-wise; deception takes immense energy and an excellent memory to maintain.

Being truthful and striving for truth is part of the journey of the Druid, knowing also that we are imperfect and often make mistakes. When those mistakes are made, the honourable Druid seeks to repair them and build bridges of reconciliation and peace. There is no state of perfected enlightenment in Druidry; a Druid's virtue is measured by the sincerity and truthfulness of their living. When we seek the truth, we act honourably and with integrity, but this is not to say that we don't fail—of course we fail; there cannot be a Druid alive that has not lied or sought to deceive another. Deception is an indication that the truth is either difficult, problematic, or something the individual simply does not want to face. Our task is to attempt to the best of our ability to express truthfulness, even if that makes one unpopular.

To know the truth is our most difficult of tasks, but there is liberation in truth—it can shatter the shackles of delusion that keep us imprisoned in our own illusions. The truth has the ability to set us free, even if the transition is painful. To love truth is to know that truth is the precursor to liberation; to love the truth is to strive to maintain it. These qualities of knowing, loving, and maintaining truth are reflected in the Druid's proclamation of peace. This is a command that is voiced as a challenging question at the commencement of rituals in the Welsh tradition, it forms the foundation for the principle of calling for peace in the English Druid traditions. As the company gathers, the Druid who is overseeing the proceedings asks,

> *Y gwir yn erbyn y byd! A oes Heddwch?* The truth against the world!
> Do you bring peace?
> *Galon wrth galon! A oes Heddwch?* Heart to heart! Do you bring peace?
> *Gwaedd uwch adwaedd! A oes Heddwch?* Shout above resounding shout!
> Do you bring peace?

The truth against the world is exactly that—there are times when the truth feels so overwhelming that it is you against the untruth! This is primarily about speaking the truth even if it opposes the dominant voices of untruths and deception. Those against the truth may sound strong and even aggressive, but the truth is strong, and at times it must be persistent. When truth is at stake, we must stand and defend it. It is active and not silent; silence can often mean approval. *Heart to heart* is knowing that the love of truth is at the heart of you speaking the truth against the world. When we strive to ensure that love is our primary motivator, we are filled with a lightness that expresses our inner nature. The New Age adage of "Love and Light" can often bring a little sick to one's mouth, yet in its derision is the betrayal of truth. Love and the light that it brings to one's countenance and being is what shines through the darkness to find truth. In the Welsh tradition, light is the energetic frequency of wisdom, and all particles of light, which are the smallest of things, contain the infinite wisdom of the universe.[37] If our primary motivator is love, then truth is its treasure. This leads to the desire to maintain the truth at all costs, for by its maintenance you bring about peace.

Truth is the tantalising yet essential first step towards finding and maintaining peace. We see this reflected in the question that the Druid asks in the proclamation:

> *A oes Heddwch?* Do you bring peace?

To which the crowd responds with a resounding *heddwch!*

This is poorly translated as "Do you bring peace?" but it requires a further note, for much is lost in its translation. The word *heddwch* consists of two syllables, the first one

---

37 Williams, *Barddas*, 255.

being *hedd*, which means "peace," but the second syllable, *wch*, changes the meaning of hedd from a concept to a verb—it transforms it into something that you do. Therefore, the accurate yet clumsy translation of it would be this: "Will you actually be the peace this world needs, will you work and strive for peace, and do you bring that peace to this place?" It is essentially a challenge that all present have a responsibility to come to that place with peaceful intentions. In doing so, they have recognised their ability to respond to unpeacefulness. It is a spell that challenges the company to either act out of truth and peace or leave if they harbour ill feeling.

Inspired by this principle, English Druid traditions have incorporated a similar sentiment into their ritual activities that may often appear like this:

Standing to face each of the cardinal directions in turn, the Druid will call out:

May there be peace in the east,
May there be peace in the south,
May there be peace in the west,
May there be peace in the north,
May there be peace throughout the whole world!

Another prayer for peace is often used in the English traditions that maintain this current:

Deep within the still centre of my being, may I find peace;
Silently within the quiet of the grove, may I share peace;
Gently within the greater circle of humankind, may I radiate peace.[38]

What started as a triad of truth has led us down the path towards peace, which is what swims at the centre point of this triad's triskele. Druids were famed as peacemakers, mediators, and adjudicators; they could bring about peace between warring tribes and quiet the aggressions of leaders. Our positions today may not carry the sweeping authority of the Iron Age Druids, but all is not hopeless. Truth and its path to peace is about focusing on your square mile. Do not be overwhelmed by the tribulations of the world; when things appear so awful or so vastly beyond your control, do what you can to shine the light of truth on your square mile of influence. Truth is a treasure that leads to peace.

38 Order of Bards, Ovates and Druids, "Peacemaking in Druidry."

The third triad is the Triad of the Three Noble Tasks. Here is the triad in full. The Druid's three noble tasks are to inspire and to be inspired, for no inspiration can be gleaned lest the Druid is thus inspired. The second is the desire and willingness to serve and be in service to those, human or otherwise, that may need the Druid's counsel. The third is the compulsion to guard, maintain, and proliferate culture and tradition, for the Druid is a guardian of the mysterious and participates in the miraculous.

To be inspired is to be inspirational, and this is the first noble task of the Druid. There can be no inspiration without joy; the Druid's task is to seek out and maintain joy. The universe in its entirety is a love song to joy; all joyous things are expressed outwardly and creatively, and each one inspires further acts of creativity. It is by being a force for inspiration in the world that the Druid has the ability to cause others to see joy, even when it feels like it's a million miles away or utterly unachievable. Inspiration is a mirror that reflects the inspirational currents in another. It stands hand in hand with love and truth and peace. When we inspire, we create and we transform. When inspiration is the most prevalent force in any situation and striving for inspiration is the primary focus, it has the ability to transform anxiety and lethargy into joy. Your task as a Druid is to seek channels of inspiration in order for you to be inspired; in doing so, you set off a chain reaction of Awen that blows through the world. Inspiration can disarm and empower; it can raise people up from apathy to confidence. Druids never underestimate the power of inspiration.

Druid are in service; they are compelled to act upon their virtues and have a direct, real-world impact. Spirituality is all very well, but it cannot and must not be one directional and serving only of the self. Inspiration spurs one into action, and when we move into service, we gift our skills and talents to the world at large. Being in service can sound somewhat vague and unachievable—what can one actually be in service to? It is tempting to always think big, to imagine one must do something incredibly grand and important, but this is not the case. Consider the earlier statement of working within your own square mile. This comes into the fore when we consider how we serve. Your service may be attending a local nursing home for the elderly and listening to their stories or it may be the erecting of bee hotels in your garden. It might be teaching a class at your local community centre or Pagan gathering. Being in service is done through a love of wanting to give, and in turn we receive a blessing and are thus blessed. But the important factor here is the wanting—it is the want to give back, to pay it forward, to share your inspiration with others, to give of yourself. It initiates a sequence of reciprocation where the more we give, the more inspired we become.

To be in service is to sacrifice elements of yourself in the true meaning of the word, to make something sacred. Turn your Druid virtues into actions that can help others reach their potential or lift a person's day from mediocrity to joy. It doesn't matter how small or how big your service is. An element of service is held in the Cymraeg (and generally Celtic) virtue of hospitality and generosity. Gerald of Wales, also known as Giraldus Cambrensis, wrote of the generous hospitality of the Welsh and how they regarded this as the greatest of all their virtues.[39] In modern Druidry this virtue is taken to heart; hospitality is perceived as a service to others who may need respite or succour, and it is always given freely and with no ulterior motive. We may see acts of presumed hospitality when we receive free gifts from various companies and corporations, but this is false hospitality, for the final aim is profit. True hospitality is in service to the virtues of Druidry.

The final task is that of guardianship. In the Welsh Bardic tradition, the function of the Bard was to preserve the culture of the people through song and poetry. In Druidry,

39 Gerald of Wales, *The Journey Through Wales*, 236–7.

the spirit of the Bard is a vital component of the Druid, and this quality is thus absorbed as a vital attribute. Through all of these triads swims the principle of wisdom, but wisdom without legacy is wasted; when our wisdom is passed on by tradition or otherwise, we achieve a state of symbolic immortality. You may read this and consider that you have nothing to pass on, but of course you do. We all carry pearls of wisdom that sing of the lives we have lived, and these pearls are treasures of the future. To guard is to protect and support the things that bring to our lives the most meaning and joy. In guarding we maintain the culture of Druidry for future generations. We can achieve this in several meaningful ways: in a community sense, our contributions to ritual, liturgy, or philosophy can be carried on by its members long after your death. You may choose to write a book to share your wisdom. You may be drawn to the art of storytelling to disseminate wisdom, or it may be as simple as journaling. This is a powerful tool where you record your thoughts and progression. Who knows? In five hundred years' time, it might be your journal, dusty and yellowed, that inspires a new generation of Druids.

* * * * * *

Consider that wisdom in the Druid tradition is taught and perpetuated in a tripartite fashion, and now consider how the various elements that make up your life and your Druidry can be transformed into triads. When things are broken down and categorised in values of three, they are easier to digest and assimilate, and provide a tidy system in which to record our wisdom. Triads are in and of themselves a tradition; therefore, when we work with triads, we are aligning ourselves with ancestral wisdom—we move into the currents of the triskele as it spins and tells the innumerable wisdoms of all things. The triads emulate the impersonal nature of the Druid tradition, for to the ancient Bards of Wales, their wisdom was not individually orientated but rather expressions of a metaphysical principle that transcended the individual and connected them to a universal consciousness. While we may act as individuals, this is an illusion of the triskele: we can see the spiralling arms spinning outwards, but they are connected and thus interlinked. This wisdom teaches us that the Druid is an integral aspect of the Awen itself, which is a single breath that blows through the universe. This is the point of all this: the alignment of yourself with the vital spirit of the Druid tradition, the Awen, and in turn the spirit of Druidry is intimately connected by threads that not only reach deep into the distant past, but also on and into the future.

10

AWEN: THE HOLY SPIRIT OF DRUIDRY

AWEN IS A term that is frequently used in Druidry, and it is one that many Druids strive to connect to, but it is often a misunderstood force that benefits from further exploration. In simplistic terms the Awen is the pervasive creative force of the universe itself. Because of its creative powers, it is made manifest through humans by means of their creativity. An analogy for the Awen is to consider the popular cosmological concept of the big bang theory, which describes how the universe expanded from a state of high temperature and density. This state measured only millimetres in size when it exploded and gave birth to the entire physical universe. The Awen can be imagined as the potential that gave impetus to that initial explosion, and it did so solely to create and expand. From that potential, the Awen moved; as the universe started to expand, the Awen—as the initial force of the expansion—proliferated the forces of creation.

Within the Bardic tradition of Cymru, the concept of Awen has long been associated as the power that blows through the Bard, and it does so by means of two conduits that direct that energy. The first conduit is the goddess Cerridwen, commonly referred to as the mother of Awen (*Mam yr Awen*).[40] The second is in the guise of the chief

---

40 See my book *Cerridwen* for in-depth exploration of this goddess and the Awen.

Bard: Taliesin, the radiant brow. From the earliest manuscripts of Cymru, the Awen is heralded as an immense force that continuously blows through the universe from the point of its origin. This original "wind" is captured in the meaning of the word Awen itself, which translates into English as "blessed or holy breath." Nothing in the universe is separate from this force, and all things are said to sing inwardly and outwardly of it. All things are a product of the creative forces of the universe and therefore cannot be separated from the Awen. This force is so expansive and all prevailing that it can at times feel too vast or too big for us to grasp it. It is for this reason that the Bards of Cymru condensed it to the expression of their creativity in the form of poetry and songs. By doing so, Bards actively participate in the act of creation; their words initiate transformation in others and can influence situations and peoples. Those who move consciously into the Awen's currents and become conductors of it are engaged in the most powerful form of magic: creation.

The awareness of Awen arises from subtle connection; rituals, magical techniques, meditation, and active imagination are all methodologies that we can utilise to become aware of the inherent force within the universe. Essentially all things in existence are windows through which the universe perceives and experiences itself; the life-force within all things is the breath of the Awen. It is an eternal force whose primary function is to cause things to "be" and to have being. In popular culture one can see the power of Awen emulated in movies. In the Star Wars franchise, the Force is described as a ubiquitous power that permeates the universe; in the fandom of Star Wars, the Force is also called the Breath of Gelgelar. Force-sensitive individuals are able to align their will and consciousness to this power and direct its current in a metaphysical sense. Movies often take seeds of cosmological and spiritual principles and incorporate them in a manner that many can appreciate and understand. Works of fiction can often reflect spiritual principles in intriguing ways that have the potential to transform one's perspective.

The Bards of Cymru were the entertainers of the time, and in their audiences many were simply there to have a good time. For others, especially apprentice Bards, the latest elements of learning were transmitted and received. Through their endeavours the Bards strived to emulate the omniscient state of their chief Bard, Taliesin, who was brought forth from the womb of the mother of Awen, Cerridwen. In doing this the Bard is magically moving into an omnipresent world-soul.[41] This triple function

---

41 Parker, *Four Branches of the Mabinogi*, 100.

of Bard, Taliesin, and Cerridwen aligns beautifully with the tripartite nature of Celtic wisdom, and by analysing it we condense the Awen into a directable stream that we can connect to. Cerridwen conducts the Awen and offers it form in the guise of the radiant brow, the prophetic spirit of Taliesin. In turn Taliesin gives the Awen a stable form that allows the Bard/Druid to move into its currents. In this analogy the third element is you. The ancient Bards are our Druidic spiritual ancestors; they carry a song that went into the making of modern Druidry. To access the Awen, we must revert to our active imaginations.

EXERCISE

Imagine an enormous cauldron that floats in an empty void. Within it is a swirling silvery cloud that spins almost like the shape of a hurricane as seen from above. The silver clouds rise up and flow over the edge of the cauldron and move in all directions. They are chaotic and unorganised—too powerful to contain. Now imagine a tall woman appearing before the cauldron. She radiates a power unlike any person you have ever encountered. She raises a hand in which she holds a wand, and she thrusts it into the swirling cauldron. As she stirs, she gathers together the momentum of the silvery clouds and controls their chaotic expulsion. Now imagine another person, younger than she, arriving on the opposite side of the cauldron to the woman. It matters not what this person looks like or what gender they are. They place their hands on the edge of the cauldron and gaze at the swirling clouds therein. They look up into the black eyes of the woman opposite. She gives a smile, and with her outstretched arm she taps her wand directly onto the centre of their forehead.

The younger person flushes with untold power and slowly turns around so their back is to the woman and the cauldron. While maintaining her hold on the wand, she cups her hands into the swirling clouds that are still spinning in the cauldron. She lifts her hands and blows the vibrant clouds from them. They move with great force across the surface of the cauldron and hit the back of the younger one's head, there to be absorbed directly into their skull. Their forehead begins to glow with a radiant light that is brighter than the cauldron's contents.

Now imagine yourself in this scene. Walk towards the younger one—you can see the light from their brow, the cauldron behind them, and the woman beyond still blowing the silver clouds. The radiant brow is shining really bright now, so you turn your back to them. The light shines through you and illuminates a forest scene before you. You can hear a breath behind you—it is coming from the woman at the cauldron in a long, steady exhalation and then it is taken by the radiant brow, and from their mouth arises a similar audible breath, but this time it carries a sound, a single note. The sound hits you like a bullet of Awen, and you begin to sing…

* * * * * *

Several things are happening all at once in that little exercise. It contains all the primary concepts and symbols that were traditionally used to bring forth the Awen. The cauldron represents the universe itself; the spinning, spiralling clouds are the vast universe coming into existence. The woman is the goddess Cerridwen, who as a conduit for the Awen has the power to direct its form long enough for it to come into being within an individual who is aligned with it. She does this by making it smaller still in the guise of Taliesin, and then by light and sound it is transmitted to the Bard/Druid. In doing so the Awen is not so vast that we are unable to conceive of it; we use occult tools to condense its power in a manner that our relatively small brains can comprehend. By taking to your imagination and creating this scene, you are actively moving into the flow of the Awen's breath. You are initiating a metaphysical conduit that is tripartite in nature, with you as an integral aspect of it. Do this exercise regularly; repetition is key.

The Awen is described in the Cymraeg tradition as containing light and sound. Medieval Bardic poetry continuously refers to the Awen as an eternal song that is propelled through the entire universe by light. Iolo Morganwg assigned a symbol to this concept that is now the most common symbol of the Druid tradition, secular and sublime. In cultural Druidry the symbol is drawn thus:

In spiritual Druidry it appears thus:

While the concept of Awen is indeed ancient, the symbol is not necessarily so and is mostly attributed to the inspiration of Iolo Morganwg. It is, however, a useful tool for meditation and imagination. Iolo devised the symbol as three lines or columns, and he offers this description of them:

> And Menw the Aged, son of Menwyd, beheld the springing of the light, and its form and appearance, not otherwise than thus, /|\, in three columns; and in the rays of light the vocalisation—for one were the hearing and seeing, one unitedly the form and sound; and one unitedly with the form and sound was life, and one unitedly with these three was power. And since each of these was one unitedly, he understood that every voice and hearing, and living and being, and sight, and seeing were one unitedly with God.[42]

The character of Menw acts as an observational metaphor for the force of Awen, allowing the reader to visualise the beginning of all things. The three rays that symbolise the Awen originate from nothing and burst forth to imbibe all of creation with life. When asked about what it is that gives life to all corporeal things enbued with life, Iolo said:

---

42 Adapted from Williams, *Barddas*, 17. The original text contains reference to God the Father as the conduit of this force. Iolo was writing in a logocentric Christian society, and while much of his ideas lie outside of Christian doctrine, his writings conform to the standard religious view of the time. In modern Druidry his works are often used with the term *Duw* (Cymraeg for "God") replaced with what is deemed appropriate to the modern reader or practitioner.

With particles of light, which are the smallest of things; and yet one particle of light
is the greatest of all things, being no less than material for all materiality that can be
understood and perceived as within the grasp of the power.[43]

His theories demonstrate that some of his thinking was years ahead of his time, exemplifying a basic understanding of what particle physicists and cosmologists align with today. In spiritual Druidry the symbol provides an emblem to connect with the Taliesin spirit by means of the three dots that appear above the main rays. These are not present in cultural Druidry and are representative of the three drops of Awen that erupted from Cerridwen's cauldron.[44] Held within the symbol you can see the three rays, upon which the triadic system can also be placed; the three dots, denoting the radiant brow; and the first circle, denoting the edge of Cerridwen's cauldron. In some Druid traditions three rings encircle the rays, which further reiterate the principle of the three worlds of existence. In the English language it is common to refer to the symbol as the Awen; however, in the Welsh tradition it has its own name: it is called *Y nod cyfrin,* meaning the mystic mark. It is a symbol that represents the powers of the Awen.

So, why use the Awen at all; of what benefit is it to the Druid? The Awen enables us to not only see the extraordinary within the ordinary, but to transcend apathy. Our individual human lives can be incredibly difficult as we attempt to juggle all the responsibilities and obligations we have to our families and societies. The race of rats that so many of us are beholden to can be exhausting and easily lead to a state of disenchantment. When we work with the Awen as the creative force of the universe, we become active participants of the universe's unfolding. To say this is not to denigrate ordinary lives, for we are all a part of the universe, but to be conscious of the Awen transforms the way in which we see our place and our function in the world. The Awen implies a constant flow of creative energy; I often imagine it as a beautiful, clear river, one of those rivers that beckons you to step into its coolness. For much of our lives we may be happy walking its banks, taking picnics along its course, but we don't necessarily want to get wet. The Awen asks you to get wet—to step into the flow of the river and be a part of it. The Awen liberates our creativity in unparalleled ways, and by working with it we are simultaneously connecting to its cultural flow, which holds within it the memories of

43 Williams, *Barddas,* 255.
44 See my book *From the Cauldron Born.*

countless Druids and Bards. It causes us to be in relationship with the great cauldron of the mother of Awen, Cerridwen. It is the blessed holy spirit of Druidry.

Working with the Awen can be as simple as carrying it with you as a talisman, perhaps drawn onto a sliver of wood or parchment in your wallet. Many Druids wear it as a piece of jewellery about their person, touching or holding it when they feel the need to be inspired. Others will sing the Awen in one of two ways, by intoning the word itself in three syllables, *Ah-oo-en*, or by using the three sacred vowels attributed to the three rays by Iolo Morganwg, which are O I W (pronounced *Oh*, *Ee*, *Oo*). Because everything sings of the Awen inwardly and outwardly, song or voicework is particularly effective when connecting to it. Visualising the three rays of light while doing so is sufficient to move your awareness into its currents. Try it when you are next outside. Sing a single vowel sound near a tree or running water; if you stand with your arms held out a little from your body with your palms facing outwards, you will effectively be emulating the pattern of the three rays of light. Lose yourself in the moment. Whatever techniques we use to become aware of the Awen, the effectiveness of working with it is found in the results yielded, with the aim of being inspired and to be inspirational.

EXERCISE

Having read the previous discourse, consider the powers of inspiration and Awen as they are made manifest in your life.

* * * * * *

☞ *Inspiration is...*

....

....

....

☞ *The things that inspire me are...*

....

....

....

☞ *The people I find inspiring are...*

....

....

....

☞ *When I am inspired, I feel...*

....

....

....

☞ *I maintain my inspiration by...*

....

....

....

☞ *I inspire other people by...*

....

....

....

☞ *Awen is...*

....

....

....

☞ *I radiate Awen by...*

....

....

....

11

AWEN AND THE
MYSTERIES OF LLEU

WHEN WE LOOKED to Pwyll earlier in this book, we learned much about our inherent abilities and aspects of our personality and wisdom. Through Pryderi we discovered what it means to be separated from the source of all things and be in a state of anxiety. Life can be exhausting. But as we traverse from the third to the fourth branch, we are in a state of flux between the worlds—in that place where nothing can ever be the same again, for the eyes of the Druid have opened onto a world filled with the vibrant, pulsating energy of the universe singing in praise of itself.

The initial sequence of the fourth branch of the Mabinogi concerns the powerful magicians of the family of Dôn, mother and earth goddess. Through impressive magical acts, a child is born of the goddess Aranrhod; it is a nameless child, known only as a *pethan*, meaning "a thing." In its childhood it is given the name Lleu, which in Cymraeg means "light, brightness, bright."[45] In Cymraeg one of the names for the moon is *lleuad*, meaning "the action of light," and there is much mystery that we can glean from this. The moon is a reflection of the light of the sun; it does not have its own source of light. In its radiancy it is utterly transformed, and its light shines onto the surface of the earth,

---

45 Lleu is cognate with the Irish Lugh; both have their origins in the early Celtic god Lugus.

illuminating our nights. It enables us to see the source of its light even when the earth has turned her face from the sun. Our universe was born from a burst of Lleu, and that light, that radiancy, sped through the young universe, causing life to spring in its wake. Most religions and spiritualities on earth have the principle of light as a metaphor for divine consciousness permeating the universe. As a metaphor, that initial light is within all things; some things shine brighter than others, but all things contain it. The light is eternally flowing, and as it moves it reveals wisdom and creativity. The function of your Lleu aspect is to reveal your radiant creative force. Within the mythological landscape of the fourth branch and the tension between the apparent forces therein, we can see light at play with Blodeuwedd the owl being the darkness to Lleu's light—she is wisdom as a treasure of darkness.[46] It is Lleu, the light, which reveals that wisdom.

Pwyll, Pryderi, and Lleu are elements of your journey through mystery, and it is here in the fourth branch that we realise the sheer power of the light that we can shine on the world. Lleu is a child of magic, betrothed to nature herself. To be Lleu is to reflect the light of the Awen into the world. Without its source of light, the sun, the moon is still there, but it is invisible—the far side of the moon has limited light cast upon its surface, and its reflective qualities are poorer, but it is there nonetheless. Lleu is a metaphor for the power of that light. Everyone has the ability to shine, but how many choose to radiate their light? This is the teaching of Lleu: that against all odds, its function is to shine and be a beacon for the Awen in the world. Light has its origin in darkness, in sheer nothingness that holds the potential for all things. Some people are unable to hold and shine their light and find themselves in a state of anxiety of being in the darkness without light. Those same people may chastise you for shining too bright and demand that you dim your light a little. Do not succumb, for your light is the brilliance of Awen and will inspire those whose lights have dimmed to turn up their vibrancy. Those who are unable to deal with your brightness—well, they must succumb to wearing sunglasses.

A Druid is filled with the shining light of Awen and becomes Lleu, the bright one, the radiant one, transformed by magical means into living, breathing manifestations

---

46 Blodeuwedd is the maiden of flowers transformed by magic into an owl. She appears in the fourth branch of the Mabinogi and is created to give Lleu a wife after his mother, Aranrhod, curses him with never having a wife of the races of the earth. She is birthed from the flowers of oak, broom, and meadowsweet, and in addition to wisdom she represents the wild, untamed nature of nature. Initially she is named *Blodeuedd*, meaning "of flower," but she is renamed as *Blodeuwedd*, meaning "flower face," when she is transformed into the form of an owl.

of eternal light-revealing wisdom. The journey towards this place of radiant Awen can be seen in mythology, and when we connect with the myths in this manner, we make them personal; we cause them to be an aspect of who we are. We can see the course of our Druidry as we travel along mythological roads towards the expression of Awen. It is a beautiful interwoven Celtic knotwork that weaves your living with a landscape that was old when the world was new. This is the true nature of a Druid, and you can tell when you see one because they shine—they crackle with the power of Awen and their inner Lleu.

In the same manner as truth, light is also a treasure of darkness. That same darkness can be seen circumambulating Lleu in the fourth branch: it is there when he is unnamed, it is there in his infancy, it remains there as he matures, and it leads to his destruction and transformation. The darkness rules over the actions and motivations of those around Lleu; ulterior motives and agendas strive to dim his light. It is a message for all of us to understand that the brighter your light is, the longer and darker are the shadows you cast. Even in the sanctuary of the forest of Druidry, there are dark shadows. We cannot be assured of the goodness of others, not even in Druidry. But all is not lost, for the darkness is the potential of the universe itself. Our ideas and our thoughts all arise from the pitch black of your cranium, where your brain sits in perpetual darkness. In becoming Lleu we move towards understanding the nature of light and the darkness that births it. In Druidry darkness is not perceived as a negative but as sheer potential; all things originate from a state of unmanifestation; before anything takes shape and form, they are truly no-thing and nothing. It is the qualities of Pwyll and Pryderi that stir the cauldron that contains the unmanifest, and it is that stirring that brings the light, that bursts forth Lleu.

Let's take a closer look and examine the nature of your light and darkness.

* * * * * *

☞ *In a physical sense, light is...*

....
....
....

☞ *As a metaphor, light is...*

....
....
....

☞ *The function of my light is to...*

....
....
....

☞ *I express my light by...*

....
....
....

☞ *I understand darkness to be...*

....
....
....

☞ *My darkness is expressed as...*

....

....

....

☞ *The treasure of my darkness is...*

....

....

....

• • • • • •

As you progress further and deeper into the mechanisms that give momentum to the Druid tradition, you will do so from the perspective of the divine child. In the guise of Pwyll you have explored the meaning and value of his virtues and in doing so tapped into your own inherent wisdom. In the guise of Pryderi you have looked at your anxieties and fears and the nature of unity. In Lleu you have identified the nature of light within you; to do so is to simultaneously understand the nature of darkness, for there can be no light without it. Pwyll, Pryderi, and Lleu are the Mabon of the Mabinogi stories; they are expressions of the divine child of the great mother. They are you. This initial exploration of these concepts is tentative. They are the first steps towards the integration of mythological mysteries into your practise. In truth, these exercises of examining and being present in your Pwyll, Pryderi, and Lleu guise never ends; it is a continual cycle of examination and assessment of your quiddity.

Armed with this knowledge and a sense that the myths of Druidry are not simply for entertainment but are transformative tools that propel the Druid into mystery, you are prepared for the dive into the tradition's profound practises. The following chapters contain profundity and questions that require a certain understanding of self in order to assimilate the information and the questions that may arise from them. As you journey on in your Druidry, foster the Pwyll, Pryderi, and Lleu aspects of yourself. Know that you are the divine child and within you, just waiting to burst forth, is the unadulterated power of the Awen.

12

BELIEVE IT OR NOT

THE PRIMARY FOCUS of Druidry is not based upon what you believe but rather on what you do. It is a tradition of doing. To make this statement is not to denigrate the power of belief, for it has considerable impact on the course one's Druidry takes. Not all Druids believe in the same things. Therefore, before we delve into the things that Druids do, it is pertinent that we take a closer look at the word *believe* because it does impact what we do and how we do it. Many of the practises that follow require a degree of belief or faith in their effectiveness and validity, otherwise why would we bother to engage with them?

However, they are not universal—not all Druids believe in the existence of gods and goddesses; some Druids are animistic, others are not. Some Druids will practise magic and others will not. There are Druids who identify as atheistic, meaning they do not actually believe in anything other than what their senses can determine as real. A theistic Druid—i.e., a Druid who accepts the existence of gods and goddesses—may also have a different experience of beliefs in the gods than another Druid. To some, the gods and goddesses are constructs that enable them to compartmentalise the natural world into bite-size pieces that cause connection. By making nature smaller, our brains can engage with it in a manner that does not overwhelm. To another Druid, the gods and goddesses have their own agency and exist as individual entities in their own right. None of the above define the correct or incorrect way of being a Druid. It ultimately reduces to the power and quality of personal connection, and this expresses a belief.

I believe that some of the deities I have a relationship with are the spirits of the natural world tied to a particular location. An example of this would be the locality-specific goddess Braint. She is the tutelary deity of the River Braint, which flows near my home on the island of Anglesey. She may have been a genius loci, or a spirit of place, at some point in the distant past, but to the modern Druids of Anglesey she expresses herself as a goddess. She is intimately tied to the river that bears her name, yet she shares a commonality of attributes that are held by other British and Irish goddesses of spring. I also believe that some of my deities transcend this locality-specific quality and exist as independent entities with their own agenda. An example of this would be the goddess Cerridwen, the divine mother of inspiration. But ultimately these definitions are determined by what I believe; a fellow Druid may disagree. The belief itself is not as important as what we do with that belief and how it defines our experience of being Druids. A Druid who does not believe in Cerridwen as an actual goddess might instead consider her as a concept or a construct within a myth that expresses the quality of inspiration. Another Druid might believe her to be a muse or the idea of divine inspiration. What unites all these Druids is the core principle that she emulates: that of inspiration and how it has the power to create wondrous things and transform lives.

What this book won't tell is what you should or should not believe in. Belief is a stepping stone across the river of knowledge. Belief guides us into experience of the numinous and the ethereal, and it is the quality of those experiences that defines our personal Druidry. However, belief does not equate to action; for this to occur, other qualities must be utilised, and the first of these is faith.

Belief and faith are used so interchangeably within the English language that we may not be able to accurately define the differences between them, yet the difference is what makes all the difference between believing in something and acting upon it. That difference is faith. This fickle and often loaded word requires a little unpacking for us to see how it works for the Druid. Faith is the impetus that takes the individual from a place of belief to acting upon it, but to do that requires another attribute: need. Many of us, myself included, believe that cutting down on food portions, eating a balanced diet, increasing your consumption of fresh fruit and vegetables, and exercising regularly is good for you. But, like countless millions of people, I did not eat healthily all the time, and I certainly did not exercise as often as I should have. I believed the facts to be true, but I had not committed to act upon it. I believed that a balanced diet would be good for me; I had faith in the facts but did not feel the need to do anything about it. This all changed when recently I discovered that I had become prediabetic; suddenly I felt a profound need to act upon that faith. Active faith was born from the need to change my fundamental and pre-packaged beliefs about food and exercise. My beliefs about my own status quo were shaken to the core and tested, and I felt an urgency to act upon a need to be healthier and take charge of my well-being.

I believe that certain applications can be employed to magically affect and effect a situation. I believe that my mind in conjunction with certain tools and methodologies can alter the course of an action. I also have faith that these techniques work. In turn, I am spurred into action when the need is significant enough to cause me to perform a spell or ritual to necessitate the outcome. This is why I often take myself to a secret grove in the dead of night with a suitcase full of candles, cauldrons, and all manner of other paraphernalia—not to be seen but to act on my belief that magic works. Another Druid may believe in magic but may not feel the need to do it. Faith is the mechanism that takes belief from the inner world to the outer world, and the motivator for this is a sense of need.

How do we move from a state of believing in something to acting upon it? This happens when we develop an inherent trust that what we believe is intrinsically true. It is real. Therefore, if it is real, we can do something to act upon it. An example of this can be seen in the popular concept of the Pagan wheel of the year. Celebrating the cycle of the seasons is not just chopping the year into bite-size pieces so that we have an excuse to party every six weeks or so. It is the knowing that human nature is an aspect of nature and that the cycles of sun and moon affect us on every level of our existence. Ritualising the seasonal festivals moves the idea of us being an integral part of nature into an actualisation. We perceive ourselves to be integral cogs in the wheel of the year as members of a global community made of more than just humans. When we act upon that belief, the resulting action has real-world consequences. Some may be moved to become more ecologically minded. Others may modify their behaviour and habits or seek out ways in which to serve other members of our global community.

It is good practise to regularly question one's beliefs; doing so creates a healthy landscape in which our beliefs reside. We can do this by looking at questions that address our beliefs.

* * * * * *

☞ *I define a belief as...*

....
....
....

☞ *I retain beliefs that were programmed or conditioned in me*
   from childhood. These are...

....
....
....

☞ *I no longer hold some beliefs because...*

....
....
....

☞ *The thing I believe in the most and that affects my life*
   the greatest is...

....
....
....

☞ *The reason for this belief is...*

....
....
....

☞ *It is validated and made real because...*

....
....
....

☞ *If the things I believe in are held to be true in my experience, how do I deal with the beliefs of others that may be in contrast or anathema to my own?*

....
....
....

☞ *The belief that I act upon the most is...*

....
....
....

☞ *I express this belief by...*

....
....
....

☞ *Are my beliefs reflected in my virtues?*

....
....
....

☞ *I believe in a number of things, some of which are...*

....

....

....

☞ *Which of my beliefs do I have the most faith in and why?*

....

....

....

☞ *How are my actions, based on belief and faith, expressed
in my life and in the world?*

....

....

....

⸭　⸭　⸭　⸭　⸭　⸭

What we believe and have faith in has enormous influence on the course of our Druidry. In turn, belief and faith cause us to align with certain practises and philosophies that are the tools and actions that many Druids engage with, and in the following chapters we shall explore in detail what they are and how we work with them.

THE ANCESTORS

WE ARE THE sum totality of all that has gone before us. The genetic heritage of count-less generations swims within our cells, carrying with it a hoard of ancestral information, memory, and disposition. Elements of our temperament, the way we appear, the colour of our hair and eyes, the diseases we are most susceptible to—all are coded within us on a genetic level. They are the influence of the ancestors on our physical being. This is the inheritance of ancestry; the stories of the past make up the songs of the present. You are the direct product of all the loves and passions and obligations of thousands if not millions of individuals that went into the making of you.

Ancestor veneration and the acknowledgment that we come to this place and time from a myriad of rivers is a popular component of modern Druidry. If you can, imagine your parents standing behind you, mother and father to your left and right, and then imagine their parents standing behind them. You may not be able to recall actual faces, but imagine the individual figures, and before long, as you progress back along that ever-increasing triangle of ancestry, it becomes too vast for your imagination to hold on to—yet all of those faceless individuals caused you to exist in the here and now; without them, you simply would not be here. At some point the line of ancestors becomes so vast that the degree of separation between families becomes smaller and smaller. It is this inheritance that is celebrated in Druidry, a veneration that is based on gratitude for the lives that we live in the here and now.

The definition of an ancestor is any deceased person from whom one is descended. Some dictionary definitions describe an ancestor as a forefather or forebear, usually categorised as a grandparent or great-grandparent. Dictionary definitions aside, in the Druid tradition an ancestor is an individual or group of individuals who are deceased and from whom we are physically or spiritually descended from. This provides a wealth of scope when it comes to how we connect with the ancestors. For instance, my grandmother who died in 2001 is an ancestor in my mind and practise, but she is one that I can remember. My paternal grandfather who died when my father was only three years old is also venerated in my practise, but I don't recall him; I only have a photograph of him, in which I look remarkably like him. I also venerate my Druid ancestors who were killed by the Romans when they invaded the Isle of Anglesey in 62 CE; I may or may not be connected to them as genetic ancestors, but they are certainly ancestors of tradition. In the same manner, if you identify as a Druid and while you may not be connected to them genetically, the Druids of the Isle of Anglesey are your spiritual ancestors.

But why do this at all; what is the point? Primarily it is the acknowledgment of the power of sum totality; we exist as the pinnacle of a stream of ancestors that reaches into the deep past. It allows us to connect with the influence of recent ancestors, those that we can remember, and offers us keys by which we can assimilate the function of grief and bereavement. Ancestor veneration enables us to make sense of our place in space and time, to perceive the strengths and troubles of the past and acknowledge them as an aspect of our ancestral stream of influence.

However, it is also important that we do not sugarcoat the ancestors and perceive them as perfect and flawless, for often the past and its inhabitants can be problematic. When we work with the memory of the ancestors, it is essential that we are honest about the past and its influence on the present, and in some circumstances we must find ways to reconcile with problematic ancestors. Just because they are dead does not mean they are beyond reproach or washed clean by the process of dying.

Intergenerational trauma affects countless people who inherit a legacy of traumatic dysfunction from their ancestors. This can present itself in behavioural, biological, and emotional problems that can have lasting effects on an individual or group. This form of trauma can present itself in one of two ways. Historical trauma can affect entire communities or groups of peoples, races, and even whole societies; examples of these can be invasion, genocide, and colonisation.[47] Collective suffering can transfer across generations. While the immediate impact of the original traumatic experience may be distanced by significant periods of time, its memory and social impact may continue to affect the present. Historical trauma, inexorably connected to ancestors, may be symptomatic in the present and expressed as depression, self-destructive behaviour, and identity crisis. These are real-time problems that have their roots in a past that cannot be changed.

In modern Druidry and other spiritual practises where the current practitioners may inhabit a land that was originally taken from indigenous groups, this can pose deep issues in ancestor veneration. Intergenerational trauma is not exclusive to those whose ancestors suffered directly at the hands of oppressors; it can also manifest itself in the descendants of the oppressors. Profound feelings of guilt over past actions that may be generations removed and to which one can do nothing to change can steer the course of ancestor veneration, making it a problematic and triggering aspect of modern spiritual practise.

The other example is transgenerational trauma, which refers to traumatic experiences that are passed down from one descendent to the other, often from parent to child. A traumatic and untreated experience is transferred from one individual to the other, with the process itself, if not interrupted, potentially continuing for generations. Inherited patterns of behaviour from past trauma can affect relationships, mental health, and general well-being through social, biological, or psychological means. Those new to the concept of ancestor veneration may be triggered and detrimentally affected if the subject is not honest and open to dialogue and discussion. How the trauma manifests will be different for each individual and unique to the original traumatic experience.

This demonstrates that ancestor veneration is not all love and light and wonder, and should not be seen through rose-colored glasses. Not all of our ancestors were good people. The vast majority of my own ancestors only two generations back from my own would strongly disapprove of my lifestyle choices. In turn, I would no doubt disagree with many of their views and perhaps even their worldview. Some of my ancestors were just bad people who did bad things to others; the majority of them would not have an

---

47 For further reading on historical trauma in indigenous peoples, see Aguiar and Halseth, "Aboriginal Peoples and Historic Trauma."

inkling of understanding towards my spiritual choices. But can they *all* have been bad? Of course not. Ancestral trauma is a subject that we must approach with honesty, openness, and a degree of acceptance, for only in acceptance of the past and our inability to change it may we strive towards healing.

In addition to intergenerational traumas, our ancestors also left a legacy of intergenerational strengths. While it is healthy to acknowledge the bad things of the past, we must simultaneously find ways of reconciling that trauma with the good things that rise from our ancestry. Not all our ancestors were assholes. Scratch the surface and you may find a great aunt who struggled as a suffragette or activists who stood up for real change.

How does this manifest in practise? An example would be a tiny pebble that I have on my ancestor altar that came from the Christopher Street Park in New York City. This was in the vicinity of the Stonewall riots that instigated a huge change in LGBTQ+ rights; those were my lifestyle ancestors. The small pebble serves to remind me of the ancestors' sacrifice. Some of our deep ancestors changed the world in innovative ways that impact us today. Others struggled to raise and nurture good children who matured to be decent human beings who cared for their kin and communities. Others strived to provide food and shelter for their families. Reconciling with the past can only realistically be a psychological and social endeavour that by channels of dialogue and action can help repair past injuries and injustices. We can do little to change the biological impact of intergenerational trauma that has informed our genetic structure, but we can help one another deal with that. Reconciling with the past is a multidisciplinary process of healing, with no one group having all the answers.

As Druids we may struggle to reconcile with the traumas of the past, but we do so by honouring the past as an integral, unchangeable component of who we are and acknowledging that we can work towards healing. Honouring that you are a product of the past does not honour or whitewash the bad people and choices of the past. If we cannot change the past, then we must find ways in which to honour it as a journey towards us; in turn, this allows progression and liberation from its many chains. By bringing into focus the strengths of our ancestors as legacy qualities, we can step into the function of veneration from a healthy platform. Our ancestors gave us significantly more than just pain and trauma. So, what can we actually do about the pains of the past without being undone in the present? For example, historical colonial trauma is being addressed in the present by a system referred to as "culture as treatment," which involves the reestablishment of cultural indicators that were vanquished and demonised by colonial influences.[48] It may seem far reaching and beyond the scope of influence of the ordinary Druid, but there are things we can do. If colonial trauma is a trigger for you, seek out the cultural innovations that aim to repair past injustices. We do this first and foremost by raising our awareness, which in and of itself arises from education. To understand the past, we must educate ourselves.

Here are some tips for dealing with intergenerational trauma from a Druid perspective that will make moves towards a path of healing.

Find Your Past. Unlearn information from the past you have received that may be flawed, skewed, or driven by agendas and ulterior motives. Use online, library, and archival resources to relearn your past from your perspective. Be your own investigator. History is often written from the oppressor's point of view, not that of the supressed, but history is a narrative that you are a part of. Learn what you can from the resources available to you to relearn the past.

Find Your Ancestry. We are fortunate to have the technology to scan our DNA for ancestral origins and traits including dispositions of health and behaviour. Start a little fund to raise the money required to discover your genetic ancestry. There are multiple online laboratories that provide this service. This can often result in surprising discoveries about who we are and where we came from.

Find Your Tribe. You may well be familiar with who your community is, but a DNA scan may well reveal other surprises. Finding your tribe is discovering support systems and structures that can make enormous moves towards intergenerational healing. Your tribe can also be those people who you have no blood relation to but who hold and support the virtues and qualities that define your life.

Find a Way to Listen. Listening to the narratives of others is powerful education. Lend your ear to those that are in sufferance of trauma. Only by listening can you hear the impact of the past. Listening is a beautiful skill for the

48 Brady, "Culture in Treatment."

oak-wise to develop, for it emulates the quality of the trees as silent sentinels who stand and listen to the world around them. In listening we learn humility and that not everything is about us.

Find a Narrative. Storytelling tools are powerful methods by which we can initiate healing. To tell one's story is to share and inspire others to understand the impact of intergenerational trauma. In ancestral veneration the past is not forgotten, it is dealt with, and in Druidry it is an aspect of the Bardic arts. Tell your story, find an audience online or in person; your story may well be just what one other person out there needs right now.[49] Changing one person's opinion or perception changes the world.

Find a Way to Repair. For historical trauma, find innovations of culture and contribute what you can, giving of your time or a donation to a charity or cause. Learn a language that the past supressed or injured. In multigenerational trauma, seek out charities or organisations to support or volunteer within that aim to educate and repair the influence of the past on the present.

Find Yourself. Multigenerational trauma can affect our genetic predisposition. Study yourself and your behaviour and habits for the genetic clues that link to your ancestry. Your body is intimately connected to the past and is the vessel that reaches forwards from the deep past into the future. By learning about our own bodies, we learn something of our ancestors' strengths and weaknesses.

Find a Way to Heal. The word *healing* is often bandied about in such a manner that it can become vague and subjective. Healing is a journey and not a destination; it is neither linear nor sequential but is often a process of oscillation. Healing requires work and constant attention to clean, stitch, and dress a wound, knowing that a little knock can reopen it. What can you do in the here and now to initiate healing for yourself or others?

---

49 Narrative Exposure Therapy is a current and effective tool in healing intergenerational trauma. For further reading, see Elbert et al., *Narrative Exposure Therapy.*

Find a Way to Reconcile. Sometimes we need to pause, feel, and say out loud, "I am sorry for what my ancestors did; what can I do to help?" and then act on that. Vocalisation is a powerful way to acknowledge past hurts and open channels of dialogue and movement. Reconciliation can take many forms, each one unique to the situation, but they require work and effort.

Find a Space. As Druids we have subtle powers at our disposal to help integrate these issues. Create an ancestor altar where you can work with the memories of your ancestors and create a positive space to focus on their strengths. Symbols, objects, photographs, candles—the list of altar items is endless, but they should connect you by whatever means to the past.

* * * * * *

These suggestions are merely the tip of the iceberg towards reconciliation, assimilation, and healing. As Druids we have a duty and a responsibility to the present and the future. Each of our ancestors dreamed and brought about a reality that was indicative of their lives at that time. Every one of those individuals planted seeds, metaphorically and literally, that grew into your present. Ancestor veneration is more than just photos on an altar; it is the profound understanding of our position as individuals who have a responsibility to the future. Our task, particularly as Druids, is to seed the future with a wisdom that comes from our living so that when we are venerated by future generations, our descendants do so with pride. The past remains unchanged and unchangeable, but the present is a gift that can keep on giving. Are you the answer that your ancestors needed? Will you be an inspiration when you are an ancestor? Stop and ask yourself these questions, for one day you will indeed be an ancestor.

In addition, consider the following questions:

* * * * * *

☞ *I define an ancestor as...*

....

....

....

☞ *I define ancestor veneration as...*

....

....

....

☞ *I will venerate the ancestors by...*

....

....

....

☞ *The ancestors who empower and inspire me the most are...*

....

....

....

☞ *The ancestors who I find problematic are...*

....

....

....

☞ *I will reconcile problematic ancestors by...*

....

....

....

☞ *How do I want to be remembered as an ancestor?*

....

....

....

14

WORKING WITH DEITIES

WITHIN ANY RELIGIOUS or spiritual practise there is an element of the numinous and the deific, but so often blind faith is necessary to connect to the primary or set of deities that that tradition may revere. In Druidry blind faith is not expected, nor is it a requirement. Druidry does not expect you to accept the existence of deities. However, at some point in your exploration, you will inevitably happen across mention of the divine in the guise of a baffling array of gods and goddesses that span the entire Celtic cultural continuum. It would be unfair to the reader for any discourse on deity to be offered without first exploring what deity is in a Druidic sense. In the West most individuals have some experience of one of the revealed religions, and therefore their understanding of what a deity is might well be informed by their connection to established monotheistic religion. This does not necessarily translate into a Pagan perception of deity. In order to understand and begin a relationship with the divine, we must first explore what is meant by the terms *gods* and *goddesses*.

Druidry allows for freedom of expression and inspiration when it comes to matters of defining what a god or goddess is or is not. The foundation of any relationship must be based on informed and direct experience. I can, of course, introduce you to the various deities within my Druid practise, but the work of connecting with them and developing relationships with them must be entirely of your doing. I can lead you by the hand to the altars and shrines of various deities and teach you something of their nature, their stories and myths, their virtues and personalities; however, I cannot teach you how to be in a relationship with them; that function must arise from your personal connection. Before we even begin to speak of connection and various ways in which deity may express itself, you must ask yourself this: Do you believe in the divine, and what has your experience of deity been like up until this point?

These are important questions to consider and answer as honestly as you possibly can, for they will define the nature of any future relationship with deity. It is also perfectly acceptable if you do not believe in the existence of gods and goddesses. Some Druids are referred to as theistic, which is characterised by a belief in deity or deities; some Druids are nontheistic in that they don't believe in the existence of deity, or at least not in the conventional sense, as we will explore shortly. What is important to consider is that neither one is better than the other, Druidry allows for freedom of expression and does not require you to believe in anything that does not fit your worldview.

Druidry is not dogmatic in its approach to the nature of the divine, and different Druids have different viewpoints and perspectives. This diversity enriches the tradition and brings a vast wealth of colour and vibrancy to it. If we were to analyse the consistencies and differences in the nature of the divine, they can be classified into seven distinct categories. This is not to imply that any other form of divine classification is unworthy of exploration, but as a general rule of thumb, the following categories are the most frequently understood and practised forms of deity definition within the Druid tradition:

- soft polytheism
- hard polytheism
- thoughtforms
- archetypes
- animistic expressions
- apotheosis/euhemerism
- inclusive and exclusive monotheism

Classifying deities in this manner may appear cumbersome or unnecessary, but we cannot meet them in person, so we must find tools by which we can know them. Consider the following discourse as the tentative steps in going on a date with a god or goddess and starting the lengthy process of getting to know them. Devotional acts to the gods are all well and good, but without a foundation of relationship we are floundering in the dark and hoping for the best. It is good practise to do what you can to learn as much about the deity that you are drawn to.

These definitions are guidelines; they are not written in stone. Worthy of note is that for many, their perception of the divine is a blend of all seven approaches. There is no right or wrong way to connect to deity; there is only your way. The first word you will encounter is *polytheism*. In simple terms this word describes the belief or worship in more than one deity. The majority of Druids I know are polytheists, but things can get complicated very quickly when we learn that there are different forms of polytheism. Now the trick here is not to be baffled by these categories. We are simply looking at the different ways by which deity can exist and come into existence, for none of them exist in a vacuum. You may read the following and discover that you sympathise with all of them or none of them, and in turn we shall deal with both issues. But first let's take a look at the seven categories of divine expression.

Soft Polytheism

This branch of the polytheistic approach refers to a belief system where the individual deities are not wholly separate. A single deity may well be choosing to manifest itself in diverse manners in order to reveal elements of its nature in differing ways. An example of soft polytheism can be seen in action in the diversity of Hinduism, with some sectors of the faith believing in one primary god being the expression and true identity of the deity. The other deities that are revered are essentially the primary deity acting within a different role; one may perceive this as personality offshoots of the one deity.

However, in practise it may not be so clear-cut. While a soft polytheist may believe that the gods they work with are, in essence, one aspect of the same being, they may still hold true that for all practical intents and purposes the gods are separate and are to be communicated with individually. For many soft polytheists, the overall überbeing may be beyond comprehension and not directly approachable. Believing instead that the myriad of personalities expressed through the pantheon of gods allows the practitioner to develop relationships in a manner that may not be possible with the over-deity.

In essence, aspects of soft polytheism break down the unfathomable into bite-size pieces, where the gods act almost as cells within the body of the primary deity. While they appear separate, this is an illusion; they are, in fact, a part of the whole. In hard polytheism the gods are separate, distinct, and have their own agency. In soft polytheism the gods appear as aspects of the same being, but in practise the division between the two is neither entirely clear nor defined.

One may perceive this within one's own physical body, for the cells that make up your body behave and act with their own agency, yet they respond and are directed by the primary system that governs the whole. They have independence and yet are an integral aspect of a collective that is overseen by a single mind or force. You also can consider the gods to be like the sparks that rise from a central bonfire, informed by the conflagration and yet maintaining an individuality. For many soft polytheists, their belief structure contains many elements of the six categories that follow, implying a fluidity to this approach that allows freedom of expression and relationship.

Hard Polytheism

In stark contrast to the principle of soft polytheism, hard polytheists perceive the gods to be individual beings with their own agency. They are distinct, separate, and real beings. The gods may interact with our world, but it is not always clear if they reside here or if they exist energetically in another dimension that interacts with our world. For many hard polytheists, the gods may occupy another world entirely and occasionally interact with our plane of existence. In Celtic mythology numerous personalities that may be identified as gods or certainly have supernatural attributions occupy the indigenous Celtic otherworld, Annwfn. In turn, this otherworld has portals and liminal places where access can be granted between the two realities. These thin places are often sites of shrines, altars, and locations of pilgrimage that serve to honour a deity.

Hard polytheists may reject the validity of other gods from other cultures as not real or inferior to their own, a discordancy that has been the blight and cause of much human strife over the millennia. Philosophical views as to the abode and function of the gods may differ from practitioner to practitioner and culture to culture. However, elements of hard polytheistic gods are often inseparable from animistic folk traditions, where tutelary spirits of certain natural landmarks became gods in their own rights. An example of this can be found in Sabrina, the British goddess of the River Severn. Human interaction with

Sabrina started beyond the mists of time, but her name is first recorded in Welsh as *Hafren*, to which various legends and myths are attributed, but this is also the native name of the river and its source. Over the centuries she morphed as townships and settlements grew along her long course from the mountains of West Wales to the Bristol Channel near present-day Gloucester. By the influence of the Celto-Romano culture, she became known as the goddess Sabrina and has persisted in human imagination and devotion for countless centuries—to the extent that some of Britain's greatest writers and poets sang her praises:

> Sabrina fair,
> Listen where thou art sitting,
> Under the glassy, cool, translucent wave,
> In twisted braids of lilies knitting,
> The loose train of the amber-dropping hair;
> Listen for dear honour's sake,
> Goddess of the silver lake,
> Listen and save!
> (Milton, 1634)[50]

In the experience of many Druids, Hafren/Sabrina is a hard polytheistic goddess, one with her own agency, and yet her origin is not clear-cut. She appears to have originated as a spirit of place, or a genius loci, but has been elevated to the position of individual deity with her own agency. Her present form conforms with the principles of hard polytheism, but how she got there remains a fickle and difficult question to answer. Is it possible for a genius loci to arise to the ranks of a hard polytheistic divinity? These are profound and difficult philosophical questions, the answers to which can only truly arise from personal connection and relationship. Perhaps Hafren/Sabrina is the combination of all the categories explored herein, bound to forces and principles beyond the scope of human understanding. It may be through examples like Sabrina that we can deduce the power of apotheosis, or to make a god—where, given enough energy, worship, and devotion, the deity becomes an independent agency.

In contrast, it is my belief that the goddess Cerridwen is an independent agent with her own existence, albeit not wholly as a part of our world. She has the ability to interact

---

50 Braithwaite, *The Book of Restoration Verse*, iii.

with our world and its inhabitants. For centuries, if not a couple thousand years, she has been revered and honoured as the source of poetic inspiration, Awen. While no shrines or altars have ever been found in honour of her, she has nonetheless persisted in spirit form within the Welsh tradition of Bards. In essence, *they* were her altars and mouthpieces. In time she developed a more Pagan persona as magical practitioners of the late nineteenth and twentieth centuries moved to connect with her, not as muse, but as goddess.

The spirit of Cerridwen has existed for countless generations, but her guise as goddess has not; this is a fairly recent development. Acts of devotion and reverence kept her alive, but the focus changed. Today she is a goddess, and to me, she belongs to this category as a hard polytheistic deity. What this example demonstrates is that an entity can exist long before its acknowledgement as a deity. It implies that the definition itself is fluid and part of a spectrum of experience and expression. It may well be that Cerridwen is actually well beyond the scope of the human mind to fully articulate, so we break it down—she was muse/inspirer, she is now a goddess. She has responded to the needs of the people, exemplifying that she has agency and the ability to respond and adapt.

Thoughtforms

In this manner the gods are created by immense human psychic focus and energy and fed by adherents and believers over time. To make this statement is not to diminish the power of thoughtforms over the other categories of definition or to believe them somehow inferior. On the contrary; thoughtform-created entities, beings, and deities can be (and often are) more powerful than those who stem from folklore or mythology. They arise from the intentionally directed thoughts of a group of people, often inspired by an individual or a kernel or seed from a body of lore or story. At times they may be in response to natural phenomena or disasters, where people seek to discover meaning and significance. In doing so, they create a mutually agreed-upon image or personality that represents the matter at hand, which is then fed, nurtured, and given life by those who connect to it. What may begin as whimsical or fantastical can evolve into powerfully constructed thoughtforms that suddenly take on a life of their own.

As human beings, we have barely scratched the surface of the human psyche and its abilities to profoundly affect the world. It may well be that some thoughtform-created deities have received enough power from their worshippers to exist independently of them. We can briefly explore an example of a thoughtform-created spirit/god in the guise of the seasonal Santa Claus.

The origins of the winter gift-bearer are lost not only in time, but to diverse cultures that fed and gave life to it. Elements of Santa Claus can be seen in the Middle East, Turkey, Scandinavia, Germany, Holland, Britain, the United States of America, and many other locations around the globe, with influences from the Christian St. Nicholas and the Germanic god Woden. With a myriad of streams influencing the figure of Santa Claus, one might consider the current thoughtform to be a cauldron of contradiction, but on the contrary, it has found a life of its own.

By whatever means and intentions, the current Santa Claus is believed by millions of children who anticipate his visit every twenty-fourth of December. Adults perpetuate this belief and continuously feed the thoughtform. To many Pagan practitioners, the figure of Santa Claus is as real a god as any other; as the bringer of light, he is the spirit of hope, warmth, and goodwill to all people. Offerings are presented to him, and there is probably not a single individual in the Western world who is unaware of the nature of those offerings—milk and cookies for Santa and a carrot for Rudolph. These offerings belie a ritual that is ingrained into the function of this thoughtform, and it is those rituals, along with countless other winter rituals, that feed and nurture the agency that is now known as Santa Claus. Each year millions of people participate in this ritual. In the twenty-first century, the ritual is extended to a period covering well over a calendar month.

If we pause to think on that for a moment—millions of people connect to this thoughtform—millions! The amount of psychic energy that is poured into this being every year is phenomenal, to the extent that upon the evening of the twenty-fourth and the day of the twenty-fifth of December, the entire world feels different. There is something tangible in the very atmosphere. The human mind, imagination, and psychic constitution can profoundly affect the physical world itself.

Beneath the whimsy of Santa Claus is a deep, ancient power that sings of meaning and significance to peoples who occupied different lands and times. He is as alive as any other thought-created deity, and we continue to perpetuate him. We may do this for a number of reasons, each one as valid as the other: for the joy of children, for familial connections, to deepen the bonds of friendships, to reinforce the principles of peace and goodwill, to acknowledge the birthing of a new year.

Santa Claus is informed by countless streams of inspiration, from an ancient winter deity to Christian associations, folk traditions, the pacification of children, commercialism, materialism, and the new Paganism. He is not one thing and one thing alone. It would be an impossible task to untangle the persona of Santa Claus and attempt to find the one true origin; it would also be foolhardy to diminish the validity and power he currently has. He exists to satisfy a need in humanity, one which is met every December 25. Loathed, despised, loved, or celebrated, the figure exists, and he exists for a simple reason: we need him to exist. He fulfils a deep-set need in the human heart. Perhaps it is the one occasion for a cynical adult to put aside all cynicism and accept that there may just be real magic in the world, even if only a hint. This thoughtform permits us to peer beyond the veil of cynicism and doubt and taste the flavour of magic beyond. He is a joyful example of the profundity inherent in thoughtforms. He is powerful and perhaps more apparent in this world than some gods who have their own independent agency.

Thoughtforms, while wonderfully mystical, are simultaneously created by the magic of ritual. They require directed thought and constant feeding; they are more often the product of meaningful ritual. But herein lies the dilemma—is the manner of their creation also potentially their downfall? If a thoughtform-created deity is given its own life and being, is its life-force forever tied to the rituals that created it? What happens when we stop believing in Santa Claus?

Archetypes

Verging close to the theories of Jungian psychology, archetypal deities represent the shadow and light of the human experience. In this case the deities are symbolic, as opposed to real beings with their own agenda and existence. But to say this is not to diminish the power these archetypes may possess and the immense influence they may have over people's lives. Critics may note that a symbolic deity in an archetypal sense is no different to a character from a work of fiction, and there may be some truth in that statement. However, it does not consider the power of the human imagination and the ability for fictionalised characters to develop into archetypes that satisfy a need.

To nontheist Druids, this category suits their needs and their ability to connect to the beings that others may perceive as deities. The gods and goddesses of the Anglesey Druid Order's family tree primarily stem from the four branches of the Mabinogi; to some of our Druids, they are archetypal energies. Rhiannon may represent the archetypal Mother or the processes of calumniation. Pwyll represents the necessity for employing caution and care in any given situation. Lleu represents one's inherent light. These archetypes inform the human condition by way of their virtues. Thus, archetypal deities are powerful representations of general complexes.

To a theist, their virtues are attributions unique to that particular deity and ones that can be emulated by a human being. To a nontheist or those who prefer the archetypal approach, the virtues of the deities represent very real human conditions. They stand as mirrored doorways through which the explorer can see oneself reflected in the virtues of the archetype. To a nontheist Druid, Rhiannon and Pwyll share the same existence as Darth Vader or Wonder Woman; they may be fictional characters, but they have the capacity to teach us valuable lessons.

Animistic Expressions

It may be said that the principles of animism can be seen to permeate all other categories of divine definition. It is likely that all religions' deities have their origin in animism.

However, the beauty of the animistic approach lies in its closeness to the earth itself and the relationships we may foster with the natural world. We all occupy a world in which reside numerous persons, only some of which are human. We perceive an element of this in the Anglesey Druid Order's civic rituals performed at the ancient monument of Bryn Celli Ddu.[51] In the cold light of day, she may appear only as a selection of stones worked by ancient hands and positioned in such a manner to create an earth-covered chamber with an approach corridor leading to an inner chamber. Aligned to the sunrise of the midsummer solstice and sunset of midwinter, she may simply be a collection of stones aligned in such a way as to have a calendrical function.

However, were we to adopt an animistic view of Bryn Celli Ddu, which the majority of our Druid members do, she is as alive as we are. Each rock, each turf, contains a spark of the divine energy that brought the entire universe into existence. The Druidic principle of Awen sings within them. Imbued with the attention, concentration, ritual, and energy of humans over countless millennia, she has developed a character and personality that are more than the sum totality of her parts. She is considerably more than a collection of stones; she has persona, presence, and even attitude and moods. The animistic

---

51 Search the internet for images of Bryn Celli Ddu.

principle within her is quite alive and tangible to the majority of people who visit her. In a secular sense this may simply be put down to the atmosphere, one created by the unusual and extraordinary efforts our ancestors went through to create her.

Bryn Celli Ddu occupies a space within a ritualistic landscape. Within yards of her mound is one of the island's most sacred rivers, the River Braint, with Braint being the tutelary goddess of the river itself. She floods in early February, coinciding with Gwyl Braint, commonly known in Pagan circles as Imbolc or Candlemas. She is our goddess of sovereignty, healing, smithcraft, and poetry; she sings in unison with Bryn Celli Ddu. She is another example of the animistic principle—the life force and divine spark within the river itself—being elevated from a genius loci to a goddess. Other monuments that have since been ploughed into oblivion surrounded Bryn Celli Ddu, but it is evident that she was one aspect of a community, a community brought into expression by the hands of human beings. We consider that we are in community with Bryn Celli Ddu, yet ironically we are the least permanent members of said community. When our stories have come to an end, she will exist thousands of years from now.

In this manner we are not simply in relationship with nonhuman personalities within the landscape; we are an inexorable aspect of the community that we all forge together. Understanding the significance and quality of this principle nurtures honourable behaviour reflective of sacred relationship. All things are inherently alive, and there are times in the course of human existence when we are compelled to elevate that aliveness. Some may be elevated to the personage of a tree, plant, well, or river and referred to as a spirit; others are elevated further and deified. The defining quality in both examples is that of relationship. It is easier for us to forge relationships with those who are the most similar: humans. But this does not suggest we are unable or incapable of moving into a relationship with nonhuman persons. All that is needed is a shift in our awareness of what defines effective communication.

Apotheosis/Euhemerism

Apotheosis means the making of a god; on the other hand, *euhemerism* is the elevation of an actual living person to the rank of a god. Both factors are relevant to the function of deity in Druidry.

For example, there is no evidence to suggest that many of the current Druidic deities were worshipped or revered as such in antiquity. No shrines or evidence of cults devoted to our deities have been found. While some—for instance, Lleu and Rhiannon—are cognate with deities in the greater European spiritual landscape, we do not have evidence of those particular names being afforded to a specific deific energy. They have become modern deities by the process of apotheosis. We have made them divine. This fact alone often lays Druidry and polytheistic practises open to criticism, and yet the critics may not fully appreciate the power of apotheosis and its usage since the beginning of human history. It is not new, nor is it extraordinary. Apotheosis usually starts with an anthropocentric figure that is fictional, mythological, or historical; it ends with a deity. Druids are quite aware and accepting of the fact that our deities exist as they do today as a result of apotheosis. They exist as deities for a simple reason: we need them to exist. They fulfil a deep need within us to connect to the virtues or attributes that they represent, and they do so as expressions of divinity.

Similarly, the euhemeristic approach is the elevating of an actual living human being to the status of a god. This mostly occurs retrospectively, where one starts with a deity and posits a human origin for it, which is exemplified by Jesus in Christianity, Siddhartha in Buddhism, and Akhenaten in ancient Egypt, along with a myriad of pharaohs who attained godhood. In the Celtic tradition, many are compelled to consider the prototypic poets Taliesin and Amergin to have been real historical people who can be elevated to the rank of gods.

Inclusive and Exclusive Monotheism

Dion Fortune, one of Britain's most prominent and influential occultists, claimed that "All gods are one god, and all goddesses are one goddess, and there is but one initiator."[52] This statement perfectly captures the essence of the inclusive monotheistic approach, which is the belief that every individual deity is an aspect of one überdeity. Elements of this may be familiar to you, for many soft polytheists are aligned to this theory, and we touched upon this in the first category of our exploration. In contrast, exclusive monotheism holds that only one deity exists; it does not accommodate the notion of the existence of other gods. This is the position of traditional Christianity, Islam, and Judaism.

52 Fortune, *The Sea Priestess*, 227.

• • • • • •

The divisions between the aforementioned categories are not written in stone and neither are they absolute. Many modern Druids swim between the different categories, coming to rest on one for a while before moving onto another or assimilating all categories into one glorious expression. There is no right or wrong way, no one and only true way, to connect to the divine. To an individual who approaches the divine from an archetypal angle, the deities are no less real to them as they would be for a soft or hard polytheist. It is the quality of the relationship that ultimately matters and the manner by which that relationship transforms and enriches both human and deity.

If you choose to believe in the existence of the gods and goddesses, you may find yourself firmly ensconced in one of the previous categories or moving between several of them. If you choose not to believe, you can still share in the wisdom that they express from an archetypal perspective. Either way, the Druid is enriched by the cauldron of the Celtic cultural continuum.

To deepen your connection to the deities of Druidry, these tips will help you:

- Find their primary sources in myths, legends, and stories, and study them.

- If the language that preserves the deity's name is alien to you, learn a little of it, enough to be able to understand the etymological significance of their names.

- Study the people that gave rise to that deity and the landscape they inhabit; learn something of their culture.

- Do not rely wholly on Neopagan sources for information; search the internet for academic and scholarly papers.

- Does the deity have a location that is specific to them? If so, explore it virtually or in person. Consider pilgrimage as part of the process of relationship.

- Amass enough information to glean the deity's attributes and qualities.

- If you are drawn to one particular deity, explore the possible reasons for that. Are there qualities you share with the deity? Do your virtues align?

- Write letters to the deity telling them about yourself.

- Create altars and find symbolic items that express the deity's attributes.

- Consider a devotional practise like daily prayers or offerings.

- Create a journal to explore the deity from an archetypal point of view, particularly if you have no interest in devotional practises.

Now consider the following questions:

☞ *I define a deity as...*

....

....

....

☞ *My understanding of the function of deity is...*

....

....

....

☞ *Deity is or is not a function of my spirituality because...*

....

....

....

☞ *What do the deities bring to my Druidry?*

....

....

....

☞ *What does my Druidry bring to the deities?*

....

....

....

☞ *I am particularly drawn to _____ as a god/goddess because...*

....

....

....

☞ *I understand the concept of worship to be...*

....

....

....

☞ *I worship the deities by...*

....

....

....

☞ *I understand the concept of veneration to be...*

....

....

....

☞ *I venerate them by...*

....

....

....

☞ *I emulate the virtues of the deities by...*

....

....

....

15

DEVOTIONAL WORK AND THE MAKING OF OFFERINGS

IN THIS CHAPTER I focus on the power of devotional activity and how to forge and deepen relationship with the deities and spirits that one is inclined to work with. Earlier we explored the three different constitutions that can initiate and kindle an inclination towards one set of traditional symbology, deities, spirits, etc., over another, so here we must unpack this a little further by exploring the mechanisms that drive a specific attraction. As an example, I shall focus specifically on deity work and the magnetic pull one might feel towards a particular god or goddess, but the examples and structures that follow can be used and adapted when working devotionally with any spirit. There may appear to be no rhyme or reason as to why you feel an attraction, which in and of itself contains mystery; we may not be able to adequately articulate why we fall in love with a human being or are immensely drawn to one person over another. The feelings that we feel, while quite real, are highly subjective and driven by forces of attraction that we may not fully understand. The same applies for our inclination to be attracted to a particular deity.

When we are drawn towards a god or goddess, we need to employ caution in the language that we use to articulate that connection, for that language has the power to inspire as well as provoke and alienate. It is common for people to say that they have been called into the service of a deity in such a way that they are unable to ignore them. For some people drawn into spiritual practise for the first time, the concept of a calling may seem alien and even spark an inferiority complex, particularly if you are unable to identify such a calling for yourself. What, in fact, is a calling? It can be as subtle as becoming aware of a plethora of symbols that are associated with a particular deity; for example, you might be finding crow or corvid feathers wherever you go. Friends may suddenly start sending cards or gifts that have corvids on them. The actual birds may make themselves more obvious to you, landing on a windowsill, moving closer towards you. A few things might be happening here: sheer coincidence, an increased awareness of corvids, or the deities associated with corvids making themselves known to you. In Welsh Druidry these might be Branwen, Bendigeidfran, and Manawydan, to name only three; in Irish Druidry it may be the Morrigan calling for your attention. In addition, you might find yourself suddenly moved by the tale of Branwen and find similarities or sympathies between yourself and her.

When a deity is not being quite as subtle, they may appear in your dreams and actively speak to you. You might be aware of them when you meditate. Their messages may be clear in that they specifically ask you to do something for them on their behalf or in service to the virtues and qualities that they embody. On the other hand, their appearance may be visionary only, with no actual direction offered. In both cases we could argue ad infinitum if this is an actual deity that is specifically calling to you or an aspect of your own self that is drawn to what they represent. We cannot prove or disprove either one. Any spiritual experience can only be subjective in nature; we are not dealing with hard scientific facts here but the numinous and ethereal. Ultimately any attraction or pull that you feel must be quantified and assessed by you and you alone, for the connection itself is deeply personal. When we speak to others who are drawn into deific devotion, we can be inspired, but it would be foolhardy to gauge one's own connection by the expressed quality of another.

The depth of connection you have to a deity is also personal to your practise. In Druidry there is no expectation that you identify yourself as a devotee of a particular god or goddess. However, some Druids may be compelled into the service of a deity and move towards aligning their virtues with them on a deeper and more intense level. The waters can become a little murky at this point, especially for a newcomer to Druidry, and often the terms *devotee* and *priest* can be bandied about almost freely, which can lead to confusion. In general terms a priest is an individual who is authorised by their community or peers to serve as a mouthpiece and often a mediator between the people and the deity/deities. The root of the word is found in the Greek *presbyter,* which means "an elder"; in Latin the word is intimately connected to the term *sacerdos,* a word used to describe the priestly function of making sacrifices or giving offerings. A priest is usually found at the centre of a community's religious or spiritual activity and often gives the greater portion of their life in service. Common in the Abrahamic religions to this day and identified by clothing or garments that set them aside or place them in a liminal position, they can also be found in folk practises and ethnic spiritualities. In Neopaganism Wicca identifies its adherents as priests and priestesses in service to that tradition. It is the depth and commitment to service that differentiates a priest from a devotee. However, choosing to use this word should come from a platform of understanding and humility, as being called into service is not the same as being called into priesthood. The words themselves can spark misunderstanding, and it is important that if you choose to identify with these terms, you do so in a manner that does not serve to erroneously elevate your perceived status.

If a priest is authorised by their community or sanctioned by other supernatural means, then a devotee may be a member of the priest's community, congregation, or enclave. An analogy of this would be that a member of a Christian congregation may be a devotee of their deity, but they are not a priest. This does not diminish their function within that religion. The same can be said for Druidry; many are content with practicing their spirituality and being a part of a wider community, while others are drawn to clergy training, teaching, and walking a path of deep commitment that can often change the course of their lives. As the current head of the Anglesey Druid Order, I serve a priestly function within that organisation: I speak on its behalf, facilitate its educational programme, and serve to build a community of Druids that share a common language. I also perpetuate the myths of our deities and stand as a mouthpiece for their stories and virtues. There are times when a member of the order might petition me to speak to the gods on their behalf, and I do so as a priest to the order and its community of human and nonhuman beings. But my function within the order is not as a priest to any individual deity. In contrast, I would say that I am a devotee of a handful of deities, and I revere and honour several more. A devotee is an individual who has strong ties to a particular deity, and this is defined by a connection that exceeds a passing interest; a devotee may have sensed a profound attraction towards a particular deity that significantly impacts the expression of their practise.

A personal example is pertinent here. In my own practise, I would identify myself as a devotee of a number of deities; to name but four, they would include the goddesses Cerridwen and Môn and the gods Llŷr and Manawydan. The devotional aspect of my connection to these deities is expressed either daily or weekly, like clockwork. Cerridwen is a goddess I honour and provide with offerings every single morning before I take to my work. A statue of her occupies the centre of my primary altar in my home office. It is accompanied by a large framed image of her on the wall above the statue. My devotional ritual begins by playing a particular Welsh song on my computer that lasts exactly four minutes. I always play the exact same song, for there is power in repetition and familiarity, and the lyrics evoke a feeling I have towards Cerridwen. I breathe with the land and the sea and the sky and then ground myself into the moment. At this point I bring her to mind and imagine her rising out of the waters of her sacred lake and walking towards me. She always appears different each time, and I take note of the details within the scene. I light three tealight candles in holders in front of her statue and then begin my devotional prayer to her, which I repeat for as long as the music lasts. In addition, I have a small branch with silver bells running down its entire length that I shake about the statue, filling the air with a glorious tinkling sound. The music, the bells, the words of the prayer—they all add to the magic of the moment that is familiar and just as routine as brushing my teeth. Once the music has ran its course, I return myself to the space of my everyday life and thank Cerridwen for her inspiration.

In the evening I honour and thank Môn, the goddess of the Isle of Anglesey, for holding me, for supporting me, and for her abundance. I tend to perform this devotional ritual outdoors unless the weather is terribly inclement. In a similar fashion to my devotionals to Cerridwen, I use a prayer that I speak in Welsh over and over for several minutes. Simultaneously I burn an incense that has been created specifically for her and made using several local ingredients. Once a week, on a Sunday, I give offerings of gin to the sea gods Llŷr and Manawydan. This particular ritual is done at the seashore, where the offerings are poured directly into the sea. In a similar fashion to the goddesses, I use words of gratitude in a prayer format to thank them for their blessings on the island and to help me always find peace within myself, even when I feel the least peaceful. If I am unable for whatever reason to be in familiar surroundings to perform these devotionals,

I have proxy symbols for each deity in a small cotton pouch that enable me to pause and consider them wherever I am.

I define these examples as devotional practises; I would not claim to be a priest to any of the deities mentioned, but I do consider myself a priest to a human community of Druids within a particular order. My reason for connecting to the deities is that they impact my daily life, and I am constantly aware of their presence and influence. As an author and someone who deals in a world that serves to inspire and be inspired, Cerridwen is my ally and my guide in seeking the powers of Awen and allowing them to blow through me. She helps me feel inspired when I feel uninspired. In return, and in her honour, I hope to inspire others by enabling them to sense the Awen that blows through them. In that spirit this book is an offering to her.

Môn is the mother of Wales, the grandmother of the world; she is a nurturer and a provider, and she holds the memories of the people of this island and the Druids who lost their lives during the Roman invasion. She is the holder of memory, the keeper of dreams, and the bread basket of Wales, and I am compelled to thank her daily and ensure that the memories she holds are shared with the world. The gods of the sea, who in my tradition are Llŷr and Manwydan, connect me to the warm currents of the Gulf Stream that keep this part of Britain temperate and fertile, but they also represent the powers of deep mystery. Manawydan straddles the sea and the land; he is the peacemaker, the arbitrator, and a powerful magician who inspires me to be the best magical practitioner that I can possibly be. In service to them, I give of myself as a teacher of the mysteries and strive to make peace where there is strife.

There is thought and connection to the reasons for devotion; they are not plucked from the air for the sake of pomp or ceremony. Devotional acts happen because we are compelled to perform them in honour of sacred relationship. They provide a space where we step into the liminal and engage with the deities in a manner that allows us to communicate with them. It is liminality that is key to listening, I hear the sea gods all the time as I live close to the sea, but my devotional acts allow me to listen to them. It is in these spaces that we move ever closer to the deities. The key to lasting relationship is repetition. Brushing your teeth once does not stop your teeth from rotting—it is doing it every day and twice a day that prevents decay. Going to the gym once will not give you that toned body—you must do it three times a week continuously or nothing will happen. Devotional acts work in the same manner—they build on the previous day or ritual, they increase awareness, they cause you to see and work with the deity in ever-increasing depths of connection. You know your friends well because you spend time with them. The same must be done with the deities that you are devoted to; each devotional act deepens your relationship.

It is important to acknowledge that a relationship is not a one-way street, and the most honourable of relationships are symbiotic, with both devotee and deity getting something. For the relationship to have integrity, we must also find ways by which we can give of ourselves in honour of them; in turn, we receive blessings or favours from them, or they help us embody their virtues in ways that are beneficial to us and them. It is easy to fall into the trap of thinking that you must do something grand and majestic to please or appease a deity, but that is not the case. Simple acts can go a long way in deepening your relationship, but always keep in mind that they are also in relationship with you. You are building a partnership. Your task is to figure out the virtues of the deity that you are drawn to and consider how your actions can emulate those virtues in this world. By doing so, you are emulating the attributes of that deity and potentially doing their work in the here and now. It can be as simple as telling their story in an online forum or writing a poem; it can be as grand as facilitating an educational day or a conference in their name. The sky is the limit. If we are doing all of this devotional work in honour of a deity, what are we taking from the experience? In some cases the deity may influence or steer areas of your life in a particular direction. Some Druids believe that the deities offer blessings on our endeavours and work. Some believe that certain wishes may be granted by a deity. But ultimately the quality of relationship is based on give and take, and devotional practises allow us the opportunity and the space to figure out what those things are.

In addition to being priests and devotees, Druids may have a casual interest in a particular deity, or an informal relationship with them. As social human beings we are accustomed to casual relationships, where we may respect another individual and admire them and yet not be that close to them. It is the person that you see once a year and you really enjoy being with them, but the connection is fleeting. It is the friend that you see once every five years, but when you catch up it is as if no time has passed at all. Casual relationships are not inferior, they are just different. To have a casual relationship with a deity is absolutely fine; you can revere and honour any one of them without feeling that you must be devoted to them.

In the tradition of Druidry that I practise, we have a family tree of deities that spans the three realms of land, sea, and sky. We have a fourth family of deities that are considered to be not of this world. That is a lot of gods and goddesses, and it would be impossible to be devoted to them in their entirety. When we become familiar with the family tree, some Druids find that they have a natural affinity towards one or more and are compelled to find out more about them and begin the first steps towards relationship. Other Druids find no great affinity with any in particular and have a casual relationship with all of them to a lesser or greater degree.

Personally, I have a love for the goddess Branwen, who is an integral part of the mythological landscape that I live in. I can visit sites that are sacred to her. Her home and her grave are places that I can physically visit. But I am not compelled to be a devotee of Branwen, which does not diminish the respect or regard I have for her; it's just that our relationship is different. Her sacred birds, the starlings, feast on the birdfeeders in my garden and when I see them, I am reminded of Branwen. There are times when I will journey to her grave to leave offerings in her memory, but these are ad hoc and at best infrequent. She feels more like a cousin rather than a sibling or a parent. We enjoy each other's company when we catch up, but we do not feel it necessary to live in each other's pockets. Branwen and I occasionally catch up, and when we do, the time spent is good. I am not compelled to be her devotee, and she seemingly has no expectations of me to be so. I could say the same for over two dozen other deities in our family tree. I will leave suitable offerings to Branwen when I visit; I know what she likes. Is this a devotional act? Possibly, but maybe not. It may be suitably defined as a gifting that acknowledges a connection that is valued but not as intense as other connections. The truth in all this is meaningful connection. All our relationships are imbued with meaning, but the value we place on that meaning can often differ from person to person and deity to deity. The trick is to remember not to be beholden to thinking you must do something when in fact you may not need to or be required to.

Listening to deity is as much a process of listening to the tides of your own being. It is never one-directional. The easiest and honest way to consider your relationship with deity is to look at the way in which you forge and maintain relationships with your fellow human beings, your animal companions, and the plant kingdom persons that you care for. In our human lives we are not devoted entirely to one individual to the exclusion of others, and the same can apply in your spiritual life. Our attraction to friends, families, our pets, the tree that grows at the bottom of the garden—they have different degrees of intensity, and the same applies to your relationship with the deities. Those who we are closer to pull at something mysterious within us or their virtues align with ours. Allow time and experience to temper your ability to gauge and act on relationship.

At this point you might be wondering what are suitable devotional practises and how do we create them? In the previous chapter I concluded with tips that enabled you to get to know the deities; here I shall focus on the nature of devotional practises. The creation of devotional acts follows from the information and knowledge that you would have gained by actively participating in the suggestions and questions posed to you previously. Developing a practise matures with time, and you may find that what was suitable at the beginning of a relationship with a deity may change as that relationship deepens. But devotional practises tend to follow a particular pattern and can be broken down into the following actions:

Preparation: Setting the intention and gathering items you require or have chosen to include.

Connecting: The stage where you ground yourself in the moment through breathwork or visualisation and then bring the deity in question to mind and visualise or imagine them in a particular landscape.

Offering: The main part of a devotional practise. Your offerings may take on a myriad of forms, but it is at this stage that you give them to the deity.

Silence: After the offering has been given, it is imperative that you be silent in order to allow any impressions or communication to occur.

Close: To conclude, you offer thanks and return to your normal, ordinary awareness.

* * * * * *

In my own devotional practises, the duration of the rituals take from approximately four minutes for my daily Cerridwen devotional to over ten minutes for Llŷr and Manawydan. They are long enough for my awareness to shift slightly and allow a moment to pause and be in the energy of the deity that I am connecting to. They are also short enough to not feel cumbersome or a burden to my day. What we choose to offer deity is a fickle and often contentious subject. In many sacred sites well-intended physical offerings become litter when they are not cleared away. Flame and soot from candles and incense can damage structures that may have existed for thousands of years. The nature of what we offer needs to reflect the respect we have for the deity and how those offerings emulate their virtues. Creating litter does not mirror the virtue of any deity; it is simply irresponsible. Therefore, it is important that you give thought and consideration to the suitability of the offerings you are inclined to make.

In the following pages I will be exploring the nature of offerings, but before we arrive there it is pertinent to address an obvious question: How do the deities receive the offerings? They don't have mouths or noses or ears, so how do they get what is being given to them? An effective offering is energetically transformed during its giving; an example of this would be the burning of incense. The original material consists of herbs, flowers, barks, and resin, each selected for their individual properties, and in burning the incense the substance is transformed: turned from earth into air and dissipating through the atmosphere. There is a sense of movement here, of something transforming from the visible to the invisible spectrum. Deities don't necessarily share the same temporal space as we do; they are invisible to our ordinary human senses. Therefore, the most effective offerings transcend the seen world and by various processes become invisible. We imagine that as this happens the offering moves from our world to a state in which they can be perceived or sensed by the deities. Just like anything in spiritual practise, it is subjective and yet it is something we have engaged in for millennia.

Candles do much the same thing. It is a solid substance that is prepared as an offering and then lit. The light, heat, and combustion combine to release an intention that is energetically sent to the deity. Spoken word or song is the movement of intention from the individual human body through air and directed towards the deity. The nature of the offering is somehow transformed from one state to another, causing its passage from intention to reception to be actualised. Therefore, setting the intention is always important to the dynamics of the devotional act. Energising an offering to make it suitable as something that will be given in a sacred manner is easy. As you create or gather your items, set your intention into them; this can be as simple as thinking of the deity and holding the item as you do so. Or you may create a small verse or a chant that expresses your intention. Or you might simply state your intention out loud. Do not be befuddled or overwhelmed by it. It is an act of devotion; fill the offering with intention that has reverence, respect, honour, and love at heart and you cannot go wrong.

Some examples of effective offerings are:

Anointed Candles: Choose candles of appropriate colour for the virtues of the deity involved. Remember that colour is energy in motion; as wavelengths of light that are perceived by the human eye, colour is alive. Various oils that the deity may like can be spread with a finger along the length of a candle. Making your own candles adds another level of depth to devotion. Small spell candles in any colour are easily available and make perfect devotional offerings because they only burn for a short period of time.

Incense: This is perhaps the oldest form of offering known to humankind and has been used in religious and spiritual practises since time immemorial. Incense can take several forms, from the burning of oils to the stick type to cone or loose/grain incense. Self-lighting incense needs only to be lit once and will burn until the material has been exhausted. Loose or grain incense must be burnt on hot charcoal blocks. Essentially, they are plant materials combined with various tree gums and resins and accentuated by essential oils or wines and honey that are then burnt. Making your own incense to reflect the qualities or virtues of the deity is a devotional act in itself. The burning of incense also quickly transforms the space where you are performing your ritual with smell and smoke. Incense is my favourite form of offering to make.

Liquid Libations: A libation is the act of pouring liquid into something or onto a specific surface. An ancient form of offering, libations have often included precious alcoholic beverages or milk and honey. These liquids can be poured over altars or into running water, the sea, or vessels that are then given to an outdoor location after the ritual is completed. Alcohol is particularly favourable for the process of creating it in the first instance is almost alchemical. Sugars are burnt ferociously by the action of yeast to transform a benign substance into one that has immense potency. Making your own wine or spirits to offer as libations is a powerful devotional act that takes you time and effort to complete. Avoid corrosive substances or liquids that contain salt, which can damage or kill plant life.

Wreaths, Bouquets, and Nosegays: These consist of flowers, usually highly scented or chosen for their specific aroma and qualities, that are then bound together with natural string as a physical offering. Other than gradual decomposition, there is no immediate transference of form in this kind of offering. Therefore, one must be mindful of its position and the risk it may pose to the environment it is in. A nosegay is usually small and highly fragrant and is my chosen offering in this category. I will create a nosegay and present it to the deity on their altar in my home space, usually in a vase with water to ensure they last for several days. When they wilt, I return them to the earth via composting.

Voice Offerings: This is perhaps the most underrated offering that one can give, and yet its power is immense. Voice offerings can take the form of spoken word, chanting, or song. They give of your energy, your vulnerability, and they are a gift that leaves no litter or residue. Writing and creating a song or a poem and then offering it to the deity is a glorious way to make yourself feel good and hopefully please the deity you have in mind. Voice work has a real effect on the physical makeup of your body, and singing in particular releases a hoard of feel-good hormones from your brain, oxytocin being amongst the most famed. It makes not a blind bit of difference if you can sing or not. Instead, learn to enjoy how singing makes you feel. If you feel good, so will the deity you are working with.

Physical Items: This category of offerings is the one that is often problematic and can invariably become litter. Physical representations that symbolise the virtues or attributes of the deity may be a tempting offering, and they are perfect for home altars. For natural locations they can become contentious, especially when they initiate a trend that others then follow. Ribbons tied to trees can severely impact the health and well-being of the tree as well as endanger wildlife. Plastics and man-made fibres can break down into microconstituents that can detrimentally affect soil and water courses. An offering at home is all well and good, but do be acutely mindful of those you might offer in the great outdoors or at sacred sites.

Oblations: An oblation can be taken to mean an offering of yourself in honour of a deity. This could be signing up for a beach litter collection scheme or volunteering at your local hospice, food bank, or homeless shelter. This is the sacrifice of time and energy that honours the deity and has a real-world impact. It is the giving of your time in honour of their virtues.

• • • • • •

This list is not intended to be exhaustive, but hopefully it serves to suggest the types of offerings that are most commonly used in Druidry. You will eventually find ones that suit you best or combine elements of all the above into your practise. Examples of devotional prayers and chants are given in chapter 22.

At the conclusion of this chapter, contemplate the nature and function of offerings and devotional practises in relation to your Druidry.

• • • • • •

☞ *What does it mean to be devoted to something?*

....
....
....

☞ *I am devoted to...*

....
....
....

☞ *I demonstrate and express my devotion by...*

....
....
....

☞ *Devotion is important or unimportant to me because...*

....

....

....

☞ *What does the deity/spirit get from my devotional practise?*

....

....

....

☞ *What do I get from devotional practise?*

....

....

....

☞ *To me an offering is...*

....

....

....

☞ *My favourite kind of offerings to give are...*

....

....

....

☞ *The reason I give them is...*

....

....

....

16

THE ART AND SCIENCE
OF MAGIC

Do Druids practise magic? This is a question that I have heard ad infinitum for decades and no doubt will continue to hear for years to come. My answer to this question is a firm yes: Druids do indeed practise magic. But before we venture into exploring how a Druid uses magic, first it is pertinent to attempt to define what magic is.

According to the infamous early twentieth-century occultist and magician Aleister Crowley in his book *Magick in Theory and Practice*, it is the "science and art of causing change to occur in conformity with will." He further elaborates on this notion by comparing the creation of his book as a magical act:

> It is my will to inform the world of certain facts within my knowledge. I therefore take magical weapons, pens, ink and paper, I write incantations—these sentences—in the magical language i.e. that which is understood by the people I wish to instruct; I call forth spirits, such as printers, publishers and booksellers, and so forth, and constrain them to convey my message to those people. The composition of this book is thus an act of Magick by which I cause changes to take place in conformity with my will.[53]

---

53 Crowley, *Magick in Theory and Practice*, xiii.

Crowley's example is effective, for it places the forces of magic into an environment that people can generally comprehend without baffling them with mysticism. While the works of figures like Crowley may seem an odd choice, considering he has been dead since 1947, he was an influential figure who wrote extensively on the art and science of magic, and his influence on occulture continues to this day. If you are unfamiliar with his works, they are readily available and are essential reading for any student of the magical arts.[54] Having a general background in magical thinking is good practise and education for the budding Druid. Crowley chose to differentiate stage magic from supernatural magic by the addition of the letter K, and the attribution of the additional letter has been connected with him ever since. However, academics, scholars, anthropologists, and historians continue to use *magic* when referring to the actions performed by peoples past or present who have a mystical quality to them. Personally, I choose to use the term magic, but you may decide to use magick; either way, it is your connection to the term that matters.

If we jump forward nearly a century, is the definition of magic in the modern world vastly different? In his book *The Path of Paganism*, author and Druid John Beckett describes magic as having three distinct functions, the first being psychological programming, the second intercessory prayer, and the third being the manipulation of unseen forces. He concludes by stating that the best form of magic makes use of all three qualities.[55] While more descriptive and not as succinct as Crowley's, the sentiment is similar. It implies a force of mind that acts on unseen energies. From the perspective of a modern traditional witch, Laura Tempest Zakroff in her book *Weave the Liminal* describes magic as "the force of action that is the essence of change combined with the spirit of influence."[56] Again, we can feel a similarity, albeit the wording is quite different, but so far it seems that our three examples are agreed that magic is a force that causes change by influences that are both intrinsic (internal forces/mind) and extrinsic (external forces). A quick internet search will yield over 2 billion pages that seek to define what magic is or is not. A glance over several of these pages results in a general consensus that magic is the influence of an individual by means of unknown forces to achieve a desired out-

---

54 For a modern biography of Crowley's life and works, read Lachman, *Aleister Crowley*.
55 Beckett, *The Path of Paganism*, 187–188.
56 Zakroff, *Weave the Liminal*, 98.

come. But what do we know of the origins of magic? Does the history of magic help us understand its function?

Magic and its practise permeate the entire human experience on every continent and in every spiritual tradition and religion, from ancient Egypt to Mesopotamia to the ancient Celts.[57] The classical author Hippolytus said that the Druids were prophets and foretellers of future events and that they used Pythagorean methods as well as magic.

This and several other examples affirm and reiterate that the Druids were involved and used magic, but frustratingly it tells us nothing about what they did or how they might have practised it. They do not elaborate on the methods and techniques used, but there is a general agreement that they did practise magic. Speculations abound as to the manner by which the Druids practised, with some evidence suggesting that the Druids walked a similar path to those of the Siberian, Nordic, and Scandinavian shamans.[58] Items in the archaeological record and in later literary sources point at practises that saw the Druids consult with disembodied spirits.[59] While classical accounts of the Druids may be problematic and layered with propaganda, there are consistent references to Druids actively consulting with inhabitants of another world for the benefit of their communities. They are often portrayed as not only learned individuals with a deep understanding of science at the time, but as a caste of individuals that engaged in natural magic. This term requires some unpacking to get to the nuts and bolts of magic and how it has evolved over millennia.

The Evolution of Magic

Back in the deep past, before the coming of the Druids, magic was in all probability perceived as something utterly supernatural, meaning beyond the laws of nature herself, and perhaps belonging only to the regions of the gods. To see an eclipse with no understanding of what it was would have been awesome beyond articulation; to have watched curtains of the aurora borealis fall from the heavens would have been to witness a magic that had no explanation. Our ancestors were making leaps and bounds in settlement and technologies for survival, but their understanding of how the universe worked was limited. And then, several thousands of years ago, some astute human beings began

---

57 For a concise history of the origins of magic, see Radin, *Real Magic*, 35–73.
58 Aldhouse-Green, *Rethinking the Ancient Druids*, 37–38.
59 Aldhouse-Green, *Rethinking the Ancient Druids*, 70–72.

to notice that things had certain patterns, ones that could be measured and then predicted. They observed that the sun moved from east to west in a repeatable pattern and its various stations could be marked within the landscape. By studying the rising and falling of the moon and its declination, they began to understand the harmony of the world they lived in. Soon after, monuments were erected that marked the passing of the seasons, making agriculture more effective. What was once magic transformed into a science.

By accident or coincidence, certain plants were known to ease infections and ailments, causing individuals to study the properties of the plant kingdom. Eventually this became understood as medicine. This is where our history becomes really interesting. If we cast our minds back to the references of the classical authors and the peculiarity of mixing science and magic in the same sentiment, we can glean wisdom. The Druids were often credited with using Pythagorean methodologies in their magical practise, which tells us something interesting about the magical and scientific dynamic of the time. By observing the natural world, it is apparent that what was once perceived as supernatural was then understood as natural phenomena.

In turn, natural magic was to split into two different functions. On the one hand, as humans deepened their knowledge and understanding of the universe and how it worked, natural magic became exoteric. This term refers to something that can be understood by anyone and can be measured or quantified by mathematics, physics, etc. In a religious or spiritual sense, exoteric can also mean something that is in the realm of the divine or outside the experience of humanity. On the other hand, natural magic also became esoteric. This term refers to something that belongs to the inner world and is often used to describe a knowledge that only a few are privy to. What we can see here is the evolution of magic. The initial supernatural component became the domain of religions who dealt with castes of spirits, gods, or an überbeing. With the bifurcation of natural magic, the exoteric aspect became what we now understand as science, whereas the esoteric evolved into occult magic, i.e., hidden from obvious view.[60] The wonder in all this is the realisation that magic and science have a common origin, captured beautifully, if a little tongue in cheek, in the popular aphorism often attributed to futurist Arthur C. Clarke: "Magic's just science that we don't understand yet."

---

60 Radin, *Real Magic*, 35–37.

Both the archaeological and classical record demonstrate that the Druids had a deep and thorough understanding of medicine and healing that included pharmacology.[61] On the surface this may appear far removed from the Pythagorean-informed magic that they claimed to utilise, but it is evident that Pythagoras also founded systems of medicine. He wrote well-developed theories on human respiratory function, sight, hearing, and the brain, combining contemporary scientific and mystical thought.[62] The medieval manuscript *Meddygon Myddvai* (The Physicians of Myddfai), while compiled over a thousand years after the Iron Age Druids, nonetheless contains older elements that may well be inspired by Druidic wisdom. While progressive for its time, many examples of medical practise within it are almost indistinguishable from magic. It is likely that the remote predecessors of the medieval physicians were the ancient Druids of Britain.[63]

We may assume that modern medicine is indisputably scientific in expression and origin, but we would be foolhardy to make such a statement. Modern medicine has its origin in European magical practise, without which it would not have developed into what we recognise as medicine today. Magic is inseparable from the human experience, and while some may be disparaging of it, the principles and belief in magic inexorably influenced the evolution of human intelligence and scientific thinking. As medicine evolved from the signatures of plants and other esoteric practises, it strived to be empirical and led by the experimental method. Jump forward from the earliest and often esoteric treatises of medicine in ancient Egypt to the advanced pharmaceutical therapies of today and the majority of ordinary people still have no idea how it all works. It retains a mystical, secretive quality to this day.

We take a pill and something happens—to the ordinary individual, it is indistinguishable from magic. The prescription is the spell, and less than a century ago it was almost always written in Latin to prevent the public from knowing what was actually being prescribed. Written in an ancient language, symbols would appear on paper that only a select few were privy to understanding. The directions given are the method by which the spell takes effect—take three times a day, etc.—and the trust or faith that the patient has is its magical energy. Medicine continues to express an echo of its magical origins. People evolved, societies progressed, and in turn many forgot the influence of

---

61 Aldhouse-Green, *Caesar's Druids*, 146–150.
62 Selcon, *The Physicians of Myddfai*, 11.
63 Selcon, *The Physicians of Myddfai*, 27.

magic on human civilisation, but, regardless of advancement, science and medicine are indebted to magic.[64]

When we examine the function of magic as a vital component of the human experience, our relationship with it is transformed. To the ancient and modern Druid, magic is not fantasy; it is not something limited to the daydreams of childhood. Rather, it is an influencer, a force that has constantly walked with humanity and taught us as much about ourselves as it has about the world we inhabit. To dismiss magic entirely would be to denigrate its influence on the evolution of science, and without it we would be ever the poorer and less enlightened as a species. When the subject of magic is raised, the never-the-twain-shall-meet attitude of many in the scientific community today is indicative of an ignorance that mocks the origins of science. With the bifurcation of natural magic into its exoteric and esoteric parts, the exoteric has developed to answer the "how" of the universe, but it is almost totally incapable of asking the "why." This is the realm of the esoteric and is where the Druid steps out of the shadows of the grove and into illumination. The role of spirituality and magic is not to explain the external world but instead to cause an interfacing of the inner world with the outer world in a manner that is conducive to transformation.

Magic offers us the experiential tools by which we can ask and answer the "why" of the universe. Magic and science are not and have never been in diametrical opposition to each other; they share a common birth, and they both serve to find significance in the human experience. There is more to unite them than there is to tear them apart.

Magical Application

It is one thing to glean an understanding of where magic came from and its use by the ancient Druids, but how does that apply to the modern world? How, when, and why do we practise magic? Having read the previous paragraphs, you will understand by now that it is in the realm of esoteric natural magic that a modern Druid practises. There is more to this than meets the eyes, for if we return to occultist Aleister Crowley once more, he said, "Magick is the science of understanding oneself and one's condition. It is the art of applying that understanding in action."[65]

64 Henry, *Magic and the Origins of Modern Science*.
65 Crowley, *Magick in Theory and Practice*, xx.

As previously explored, magic is not hot air and wishful thinking; it is an application of the forces of nature that are directed by the function of will in conjunction with intention. Having an understanding of oneself is essential to the effectiveness of magic. How can we hope to influence the world if we have little influence over ourselves? In most modern magical traditions, there is a period of training and education that involves an inwardly directed focus. To know oneself is to know the universe, for we are a miniature representation of it. This is what Crowley is hinting at—by understanding the forces that drive the human condition, by proxy we learn how to apply that knowledge in a practical manner upon the universe. It is tempting at this point to venture off into pseudoscience and the world of quantum and particle physics and its narrative of interconnectivity of everything at an atomic level, and for some people the study of such things enriches their understanding of magic. Alas, it is not my expertise, but on a magical level I do understand that it is interconnectivity that allows magic to have influence, that on a level beyond my ability to articulate everything is linked one to the other. Magic and its direction at a subtle, energetic level causes a disruption or a manipulation of the strands that hold all things together.

In my musings I visualise the magical currents of the universe as a spider's web. Sensitive to any movement, each strand is interconnected—a tiny plucking on one end will ripple and affect the whole. For this to be an effective visualisation for my practise, I need to understand my place in it all, and I believe it is this Crowley was referring to. Understand yourself and you will glean an understanding of magic and how to use it.

When we examine the application of magic, it can be deduced that the practise of esoteric magic is dependent on three abilities.

The Power of Three

The Power of Mind

The first is mental and is indicative of willpower and the ability to direct that influence in a particular and preselected trajectory. This is not as easy as it sounds; the mental agility required to sustain prolonged periods of focus and direction takes practise. It is not something that happens overnight, which is why so many magical traditions provide intense training for their students to master the power of the human mind. This skill is essential for the effective casting of spells and other works. To an extent we are all familiar with techniques that employ mental forces and agility in a secular manner. Daily affirmations and positive thinking are proven to increase well-being. One discipline in this spectrum is mindfulness, which is proven to have significant and positive influences on both mind and body.[66] Meditation, visualisation, and other techniques that actively work on the human mind are important practises that enable us to understand our own mental powers. In addition, the effects of such methods are not purely limited to the ethereal regions of the mind; on the contrary, they have a measurable effect on the wellness of the physical body. In any exploration of mental forces, it is inevitable that we encounter its ability to affect the real world, yet it continues to be invisible.

The more precise you are at using your mind, the more effective your magic will be. Magic calls for intense periods of concentration, and honing your mind's ability to be able to do this with ease is the first task of any budding Druid's tentative footsteps into magic. Therefore, if you are attracted to the concept of magic and its practise, take up a meditation routine or focus your mind on a new skill. Learning a new language is an excellent way to direct your ability to concentrate. Use the art of writing to direct your mental energy. Take to your imagination in creative ways that direct the flow of your mind and your will in a particular direction.

If you are anything like myself, your head is a hot mess for a good portion of the day. I have to really focus to get things done, and this includes magic. I may well be a Druid with decades of magical experience, but I am also easily distracted by nice shoes, anything colourful, and a mundane TV show. But I have learnt that when needed my mind can be directed with pinpoint accuracy. The manner by which I describe my mind is as a vast lake—there are rivers and streams running into it from all directions, there are shallow bits, rocky bits, unfathomable depths, and an occasional island. There are fish swimming about within it, there's the occasional heron that dive-bombs the surface, and the ducks are just a hot flapping mess that break the surface tension (my concentration) all the time. There's a kid over there skimming flat stones over its surface and one of those wild swimmers with a bright orange float trailing behind them so that we can identify the location of the body if they drown. It is a beguiling, belligerent, bemused mess. But I have to work, write books, and do magic, so I focus on that lake and hone in on a section where the water runs into the mouth of a river, and that river becomes narrower and narrower, and the water is crushed by the rocky banks; it can barely contain it. The

66 Williams and Penman, *Mindfulness*, 5–7.

narrower the river becomes, the greater my concentration, so I follow it consciously and with great effort. The lake is still there, but it is behind my concentration. My only focus is on the narrow stream that I allow to leave it. This stream could represent anything in my magical arsenal: healing, clarity, change, retribution. But tantamount to its effectiveness is that I maintain a hold on its trajectory and do not allow the lake to interfere. This is magical focus and the influence of my force of will.

The Power of Divination

The second ability is divination. In a traditional sense this is the using of tools that enable or facilitate clarity and guidance. These tools can be anything from the casting of bone fragments to runes or tarot cards—the methods are endless. But these methods also come with sensationalistic baggage. We can make assumptions about them, and often they can be incorrect or misinformed. Quite often divination is assumed as being entertainment; it is the futile search for the tall dark handsome stranger that probably does not exist. In a fairground sense, it is the search for a future that is absolute. In this example nothing is learned and no meaning is derived from the action. Human beings have a tendency to believe that the future is unchangeable, and its absolution may provide a degree of comfort, knowing that you can do nothing about it. In truth, the future is not fixed; instead, the future is an unfolding that is based on the trajectory of present events. True divination is not simply a fortunetelling device but a system by which we may determine the outcome of certain actions based on their current or altered trajectories. It differs from prognostication, which is based on the calculation of risks and the determination of possible outcomes based on your knowledge of the situation. In contrast, divination is the gleaning of information that suggests a hidden knowledge or the aid of powers that are occult, hidden from plain view.

The word *divination* means to summon or conjure or make something out by magical means. Its etymological roots are in the Old French term *divination* and the Latin *divinationem*; both terms mean to discover something that is hidden or obscure. You will also note that the word contains an element of "divine" from the Latin *divinare,* which literally translates as "to be inspired by a god." There is a lot to unpack in a word that comes with a tremendous amount of preconceived and often erroneous associations. Divination allows one to perceive the visible and invisible worlds in a manner that encourages clarity or to foresee how current actions may affect the future. It is not absolute; even in the most well-thought-out actions, there are variables that cannot be predicted.

Divination provides a tool by which the Druid can analyse the details of the act of magic to ensure its validity and effectiveness. Essentially divination is the creating of lists for and against, with arguments for both. The ancient Druids were renowned for their ability to prophesise and to counsel the decisions of kings. Taliesin, the prototypic Bard and prophetic spirit, frequently expresses this quality, in the Book of Taliesin there are ten poems concerned with *darogan*, meaning "prophesy." In a conversation with Taliesin, the renowned magician Merlin takes to divination by turning to gaze at the stars, and in doing so he says:

> I was carried away from myself and like a spirit I knew the acts of past peoples and could see the future. Then since I knew the secrets of things and flight of birds and the wandering motions of the stars and the gliding of the fishes.[67]

Merlin is describing the state of mind one can achieve in divination, which is to clearly see, hear, and sense. You may be familiar with other terms that describe these faculties in the form of clairvoyance (to see clearly), clairaudience (to hear clearly), and clairsentience (to feel clearly). Often associated with mediumistic and psychic pursuits, they are nonetheless words that describe the skills one develops through the practise of divination. In the Fourth Branch of the Mabinogi, the Druid and magician King Math was able to hear any whispering between people, however quiet, if the wind got hold of it. Examples abound throughout Celtic mythology and poetry of the wonder of divination and the ability to see clearly by occult insight and intuitive perception. As we look for examples in the past, what we discover is the propensity for Druids to make use of divination as a function of magic.

Divination provides a pathway to see the shadows of what might be, but not necessarily what will be. It informs the manner by which we work our magic. The Druid is a manipulator of these shadows, able to feel their way through the murky and unclear future and pull forth the shadows that are most likely to lead to the desired outcome. Then, in a process of working backwards from that shadow, the Druid finds the link to the present decision that will most likely yield the future result. In the art of divination, the Druid becomes the conductor of time and space, with their baton directing the threads between the past, the present, and the future.

67 Parry, *The Life of Merlin*, 33.

There are a number of tools that the Druid can employ to achieve this. In my practise my go-to tools are a set of bones from wild animals I have found deceased in my vicinity that I use as an oracle. To do this, I cast the bones, nine in total, onto a cloth that has a pattern upon it that allows me to read their positions. My first divination love was tarot; I discovered it as a teenager, and it continues to be my preferred method. Both these tools enable me to see the shadows of outcomes, and by playing with them I can bring them into focus and clear a path towards an outcome that is desired or necessary.

In magic this is useful, for the purpose of the magic might be unintentionally skewed or misdirected. Clarity may be needed to ensure that the right form of magic is being done for the right reasons. Divination provides us with the opportunity to analyse our intentions and determine the right cause of magical action. In addition, divination serves to inform and transform the matter at hand, even if it is only one's perception that is being transformed. If you are new to the divinatory arts or have had limited exposure to it, my hope is that this short discourse has served to transform your perception of what it actually is. In turn, it is your task to seek out a divination method that best suits you. What suits one individual may not suit another, but when you do find one that resonates with you, honour it by learning as much as you possibly can about it so that you have the best grounding in that particular system.

The Power of Theurgy

The third ability for effective magic is a process called theurgy, literally meaning "god working." This is the Druid's ability to communicate with nonhuman spirits or deities. That seemingly small sentence can be extremely problematic to anyone who is perplexed or has little understanding of what that means in a real-world sense. Essentially, theurgical work is the employing of specific deities or spirits that act as magical allies, i.e., powerful and experienced assistants that guide the practitioner and lend their power to the magical act. In addition, you may simply wish to seek the counsel or guidance of a particular deity. In the Welsh tradition there are patron deities that govern the forces and powers of magic: Manawydan, Cerridwen, Gwydion, and Math. Cerridwen represents the undercurrent of magic and our understanding of it, whereas Gwydion and Math represent that act of practical magic. Manawydan represents its application. The previous chapters will have offered you the groundwork in developing the necessary connection for theurgical work to be a component of your magical practise.

In the Spirit of Things

Many Druids work with nonhuman spirits that do not fall into the category of deity, so what is a spirit? Traditional dictionary definitions interpret a spirit as the animating or vital principle that gives life to an organism, and it is often described as the seat of emotions and character. In many religions and folk traditions, the spirit is believed to be the invisible component of an individual that is connected ethereally to the divine. In any definition of spirit, it is apparent that it does not refer to something solid or material but rather to the mind or the emotions. When one is new to Druidry, talk of spirits and gods may be baffling or even uncomfortable, particularly when they are often spoken almost as fact, with a presumption that everybody knows what we are talking about. This can be problematic, and often in those situations folks need to have an honest discussion about what that actually means. Scour any bookseller's titles of New Age, spiritual, or metaphysical books and you will find very little talk of "What is a spirit?" It is as if the foundation of the statement itself is taken as a given—that we all have a basic understanding and acceptance of what that is—and yet this is far from the truth.

I recall giving a presentation in the late 1990s where the subject was Welsh mythology in Pagan practise, and I talked of the characters as spirits and gods. Someone asked, "Can you tell me what you mean by a spirit?" The question floored me. I had no real answer and was suddenly aware of an enormous hole in my practise that I had not previously addressed. I felt I had an understanding of what a spirit was, but I had never had to articulate that to another person. Ask a hundred people that same question and you are likely to receive a hundred different answers, but it is important that as practitioners we have an understanding and an experiential knowledge of what that means. Realistically I can only offer you what I believe a spirit to be and how we might work with them.

In modern magical practise we are led to believe and often asked to believe that the entire world is populated with nonhuman entities—from elementals to fairies and all manner of other spiritual beings—that usually we cannot see with our physical eyes. So, if we can't see them, are they actually there? If they are there, how do we detect them? If we can't see them, are we somehow inferior to our peers and those who claim to see them all the time? I have worked in mortuaries and morgues my entire adult life, and you would think that in an environment like that there would be spirits aplenty. Surely a house of the dead must be like the departure zone of a busy airport? In truth, it isn't; any anomaly that does happen in those kinds of places is the exception and not the rule. Are there disembodied spirits of dead people wandering around the world intact and acting as they were in life, only invisible? It is my belief that is not so, but I do believe that the emotional energy expressed in life may remain and be detectable as an echo after death.

In my belief and practise, a spirit is the energetic and emotional expression of the animistic principle. I believe that everything is alive and contains within it a spark from the source, a universal principle that sings of the origin of all things. I believe that this energetic principle is in relationship with the world around it and is moulded and formed into an identity that sings of its uniqueness. I also believe that all things contain this—from a small daisy to a tree to a cat to a mountain. Druids tend to have an obsession with trees, and in turn they are believed to have spirits that we can communicate with, which might be useful when working magic, particularly if we need the assistance of an attribute unique to a specific species of tree. So does a tree spirit have two legs, two arms, and a head? No, not at all, but it can appear as such to someone who is wanting to connect with it. Humans have a tendency to anthropomorphise their environment, so we see shapes that emulate our form—this is why we see a man in the moon. Who knows what a squirrel sees? Possibly a squirrel.

We can all read a room. We have an inherent and instinctive ability to read a room's mood and energy. We can feel the atmosphere of a place and may often comment that it feels thick or oppressive. We can tell if someone has had an argument or if a person's mood is off. While there are subtle physical clues that give these things away, there is no doubt that most of us have experienced a deep sense and sometimes an unease from reading a room. What we are actually doing is sensing the invisible, and the most obvious are those that are driven by emotion. All these components are traditionally associated with spirits.

While we are composed of matter, we are driven by energy, and emotion is the one we are most programmed to sense and respond to. In essence, when you read a room, you are reading the spiritual output of a person or persons. In a Druidic sense, when I enter the grove that I am most accustomed to practising in, I read the room. The trees in this grove are old. They have moods, they respond to their environment, they communicate with one another. They are alive. I sense their spirit through my emotions and I reach out to them through my emotions. I find a place within me that is still and quiet, and then I raise my emotions in accordance to the magic I am practising—this might be love or compassion for healing, passion for change, anger for shifting blockages, or joy for transformation. I may use words to tell the trees what I am doing and ask for their help, but it is my emotions that I am convinced they sense the most. Do they reply? Yes. They do so by means of their energetic or emotional field, and in the stillness I open myself to detect emotion. Invariably a tree will respond to you through emotion; the task of a Druid is to detect and interpret that. This is the reason why it is said Druids can talk to trees.

The more we communicate emotionally, the better we become at it. Always read the room! If you are not accustomed to this, then start by observing something in the natural world—a tree, a plant, etc.—and watch it closely for a period of several months and preferably over the course of an entire year. Take note of the passing of the seasons and the effect it has, form a relationship, and learn to read the subtle signs of that being as it communicates with its surroundings. It is a member of a community of organisms, with one of those organisms being you. We are not separate, we are not distanced: we are all kin. Knowing this on a deep level is the key to opening channels of communication. We all have something in common. We can all feel and sense our environments.

In contrast, heightened states of awareness and ecstatic ritual activity can also enable you to be more perceptive to the invisible energies around you. Ecstatic rituals are techniques that involve drumming, dancing, chanting, or singing in a repetitive and prolonged manner that causes you to lose your inhibitions and limitations. They are immensely powerful techniques that have the ability to completely transform your perception of reality. It is often in these altered states that people will recount feeling intense emotions that they are receiving rather than expressing. Other people will see things from the corners of their eyes, indicating the presence of something or someone "other." Ecstatic techniques all serve to heighten your energy—your spirit, if you like—and in doing so, the rational and logical part of your being is forced to take a back seat, making you more receptive to the emotional energies around you.

This is how I communicate with spirits and the gods, either through still and silent emotional connection or heightened states of awareness. In either case, I am not striving to "see" a spirit, but to communicate. Often my encounters with spirits is not clear in the moment; there are times I must journal about it or sleep on it and other times I am able to feel a response within the duration of the practise. But we must be honest with ourselves here and accept that spirit communication is subjective and personal. It is a practise that we must engage with ourselves and fathom for ourselves, and it often involves assessing the nature of your reality and how you perceive the world around you. Essentially, nobody can do it for you. We can inspire one another, but we cannot and must not dictate what a spirit may or may not be.

In the folk traditions of my land, we have castes of spirits that are not nature orientated and appear entirely other, as if occupying the same world but on a different dimensional level that we are unable to comprehend. Some of them are associated with certain natural features, and our mythology offers tantalising glimpses of another reality that occupies the same space as we do, and yet they are cleft in twain, separated by a gossamer-thin veil that obscures one reality from another. Liminal times of the year like Mayday or Halloween are each called an *ysbrydnos,* or spirit night, where the veils thin enough for the different worlds to become aware of each other. In almost all cases of the fair folk in Wales, liminality is the key to perceiving them, meaning times and places that are betwixt and between. Magic and its practise often intentionally create liminal spaces in which we can become aware of the subtle forces around us. In my experience, it is emotion that is the conduit for communication and connection. My magical practise intentionally acts upon my emotions to be receptive to the emotions that surround me. In doing so, I am more able to sense that which is called spirit.

The Skills of Magic

According to author Dean Radin in his book *Real Magic*, which I highly recommend that you read, magic is the application of two skills, namely attention and intention; in turn, these are modulated by belief, imagination, emotion, and clarity.[68] While subjective in and of themselves, each modulator can be seen as cogs in the wheels of the three abilities necessary for effective magical work: our mental abilities, our divinatory skills, and our ability to communicate with the spiritual principle. In addition to these, the act of magic is often ritualised into patterns of actions that reinforce the intention and maintain attention. While the accoutrements of magic are not wholly necessary—as in altars and incense burners, candles and cloaks, etc.—they do have their place. The intention of any magical tool or item is to liminalise the proceedings; they add an air of the extraordinary and affect our senses and, in turn, our emotions. Some like the accoutrements and others do not. I fall into the first camp; I adore them. I have an old wicker

---

68 Radin, *Real Magic*, 73.

picnic basket packed with all manner of magical tools, wands, incense, candles, lighters, votives, cauldrons, and all sorts of delights. I have a particular love for incense as a magical and devotional tool. I find that working in a space that is slightly obscured by fragrant smoke is conducive to emotional connection. It transforms a space and makes it appear liminal.

In addition to the above qualities, a further three practical tasks accentuate and give substance to any magical work. The first is visualisation, where we imagine or bring to mind the outcome of the magic and maintain our attention upon it. The second is gesticulation, where bodily movements are used to direct the intention in a certain pattern; these can be ritual gestures or the repetitive beating of a drum. The third task is vocalisation. Our voices are energy, and voice modulation can intensely affect the space you occupy and reaffirm your intention. To a Druid, vocalisation intimately connects us to the cauldron of the Bardic spirit.

* * * * * *

To come full circle, do Druids practise magic? Some do and some don't. This Druid certainly does! You may choose not to, and it will make you no less of a Druid. The magic that I practise is predominantly a form of folk magic that is inspired by Welsh culture. Much of it involves the making of a *swyn* (singular) or *swynion* (plural), which translates to mean a spell, a charm, or a magical remedy. Regardless of whether the magic I practise is the simple lighting of a single candle or a full-blown two-hour-long ritual with fanfare and pomp, both contain all elements described in this chapter. On face value these might appear indistinguishable from Witchcraft practises, and indeed many Druids are also practising witches. Druidry is my spirituality. It is simultaneously devotional, philosophical, and cultural, with magic being an important cornerstone of my practise.

So, where do you go from here? If you are new to the magical arts, your first task is to educate yourself on the various methods of practising magic. A glance at any metaphysical publisher's catalogue will yield an overwhelming array of books on magical practise. To begin with, keep it simple and do not be overwhelmed. The information contained in this chapter coupled with the suggested reading list at the end of this book should hold you in good stead.

Let's pause here and consider the nature and function of magic in your potential practise.

· · · · · ·

☞ *Magic is...*

....
....
....

☞ *Is magic necessary for the practise of Druidry?*

....
....
....

☞ *I believe or do not believe in magic because...*

....
....
....

☞ *Magic will or will not have a function in my Druid practise because...*

....
....
....

☞ *I believe that magic works because...*

....
....
....

☞ *I have experienced the result of magic by...*

....
....
....

☞ *The skills I require for effective magical practise are...*

....
....
....

☞ *I am or am not drawn to divination because...*

....
....
....

☞ *The type/s of divination I am drawn to is/are...*

....
....
....

☞ *Magic will or will not enhance my Druidry because...*

....
....
....

☞ *I define a spell as...*

....

....

....

☞ *I want to practise magic because...*

....

....

....

FOLLOWING THE CYCLE
OF THE SEASONS

THE CYCLE OF the seasons are the stage upon which the Druid dances with the sun, moon, and stars, and it is often referred to as the wheel of the year. In a secular sense, people are generally familiar with seasonal festivals that punctuate the year and give reason for pause or celebration. To the Druid, the turning of the wheel of the seasons offers more than an opportunity for celebration; they provide a way in which we sense our part in the drama of the seasons and move deeper into relationship with the forces that govern all life on earth.

We live on a planet in a Goldilocks zone, not too hot and not too cold, with a moon that is precisely placed to occasionally totally obscure the sun's light. We can experience seasonal phenomena that remind us of the mysteries and magic of life and the interconnected systems we are a part of. We are surrounded by so much magic that often the mundanity of life can shroud our vision of the wonder we are a part of. The wheel of the year provides us with precious opportunities to pause and be active participants in the ever-turning cycles. With each passing year we are reminded of the cycles of our living, reflected in the seasons, from birth through maturity, into old age, to death and rebirth. The seasons offer opportunities for us to gather as a community of fellow Druids, deepening the connections we have between each other. And all of this happens like clockwork, all around us, all of the time.

It is so easy to become bogged down with the humdrum of everyday living—we are busy balancing jobs, careers, family obligations, social lives, the laundry! It is no surprise that we often feel the need to jet off to other climes in order to stop and recharge our batteries. I used to feel that the year was running away from me, and I am certain time is accelerating at an alarming pace as I get older. When I began my own journey into Druidry and Paganism, I found that attuning to the cycles of the seasons helped transform the relationship I had with the world around me. In my youth I had barely paid it any heed or attention other than being grateful for gifts at Christmas and the opportunity to dress up at Halloween.

When my focus shifted as I deepened my studies and Pagan practise, I began to see the world through very different eyes. The transformation was subtle, but within a couple of years of having stopped to ritualise and celebrate the wheel of the year, I was changing as a person. On the surface this may appear simplistic—just taking notice of what is happening around you—but its ability to transform is immensely powerful. When we observe and listen deeply to the moods of our planet and the behaviour of our locality, our perception of our place within it begins to change. For the majority of my formative and early adult life, nature was something that happened around me; as a Druid I understand that human nature is an integral part of nature. We are not separate beings to whom nature is something that occasionally happens or impedes upon. Humankind has long since tried to control and govern nature, and yet we cannot. Like the cells within our own bodies, we are working parts of a whole.

As I started on my journey, actively observing the cycles of the seasons was my first step into a life of ritual and magic, and to this day it forms an integral aspect of who I am as a Druid. Divided into bite-size pieces, the Druid wheel of the year offers us something to celebrate and connect to approximately every six weeks or so, sometimes even more often, and we shall explore what these are in the coming pages. However, it must be understood that the cycle of the seasons as presented in this book is not an antiquated system. There is no archaeological or literal evidence to suggest that the Druids observed them all, but there is evidence to suggest that our Neolithic ancestors certainly marked the stations of the sun by aligning their monuments to the sunrise or sunsets of the midsummer and midwinter solstices. In Welsh mythology *Calan Mai* (Mayday) and *Calan Gaeaf* (Halloween) are significant periods in the year, marked as *Ysbrydnos* (spirit nights), in which the people believed the veils between this world and the other was at its thinnest.

The popularity of the wheel of the year in its totality, usually composed of eight stations, is fairly new and attributed to various influences: Iolo Morganwg, Jacob Grimm and his work *Teutonic Mythology*, Margaret Murray's *The Witch-Cult in Western Europe*, and Robert Graves (famed for creating the Celtic tree year) and his book *The White Goddess*. By the mid-twentieth century, the idea of an ancient Celtic year had become increasingly popular and influenced the pioneering fathers of modern Druidry and Wicca, Ross Nichols and Gerald Gardner. By the '60s the idea was given further credence by the philologist Nora Chadwick[69] and archaeologist Ann Ross.[70] Chadwick declared that the ancient Celts only celebrated four primary stations of the year that corresponded to agricultural cycles. She also suggested that the ancient Celtic year commenced at Samhain (on or around November 1 in the modern calendar); however, there is no firm evidence to suggest this was the case. In contrast, Wales has literal sources that actively refute this notion.[71]

These ideas quickly took on a life of their own, with the new Druids, witches, and Wiccans keen to lap up any information that appeared to arise from reputable sources. While the previously mentioned authors were experts in their field, they alas made incorrect assumptions of a uniformed "Celtic year." As a new age of Pagan writing was spawned through the 1960s, '70s, and '80s, a general assumption was made based on the available material of the time; Pagan authors were informed by the conclusions of earlier authors. A general consensus soon arose that the Celtic year bore names that were distinctly Irish Gaelic, and these were quickly adopted into general Pagan practise. Regardless of location, Samhain was the name for Halloween wherever one lived, Beltane for Mayday, and so forth. With little question, Pagan authors took to these names like ducks to water, and by the end of the twentieth century the Celtic year, with its beautiful antiquated names, had stuck. The influence of this was so great that as I embarked on my Pagan and Druidic studies, I too adopted these titles, which were not in my native tongue nor the tongue of the ancient British Celts. It was years before I questioned this.

69 Chadwick and Dillon, *The Celtic Realms*, 108.
70 Ross, *Everyday Life of the Pagan Celts*, 151–154.
71 Hutton, *Stations of the Sun*, 408–412.

Reach for any book in the general New Age or Pagan genre and the wheel of the year will generally run in this order using these words: Samhain, Imbolc, Beltane, Lughnasadh. Commonly referred to as fire festivals or agricultural feasts, they are punctuated at their midpoints by the solstices and the equinoxes. In total, eight festivals or feast days mark the passage of the Pagan wheel of the year. The nature of the names arises from the Goidelic language of Ireland with similarities in Manx and Scots Gaelic; these are linguistically distinct from Brythonic Celtic languages of mainland Britain. By the mid- to late-twentieth century, the idea of a wheel of the year offered the new Paganism a modern method that incorporated ancient and folkloric components and provided a cohesive system that punctuated the year into a structure that could easily be ritualised. Time has passed, and now we must step away from long-standing erroneous traditions that made sweeping assumptions about the usage and function of seasonal festivals and reclaim the sovereignty of the festivals as they were and are practised in one's own land and within one's own ancestral stream. These names are deeply special and indicative of the Goidelic/Irish culture. For me to use them as a generalisation of a pan-Celtic wheel of the year is to do a disservice to that culture and their language and ignore the value of my own cultural connection to the cycle of the seasons.

What is important to consider here is the often-erroneous thought that ancient must be better. Modern Druidry is precisely that—modern—and it is inspired by the past, not defined by it. The fact that in its current form there is a cohesive structure to the year has served to empower and build community, as the wheel of the year has become a valued practise. In Welsh Druidry the influences for the modern wheel of the year come primarily from three distinct sources: the archaeological record, mythology, and Iolo Morganwg.

The archaeological record demonstrates that several surviving monuments in the British Isles are aligned to the sunrise of midsummer and the sunset of the midwinter solstice. This hints at a calendrical function that may have been necessary to provide the ancestors with guidance of agricultural relevance. In contrast, Welsh mythology does not mention any of the solstices or equinoxes, only the festivals of Calan Mai (May Day) and Calan Gaeaf (Halloween). Fast forward to the late eigthteenth century: Iolo Morganwg omits any mention of the four agricultural festivals, focusing instead on the solstices and equinoxes. We cannot be entirely certain of Morganwg's sources, much of which probably stemmed from his own imagination, but he is an important figure in both modern Druidry and Welsh culture. He is credited for giving the Welsh people a cultural and historical reawakening that we are indebted to, and the terms assigned to the wheel of the year by Iolo are now generally accepted in many modern Druid groups and orders.

According to Morganwg in his collection of work called *Barddas*:

> *Yr hên Gymry a ddechreynt y flwyddyn drannoeth i'r dydd byrraf o'r gaeaf, sef ar droad yr haul*. The ancient Cymry began the year on the morrow of the shortest day of the winter, that is on the turn of the sun.[72]

With that in mind, modern Welsh Druidry commences the wheel of the year at Midwinter and is presented thus[73]:

FESTIVAL NAME	SECULAR NAME	COMMON PAGAN NAME	APPROXIMATE DATE
Alban Arthan	Winter Solstice	Yule or Midwinter	On or around December 21
Diwrnod Santes Dwynwen	St. Dwynwen's Day	Dwynwen's Day	January 25
Calan or Gwyl Braint/Ffraid	Candlemas	Imbolc	On or around February 2
St. David's Day	St. David's Day	St. David's Day	March 1
Alban Eilir	Vernal Equinox	Eostra or Ostara	On or around March 21
Calan Mai	May Day	Beltane	April 30–May 1
Alban Hefin	Summer Solstice	Midsummer or Litha	On or around June 21
Calan or Gwyl Awst	First Harvest or Lammas	Lughnasadh or Lammas	August 1
Alban Elfed	Autumn Equinox or second harvest	Autumn Equinox or Mabon	On or around September 21
Calan Gaeaf	Halloween	Samhain	October 31– November 1

72 Williams, *Barddas*, 416–417.
73 The wheel as presented in this book is pertinent to the Northern Hemisphere. In the Southern Hemisphere the festivals are reversed; i.e., Calan Gaeaf would be celebrated on April 30, Midwinter on June 21, and so forth.

You will note in the calendar that there are four seasonal festivals that begin with the word *Alban*, which means a period of three months, a quarter, equinox, and solstice. Poetically they can be taken to mean the high point or zenith of each season.

Iolo Morganwg defines them like this:

- Alban Arthan is the calend of January
- Alban Eilir is the calend of spring
- Alban Hefin is the calend of summer
- Alban Elfed is the calend of October[74]

Arthan is derived from the term little bear and may be a reference to the birth of Arthur as a representation of the divine child. This is the time of midwinter solstice and the rebirth of the sun as he begins his journey back towards summer. It is the shortest day and longest night of the year, but all that darkness contains a seed of hope. It is that seed, the promise and potential for new life, that penetrates all the festivals that circumambulate or are directly inspired by the midwinter solstice. Christmas, Yule, Hanukkah—they all celebrate light and hope. At this time Druids acknowledge this tipping point, after which the days will begin to lengthen.

Eilir means the season of spring, it is the vernal equinox, when day and night share equal time. While spring storms can still cause havoc and eastern winds can bring snow and cold to the British Isles, the sun is stronger and the plant kingdom is responding to his warming rays; the trees bud, and we generally begin to feel better within ourselves as we receive more radiation from the sun. At this time the Druid celebrates this balance and the battle between light and dark.

Hefin is summer, and Alban Hefin is the feast of midsummer, and although we are only in June, it feels as if there is so much more summer to come. In truth, the sun turns on his heels at this point in the year and begins his journey back towards winter. The days begin to shorten once more, with each day following the summer solstice holding a little less light than the day before, and yet the sun is at his most powerful. There is much to celebrate as his heat continues to bake the earth and her larder. It is a time when the Druid celebrates the intensity and vibrancy of life in its prime and simultaneously acknowledges that at its zenith, life must slowly begin the journey towards death.

74 Williams, *Barddas*, 418–419.

Elfed means autumn; this is the final harvest. The earth has provided all she can give to sustain life. The golden fields are now empty, decorated only with bare stalks. But in the woodlands and hedgerows nature offers one last hurrah, with branches straining under the weight of fruit. It is the earth's final gift before winter. It is the time when the Druid takes stock, contemplates the message of maturity, and prepares the larder for the coming winter. In a practical sense it is the time when the Druid is at their busiest, foraging and creating magical elixirs, medicines, wines, and preserves that hold within them the powers of all the seasons.

To complement his stations of the sun, Iolo also offered advice regarding suitable offerings for each station in the form of a triad, which reads thus:

> The three common oblations of a Bard/Druid, one is milk contribution which is offered on Alban Hefin; the second is meal contribution on Alban Elfed; the third is honey contribution which is offered on Alban Arthan, and portions of each of the three on Alban Eilir, that is when new songs are privileged. And the poor, aliens and strangers are to have their portions from the three oblations at those times, since they have no due maintenance from land and chattels.[75]

In addition to the four Albanau (plural of Alban) are the four Calan festivals. *Calan* is derived from the Latin word *calends,* meaning the first day of a month. Often in Cymraeg the term *gwyl,* meaning a holiday or a feast, is also used to describe these festivals. It is not clear why Iolo Morganwg chose to define the Albanau as the calends of a particular month.

Calan or Gwyl Braint/Ffraid

After Alban Arthan, the first Calan we arrive at is that of *Calan* or *Gwyl Braint/Ffraid.* Both these nouns are feminine and cognate with the Irish Brigit. Legends attest that Brigit of Ireland, or perhaps a version of her in a metaphorical sense, travelled to Wales across the sea on a small square turf of grass. She settled here and a church was established in her name, where she was known as St. Ffraid. On the Island of Anglesey, she appears in another guise as the tutelary spirit/deity of the River Braint. Braint is also cognate with Brig, Brigit, and Brittania. Her feast day on or around the second of February is usually marked by rivers flooding and breaking their banks and the arrival

---

75 Williams, *Barddas* part 2, 55.

of snowdrops. During this time Druids will celebrate the first stirrings of spring. Albeit snow, ice, and tempests may continue for some weeks, her festival is one of hope that soon the sun will shine brighter. In addition, Ffraid/Braint in her guise as a goddess emulates the qualities of healing, poetry, and smithcraft. The significance of this festival is its ability to awaken within us an understanding of how subtle the regenerative powers of the earth are. The smallest bulbs, deep underground, can sense the pull of the growing sun and stretch their stems up to break the surface and burst into flower. In particular, snowdrops symbolise resilience and hope; they contain the promise of summer. Devotional or ritualistic work during this time would focus on the regenerative powers of nature and those within ourselves.

Calan Mai

Calan Mai, derived from the name of the month of May, heralds the true arrival of summer and its fertile and fruitful energies. By this point in the wheel, the earth has greened, and the blossoms of late spring and early summer decorate the landscape. It is traditionally a time for communal celebrations that usually involved fire, perhaps to symbolise the heat and passion of fertility. In mythology it is the day when the figures of Gwyn ap Nudd (winter) and Gwythyr (summer) fight an eternal battle for the hand of the maiden Creiddylad. In lore this battle is seen in the seasonal positions of the twins depicted in the constellation of Gemini as they turn through the cosmos. For the Druid, Calan Mai represents the life-giving forces of nature in action and sexuality in all its wonder and magic.

Calan Awst

This feast is derived from Awst to mean the eighth month of the year and the equivalent of August. If the previous two Calans are the seeding and bursting forth of the forces of summer, Calan Awst is the point at which they are baked into something that can be transformed to sustain us through the coming months. The sun's power has literally cooked the earth. It is ripe for the harvest, but at this point it is not in a form that can immediately nourish; it must be worked and transformed by busy hands into a state by which it can be digested. It is the point of sacrifice in its literal sense of "to make something sacred." The golden earth is reaped and the heads of wheat cut to be ground and milled into flour. It is perhaps the season that we are most alienated from, as the processes of modern agriculture have removed the harvest from the majority of our lives. We take it for granted that fruits and produce are available out of season, on demand. The majority of people no longer work the fields; we have lost the appreciation for the sacrifice of nature and the bounty of the harvest. The Druid attempts to realign this discordance in a way that brings the sacred nature of the harvest back into focus. We may do this by learning about agricultural methods or working an allotment or garden to glean an understanding of what the earth provides.

Calan Gaeaf

The final Calan is that of Calan Gaeaf, the calends of winter. The earth can provide no more sustenance, and all that can be harvested has been called in. It was the time of year that our ancestors feared the most, uncertain whether they would survive the winter. Historical associations with this time of year express the mysteries of death and memory and the descent into darkness. As the earth turns skeletal and appears dead, we are reminded of our own inevitable deaths. All Hallows Eve, All Soul's Day, All Saint's Day, Halloween—all these festivals have at their heart a function of remembrance and honouring of those who have gone before us, or the acknowledgement of someone who has been elevated by the process of death into something other, like a saint. At Calan Gaeaf the Druid honours the ancestors and the necessary forces of death and decay.

* * * * * *

In common practise the wheel of the year is divided into eight portions. You will note in the chart on page 181 an additional two dates exist in the Welsh tradition, namely Dwynwen's Day on January 25 and St. David's Day on March 1. Dwynwen is the Welsh patron saint of love and sick animals. Her shrine is located on the island of Llanddwyn, off the southwest coast of Anglesey. She has been adopted in a Neopagan sense as a goddess. On her feast day, the Druid acknowledges and honours the forces of love. In secular Wales, her day is celebrated in a manner similar to Valentine's Day. March 1 is the festival of St. David's Day, the patron saint of Wales. In a secular and spiritual sense we celebrate the nation and language of Cymru. For a Druid it offers the opportunity to pause and honour the struggles that Cymru as a country and her people have faced, the sacrifices we have made, and our achievements. In my personal practise, it is a day where I work with the Red Dragon of Wales as an archetype for the tenacity of Welsh people's spirit.

In addition to the divisions demonstrated previously, the Welsh tradition also actively acknowledges two phases of the moon, the full moon of each month and the sixth day of the new moon. The latter has its roots in a statement by Pliny, who wrote that the ancient Druids harvested the mistletoe, believed to be their most sacred plant, on the sixth day of the moon.[76] Immortalised in the exquisite oil painting by Henri Paul Motte, the image of the Druids high up in the great oak trees cutting the sacred mistletoe with a golden sickle remains a powerful image to this day, one that has since influenced the popular perception of the Druids. Colloquial traditions on the Isle of Anglesey have perpetuated this tradition, with the mid-twentieth-century magical group Y Cylch Cyfrin ("the mystic circle") maintaining this practise, one which the Anglesey Druid Order continues to observe. In his influential book *The Triumph of the Moon*, Professor Ronald Hutton briefly recounts his involvement with a Welsh-language television documentary about the Y Cylch Cyfrin in the mid 1990s, when the last surviving member of that group was still alive. Hutton confirmed the existence of the group as a genuine local spiritual tradition.[77] It is believed that their greatest festival was the Thursday after the January full moon, though nothing remains in writing or the vernacular to explain the reason or significance of this date. In the current tradition of the Anglesey Druid Order, the sixth day of the new moon is auspicious for the practising of magic. During the full moon, many modern Druid orders and groups use this time to focus on the principles of peace—of finding peace within ourselves and the wish for peace throughout the world.

At the conclusion of this chapter, consider the following questions:

⁕ ⁕ ⁕ ⁕ ⁕ ⁕

---

76 Hutton, *Blood and Mistletoe*, 14.
77 Hutton, *Triumph of the Moon*, 303–305.

☞ *My favourite season is...*

....

....

....

☞ *My favourite festival is...*

....

....

....

☞ *I value or do not value the wheel of the year because...*

....

....

....

☞ *I mark or celebrate the wheel of the year by...*

....

....

....

☞ *Why should I observe the wheel of the year?*

....

....

....

18

MEDITATION

MEDITATION IS A peculiar subject for many, filled with misconceptions and heightened expectations of 3D, super-high-definition visions of another world or landscape. There may be some people who truly do perceive their visions in 8K and super surround sound, but they are few and far between, and you must not lose heart if your visions do not live up to those experiences. In my early days of exploring Druidry, it was apparent that the precursor to any Druidic work or ritual involved a form of meditation—a practise that continues to this day. Alas, I did not entirely know what a meditation was or indeed what would happen within one. As a young explorer of the magical arts, I recall most vividly being mortified that my inner visions were nothing like the crisp, clear versions of my peers at the time. It left me feeling dejected and inferior. I felt I had fundamentally failed at one of the go-to-methods that I perceived as essential to Druidry. It led me to a place where whenever someone would utter the words "Now close your eyes and relax," the most common introduction to initiate a meditation session, my heart would literally sink. In fact, the opposite of relaxation would happen. I found myself becoming agitated and stressed by the mere thought of having to meditate.

I knew that I could not do it for love nor money, not that I entirely knew what I was meant to be doing or what was expected of me in the first place. It left me feeling like a charlatan, sitting there and going along with the group—keeping up with the Joneses, if you like, for the sake of toeing the line. But what was this line, and why on earth was I toeing it? I had to get to the bottom of what was becoming an irritation and a fiasco. I turned to my trusted Oxford Dictionary to see what they had to say about the definition of meditation: "The action or practice of meditating."

That was not at all useful. In turn, they defined the word *meditate* as "To focus one's mind for a time for spiritual purposes and for relaxation."

I could certainly appreciate the first part of that sentence, but for relaxation? It was having the opposite effect for me. So, quietly and assuredly, I went off to explore what all this meant and why it was and is such an inexorable aspect of modern-day spiritual expression. It is important at this juncture to say that this was happening thirty years ago and was a task easier said than done. With no Google to help, the local library was my only source of inspiration, and very little was yielded other than the odd book on yoga that served only to baffle me further and a small book on Transcendental Meditation that appeared quite different to what was happening in Pagan circles.

In 1990, finding good books on magical traditions and the occult was rare in Wales; one needed to hunt far and wide for them. I eventually came across a copy of the book that I believe changed the course of my spiritual path forever. In a small tome by American author Scott Cunningham called *Magical Herbalism*, he claims that meditation "stills the conscious mind to the point that psychic messages may become known."[78]

I believe it was the manner that he stated the function of meditation that struck a chord within me. "The point that psychic messages may become known" implied that the process itself is subtle, not cinematic; powerful, yes, but not dramatic; ethereal, not earthly. I understood what was meant by *psychic*, which in itself is a fairly loaded term, but I took it to mean the opposite of that which is physical, instead relating directly to the experience of the spirit. Psychic is a term that refers to experiences that are outside or beyond the articulation of natural and scientific principles. It is not, as common lore would have you believe, a power that only a few possess, and it is not limited to impressive expressions of prediction or dramatic supernatural powers. It is subtle and engages the senses in a way that we are actually quite accustomed and programmed to achieve.

However, my sojourns into various Pagan circles had implied that visions in meditation would appear very much like an observation of the real world, and that was not my experience at all. Others could see and taste and feel, while I felt nothing other than

---

78 Cunningham, *Magical Herbalism*, 58.

foolish. How could the visions be as real and solid as the world I physically occupied? Shouldn't I be relaxing and emptying my mind, not wandering in flowery otherworldly fields? What on earth was going on?

I concluded from what little information I could find that the art of meditation began with a relaxation technique, often involving a focus on one's breathing, followed by concentrating on a specific intention or visualised journey to allow certain influences the ability to communicate with one's mind. But was this meditation or imagination or both?

Eventually I realised that while every good intention was utilised in the application of these "meditation" sessions, they were, in fact, a jumbled yet well-intended concoction of various techniques. A general internet search on the subject of meditation today will yield a million results, but very quickly one will discover that meditation falls into various classifications:

- relaxation

- gratitude

- spiritual

- focused

- transcendental

- mindfulness

- movement

- visualisation

The final entry, visualisation meditation, felt more akin to what I was experiencing in New Age and Pagan circles, where one was required to follow a storyline or narrative. These storylines followed a set pattern—an introduction, an action, and an exit. Within the action sequence, one would often meet or converse with an otherworldly being or deity and receive advice, guidance, or be given an object or symbol pertinent to one's experience. This was never a part of my experience. Generally, I would fall asleep during the relaxation process or my mind would wander to places I could not steer it back from. It felt pointless and stupid and left me quite bereft that I was failing at what was seemingly a fundamental practise of modern spirituality. It transpired that it was all a matter of perspective, and what my mind needed were boxes into which I could place and label the various techniques and methods and thus make sense of them.

I concluded that what I required within my practise were three distinct forms of meditation:

- relaxation

- visualisation

- walking

Relaxation meditation is focusing on a technique that brings about a profound sense of stillness, calm, and serenity, the result of which dramatically affects your mind and body. On a physical level, this technique will lower your blood pressure and allow your body to achieve a state of healing rest that is akin to the deepest patterns of sleep but without the loss of your conscious mind. You are essentially still in control. Several methods can be utilised to achieve this state of meditative consciousness, from focusing on one's breath, music, subtle natural sounds, etc. In my own practise of relaxation meditation, I utilise a modern phenomenon called ASMR, an acronym for Autonomous Sensory Meridian Response. My mind tends to wander anywhere but that which I wish to focus upon, therefore I determined that I required an aid to assist my efforts, with the most effective one being ASMR.

ASMR has a physical component where one feels a tingling sensation that usually runs from the crown of the head and down the back of the neck and spine. In moments it can lead to a slowing of the breath and heart rate and lead into a profound state of relaxation. Consider the sound and physical reaction to someone running their fingernails down a blackboard or grinding one's teeth against wool; these are the unpleasant aspects of ASMR, a physical and mental reaction to external stimuli. Studies into the phenomenon are still in their infancy, but as of 2018 over 13 million ASMR videos had been uploaded to YouTube. These videos reproduce common ASMR triggers that initiate the response. The triggers are many and varied, from whispering to chewing to brushing, stroking, and page turning. Trigger videos can be found by searching for "ASMR Triggers" on YouTube.

The majority of ASMR videos and sound files make use of binaural microphones, which enable the sounds recorded to move from one ear to the other and back again. In my own experience they lead to a profound state of relaxation where I connect to my own body and, by proxy, the very source of the universe itself. I utilise ASMR for deep relaxation. With an arsenal of favourite videos at my fingertips and noise-cancelling headphones to heighten the experience, I use this method at least once a day. I find the physical and mental reaction to ASMR a powerful tool for relaxation.

Visualisation meditation is an active process. It may begin with an introductory sequence that causes the body to relax but leads to actively seeing the subject or journey that is being undertaken. Having grandiose expectations about the vitality and vividness of the experience may lead you, as it did me, to disappointment. But do not lose heart, for in the twenty-first century we have a myriad of technologies that can assist us in exploring the subtle. In my own practise, I make use of noise-cancelling headphones for any visualisation work I undertake, unless I am in a group session and need to listen to the facilitator. Listening to a pre-recorded guided visualisation through headphones certainly works better for me. If I have memorised the journey beforehand, I will often make use of white or pink noise files, again from YouTube, to assist my focus. Many of these files are well over an hour long and provide an excellent resource for shifting the patterns of one's consciousness.

The third example is walking meditation, a particular favourite practise of mine. It is, as you would expect, meditating while walking. It is perhaps the simplest technique, yet its simplicity does not denigrate its effectiveness. I am fortunate to live by a forest in which I am at liberty to walk in at any time of the day or night. There are times when I walk there for no reason other than to take in the peace and serenity and enjoy some good fresh air and exercise. At other times I will embark on my walk with the sole intention of gleaning insight or clarity to a problem or an issue in my life, or to seek inspiration from the subtle realms beyond the ordinary senses. To do this I prepare beforehand by journaling the issue at hand and what particular outcome I desire. "Should I take this new job?" might be an example of a clear and concise question to ponder. "What is the nature of inspiration?" might be vaguer and yet equally as transformative.

For the first seven minutes of my walk, I listen to an ASMR file of my choosing through my noise-cancelling headphones. This enables my mind to still from the humdrum of my day while my body is busily engaged in the automatic function of walking. As my mind settles and my body warms to the physical exercise, I begin to ponder the issue at hand and maintain my awareness on it. At the conclusion of the seven minutes, I disengage the sound file, remove the headphones, and continue to walk. In this relaxed state, with my issue in mind, I walk purposefully through the landscape, allowing any input from the natural world to pass through me but without hindering active thought. Instead, I allow them to contribute to the experience with the croak of a raven, the creaking of trees, the whistle of the wind through branches. A walking meditation is the assimilation of all these things into the mind to meld and blend with the swirling thoughts that express the intended question or issue. It is a form of immersion that is slightly beyond the ordinary—an acute awareness of your environment but in a manner that does not distract from the power of thought. At the conclusion of the walk, I return home, go about my business, and then hours later I journal the memory of the walk.

Is visualisation meditation the same as imagination?

The lines between the imagination and active visualization meditation are blurred and perhaps a matter of semantics. However, in any study of the subtle and the psychic, one must not be disparaging of imagination or simply put the experience down to the fronds of imagination alone. For it is indeed through our imagination that we begin to perceive the vitality and reality of the subtle planes of being. By honing one's imaginative skills, your ability to engage in visualisation meditation will significantly improve. The images and visions that one "sees" during a visualised meditative journey are in essence the same forms as that which you see in your imagination. Images in imagination or meditation have neither volume nor mass—they share that same commonality—and yet the results of imagination can lead to expression that has both volume and mass.

Read the following short instructions and then pause your reading and perform the following exercises.

EXERCISE

Close your eyes and take your imagination into your kitchen. Go immediately to the nearest drawer or cupboard that is the closest to your sink; left or right, it matters not. Open it and tell yourself what it contains. Describe the contents as thoroughly as you can.

Now take your imagination to your bedroom and do the same thing with whatever you have next to the side of the bed you are accustomed to sleeping on. Is it a bedside cabinet? A table? A shelf? A wall? Whatever it is, describe it out loud and to yourself.

Now open your eyes and cast your mind to the contents of your purse or wallet or personal bag. Describe its contents as thoroughly as you can, including colours and textures.

. . . . . .

For the majority of people, the above exercise is easily achievable, for it relies on a combination of factors: memory, recall, emotional connection, and imagination. The first three factors are functions of the brain's ability to memorise things and places and bridge the connection between your conscious and subconscious mind. The fourth element, the imagination, brings it all to life. The more you consider the contents of the kitchen drawer or cupboard, the more descriptive and accurate your vision will be. But the question is, are you actually seeing these things or simply recalling them from memory? A neurologist would tell that you are simply recalling them; a Druid would tell you that you are seeing them in your mind by the power of your imagination and subtle senses.

Your emotional connection to this exercise is personal and indicative of your everyday living. They are in all likelihood fairly neutral in expression, and any emotional association you have to these objects are familiar and benign. But there is significantly more to the power of imagination...

EXERCISE

Close your eyes and imagine a large mountain range before you. These are your own created mountains, so you decide what they actually look like. There are thick gray clouds above them, possibly heralding rain. Now imagine what it would look like if a sailing ship, complete with billowing sails, was to sail right out of those clouds and float gracefully towards you. Mountains, clouds, and a flying ship. Add colour and movement to the scene. If it helps, speak it out loud as you describe to yourself what you are seeing. Can you see any people on the ship's decks waving to you? Play with it. This is your created world; make it fabulous!

. . . . . .

Our imagination allows us to create imagery of things that exist and don't exist in the ordinary world. Most people are capable of generating an imagined image of their dinner last night, or they can equally and just as effectively imagine the impossible sight of a sailing ship flying out of a cloud bank. In both cases the imagery that you have created is just as real, albeit one is created from memory, whereas the other is created by cognitive processes not entirely understood by the scientific community. What is relevant here is that you can actually "see" them.

In addition to visual imagery, the imagination can also initiate powerful emotional responses that can lead to elation, joy, or terror. We are equally capable of imagining a flying ship as we are a dark and foreboding apparition that hovers at the bottom of the bed. The majority of people may well have experienced the sense of deep foreboding from the appearance of a dark human-shaped entity lurking in the corner of a room that one may not be wholly familiar with. By the flick of a light switch we discover the figure is merely a dressing gown hanging from a coat hook on the back of a door. But for a moment, if not several, the apparition was real and filled with vitality and energy. The more we fuel such an apparition, the more real it becomes. The power of one's imagination is limitless in its ability to affect the mind and the body. Fear and joy are opposite sides of the same coin; the coin itself is the imagination. What is important to note here is that what you actually "see" during a visualised meditation is in essence exactly the same as the images that you have just imagined in the previous little exercises. They are subtle, but do not confuse subtlety with vagueness; their ability to affect and effect you are indisputable.

Now let's look at your imagination with your eyes wide open.

Again, familiarise yourself with the following words or speak them into a recording or smart device and play them back as you perform the exercise.

EXERCISE

You may sit or stand. Focus your attention on a single spot on the wall before you. You may blink as you would ordinarily. Take a deep breath in through your nose and exhale sharply through your mouth. Slowly become aware of your periphery—I don't want you to actually look at it, just become aware of it. You are still focusing on the same spot on the wall. Now be aware of 180 degrees.

Drop your jaw, relaxing the muscles thereabouts, and inhale and exhale through your mouth.

Now extend your awareness to what is behind you. See it as you did the previous exercises, but continue to focus on that spot on the wall. With your awareness now extended to 360 degrees, I want you to imagine that there is a ball floating just behind your head, a few inches away from you. It can be any kind of ball; this is your imagination. Move that ball closer to the back of your head until you start feeling the tell-tale tingles of something coming at you. You are no doubt familiar with that spider sense that tells you something is right behind you, almost touching you, or watching you from a distance. It invariably leads to a physical sensation akin to a tingle. Allow yourself to feel this tingle as you move the ball closer and then farther and then closer to the back of your head.

Now play with that sensation, but remember, you are still focused on that spot on the wall, the only difference being you can also "see" everything else around you, including the ball.

. . . . . .

Consequently, you have expanded your awareness beyond the assumed limitations of the human senses and instead utilised other senses and abilities that are supernatural. You just used your imagination to get there. It is in this state, in this awareness, that you can also journey to the invisible worlds of gods and spirits and ancestors and explore your own psychic and subtle skills. The subtle worlds are available to you whether your eyes are open or closed. Others may tell you that you are simply imagining it all, and you may relish in knowing that they are quite correct. You did imagine it all—that is what is so wonderful about it! Whether we are meditating, pathworking, journeying, or engaged in relaxation or mindfulness, our imagination is key to opening the doors of experience. It is your primary tool for exploring the other.

The Occulted Mind

If we venture further into the subjective world of the mind and imagination, we can discover the potential for a whole world of magic that is hidden from our ordinary sense: the occult world. That word in itself may trigger a reaction in you: on the one hand, it may be something you are familiar with; on the other hand, this is an introductory book, so you may have little experience of what that word means. It is a fairly loaded word, "occult"—it sings of dark movies and magic, of wizards and witches and magical powers. In truth, the word simply means that which is hidden or a secret that is yet to be divulged. That which is occult is just out of sight, around the corner—it lies between the lines of a book or is hidden in the riddles of poems and the wisdom of myth. Meditation and imagination allow us to circumvent the mechanisms that cause things to be hidden. They are the tools that we utilise to glean wisdom from sources that are beyond the ordinary. They cause the curtains that occlude us from mystery to be peeled back, allowing us to peer beyond them and into the face of mystery.

With this in mind, we can now consider the possibility for stable imaginative realities to exist, ones that have been created by magical practitioners and nurtured and nourished by subsequent practice. In many magical traditions, these thought realities are referred to as pathworkings. Essentially, they are journeys that have established sets of symbols and paths that direct the mind towards a particular location, destination, or potential outcome. By offering the mind a map, it frees the periphery of the mind to absorb details that are extrinsic to the experience itself. In other words, a journey through an established world made entirely of thought allows for images, information, or knowledge to be dropped into the mind almost like a file. This method utilises an occult principle called thoughtforms, which you encountered earlier in the chapter that explored the nature of deity. These are forms of imaginative creation that arise from the thought of an individual or the collective thoughts of a number of individuals who are engaged in creating something beyond the ordinary senses. In turn, these thought landscapes are continuously fed by the individuals who engage with them and in essence become realities of their own making. When you embark on a guided journey into a meditative/imaginative realm or world, this is essentially what you are working with.

With the trajectory of your mind being directed towards a particular direction, it allows for input to occur from the surrounding inner landscape—a world that was hidden (occult) from you only moments before. This journey may be one in which the intention is to meet with a particular ancestor or a spirit of a tree or a deity; the possibilities are endless. In my own journeys, I may use the guided meditations of another person or I may have written the journey myself ahead of time. I will then partially memorise the details and take to my imagination. There is an element of acceptance that is necessary for the input one receives from a meditative state or a state of active imagination to be assimilated into information or knowledge. In my experience, this insight comes with hindsight. I will journey, return, go about my ordinary business for a few hours, and then journal the encounter. The act of journaling relies on my memory of the events that took place, and it is in this recollection where I find I have memories of events that were unplanned, implying to my magical mind that I had received information from something or someone beyond and yet tied to the experience itself.

Finding your way through the practise of meditation, particularly if you find it difficult, may require you to utilise tools to circumvent those issues. Often, as demonstrated, it may only need to be a shift in the use of words; I am far more comfortable with thinking of it as "active imagination." I prefer to take to the imaginary worlds rather than to a state of meditation per se. These are, of course, semantics—they do the same thing, and yet words and the constructs they create are immensely powerful and can either hinder or help our experience.

Ultimately, meditation in whatever form we use or prefer is a method by which we stop to observe and listen to the tides of ourselves and those of the world around us. They enable us to tap into the subtle places between the worlds where mystery abounds. Do not be discouraged if direct input does not happen at the time of your meditation or journey; do not dismay if nothing seemingly happens at all. The trick with meditation is to have as few expectations as possible and learn what it means to simply be in the moment. In a world of "I want it now!" mentality, meditation enables us to pause and witness the ebb and flow of our own tides in unison with the worlds around us.

With this in mind, answer the following questions:

* * * * * *

☞ *I define meditation as…*

....

....

....

☞ *The function of meditation is…*

....

....

....

☞ *Do I need to meditate? Why?*

....

....

....

☞ *My preferred method of meditation is...*

....

....

....

☞ *I maintain a meditation practise by...*

....

....

....

PRAYER

IN ITS VARIOUS forms, meditation can be defined as an act of listening to the tides of oneself and the universe. Prayer, on the other hand, can be articulated as actively speaking to a deity or spiritual entity. The word may come loaded with past baggage, but it is important to note that prayer does not belong exclusively to the revealed religions. Humans have been praying and entreating deity and spirits since time immemorial.

For many, the function of prayer is to occasionally clasp the hands together and ask an invisible being for favours or certain wishes to be granted. For millions of people, their only point of prayer reference comes in the form of emergency prayer, when one finds oneself at a point of crisis or personal challenge. Emergency prayers happen when things appear hopeless, and usually that individual has never prayed or given a single thought to a deity in years. It occurs almost like a factory setting, concluding that nothing in the physical world can help, therefore one turns to the supernatural. Often the nature of emergency prayer comes in the form of a bribe—"Do this for me and I shall do this in return"—in the hope that the entreated deity will pity the petitioner and grant their wish.

Our relationship with prayer is complicated and often contradictory and confused. As children many of us were taught the prose of prayer to be repeated before bedtime or prior to eating. These prayers are taught, as is the ritualistic behaviour that accompanies them: on one's knees with the hands pressed together and the fingers pointed upwards towards the heavens. I grew up in a Welsh Methodist chapel community where Christian ritual practise and theology was the primary religious education at school, and it was here where we were taught to pray. However, what we were not taught as children was the reason and function of prayer; it was simply something that you just did. As a child, I was never entirely convinced by Christianity—it felt alien, not of this land, and somehow jarring even to the innocence of a young Welsh child. But I did enjoy the rhyme and prose of prayer, and I had the sense that whenever the entire class was in the act of prayer, something else was happening just under the surface or just out of sight. I was too young to articulate or make sense of what was actually happening, but I did relish in the space and the sense of otherness that happened when we all prayed in unison. In seconds we moved from being curious and sometimes naughty children, passing remarks and prods and notes to one another, to suddenly being a company engaged in something extraordinary.

In the Welsh schooling system, the day would begin with what is called an assembly; all pupils and teachers would gather at the main communal area to begin the day. News, events, and some housekeeping would occur, and the entire company would fall into prayer either at the assembly's beginning or end. The prayer would be structured, and all pupils would know it by rote. But what was the point of it all? Why did we do it? Prayer has multiple functions: it brings people together through the use of a common language. It unifies, strengthens, and reinforces commonly held beliefs and reiterates the group's faith. It allows the practitioners to actively speak to the deity at hand.

The latter sentence is perhaps the most important point when it comes to understanding the function of prayer within a Pagan Druid context; prayer enables and nurtures relationship. When we actively speak to a deity or spirit, we are reinforcing and maintaining the principles that go into the making of sustainable relationships. In my own practise, many of my prayers are immediately followed by a state of relaxed meditation or silence. In prayer I speak to the deity in question; in meditation I listen for their reply or answer. Prayer fosters the relationship that I am developing with the unseen. I can converse with my friends and family—we have vocal cords, we live in an atmosphere that carries sound to eardrums—but the same cannot be said for the unseen. The gods and spirits and the ancestors do not possess the same physiology as we do, therefore our method of communication with them cannot be the same as that with our human kin. We require a shift in perspective, so we revaluate the methods of communication available to us. Prayer is the gateway.

If we consider the most used prayer in the Christian religion—the Lord's Prayer—we can see a pattern that is common to all religions and spiritualties. It begins with an invocation, stating who and what is being entreated within the structure of the prayer, and it is followed quickly by praising the deity and offering thanksgiving. Thereafter a petition is made for the needs of the petitioner and their communities or families to be met, followed by a supplication, where the prayer asks for a specific blessing or petitions a specific request. The prayer ends with words of devotion that reinforce the role of the deity within the supplicant's life. Quite often the Christian Lord's Prayer acts as an initiator for personal prayer—a bookend, if you like, that marks the beginning of the process. It is common that after the set prayer, the adherent will move into personal dialogue with the deity at hand.

Within my practise of Druidry, if we look at a prayer to the earth mother goddess Dôn, we can see similarities in style, intent, and narrative:

> Dôn, mother of earth, fruitful womb of all that lives,
> And our rest at the end of life,
> We call to you, arise and come unto us.
> You of the bountiful earth, our nourisher and keeper,
> To you we sing our praises.
> Bless our fields and crops with abundance and plenty,
> Cover us in your mantle of protection.
> May your mountains give us shelter,
> Your rivers sustain us.
> Blessed are you amongst the gods,
> O great Mother, to you we give praise for the wonder of earth.

· · · · · ·

If we look at the various aspects of both the Lord's Prayer and the prayer to Dôn, we can list common threads therein:

- invocation

- praise/thanksgiving

- petition

- supplication

- devotion/reinforcement

This pattern is common to most prayers that are used in spiritualities the world over, and for good reason: they are effective. The trick is to move away from any previous baggage one might have with the function of prayer and develop a new and fresh connection to it. This is not as easy a task as it may sound and will take months if not years of new practise to cause the experience to feel authentic and valid. I felt at odds with prayer for a long time because a part of me felt that I was just transferring one tool from one system to another—it felt almost disingenuous. Eventually I began to understand that prayer and its effectiveness works hand in hand with listening, much like meditation. Moving from one spiritual or religious system to another is tricky, and it requires attentive deconstruction of one system and the construction of another. Certain techniques of spiritual practise have a universal component to them and are not indicative of possession. Christianity or Islam do not own the rights to prayer. People have been praying for as long as people have existed. The act of prayer does not identify the religion or system; instead, it is the manner by which an individual or a group forge and maintain their relationship with the invisible nonhuman aspect of their spiritual practise.

In any form of spiritual practise, we are working with the invisible. Prayer and meditation work in harmony to open channels of dialogue with that which cannot be seen, at least not by the ordinary senses. In my own personal practise, I offer prayers each morning to Cerridwen, the goddess of inspiration, so that I may be conscious of opportunities to inspire and be inspired. In the evening I offer prayers to the mother of the land I live upon. The prayers are simple. The words often change to reflect my mood or the current of the day itself; they are sometimes brief and at times lengthy, but above all they are deeply personal. In your own practise, you may choose to incorporate prayer into your daily practise, but understand that it is not a necessity nor a requirement of being a Druid.

As you reach the conclusion of this chapter, consider the following questions.

· · · · · · ·

☞ *A prayer is...*

....
....
....

☞ *The purpose of a prayer is...*

....
....
....

☞ *I find the word "prayer" problematic because...*

....
....
....

☞ *I am comfortable using the word "prayer" because...*

....
....
....

☞ *I deem prayer necessary or unnecessary for my practise because...*

....
....
....

☞ *The power of prayer is in its ability to...*

....

....

....

☞ *I will develop a practise of consistent prayer because...*

....

....

....

ELEMENTAL POWERS

IN DRUID RITUAL it is common for the elemental powers of our planet to be acknowledged and called upon to either attend, witness, or protect the rite. But what does that actually mean?

There are two distinct Druidic ritual methodologies of working with the natural energies of our planet. One may choose to work within the system of land, sea, and sky or with the more traditional four classical elements of earth, air, fire, and water. Neither one is more correct than the other, but they do offer a slightly different approach to connecting with the powers that exist around and within us. If you have some experience of ritual practise, these may not be entirely alien to you. If you are new to the world of ritual, it is required that you have an understanding as to what is being called into a ritual space and why. To begin with, we will look at the system of working with the three realms of land and sea and sky.

The Three Realms System

How this system differs from the classical four elements is in its overtly animistic nature as opposed to primarily occult nature. However, to make that statement is not to suggest that the three realms are devoid of any occult attributions; on the contrary, they certainly do, for they contain within them all that is seen and unseen, visible and invisible, to the human eye. But the overall approach is primarily locality specific, whereas the four elements approach contains a universality that is intimately connected to traditional occultism. I shall explore more on this in the relevant section.

Some Druid groups, groves, and orders will have a preference to practise either the three realms system or the four elements system. Most experienced Druids are comfortable flitting between both systems. For now, our attention will focus on the three realms of land and sea and sky. In this system, most groups utilise a triskelion to organise the foundations of the three realms into a physical space where they may then be used for ritual or practise. A triskelion (triskele, triple spiral) is a Celtic pattern of three spirals that spin from a central point. Examples were given earlier, but for ease of reference it looks like this:

An example of its use ritualistically can be found in the practise chapter. The function of the three realms system is to attune the individual or group to the specific expression of the landscape in which they find themselves. It pinpoints the energies of the natural world to the immediate sensory environment, and in doing so it causes the participants to become ultra aware of the landscape and who they are sharing it with. This system relies on an animistic approach to the natural world, where everything is seen as alive, or containing a spark of the divine within it. The world is perceived to be full of individual lives other than humans. In ritual practise we take time out to stop, observe, and be immersed in the world around us. This is quite different to traditional magical practise, where a bubble is created to contain energies within it and seal the participants from the world beyond the created circle. A Druid ceremony of the three realms invites all beings of the natural world to be aware of the Druids' actions and, if compelled, to witness and participate in the ceremony itself. Simultaneously the Druids will acknowledge the subtle or magical powers of the realms. But what does that actually mean in reality?

Let's consider each of the realms in turn and how we might engage with them. First and foremost, as land-based creatures, where most of our physical experiences arise from the material world around us, we consider the realm of land.

The Realm of Land

Regardless of where you are in the world, every segment of earth will contain its own complex organisation of life-forms, each one striving and often struggling to survive. All things are connected through the soil and rock that make up the foundations of land, and those in turn reach down through the depths of dirt and into clay, bedrock, and further still into the very depths of the earth's crust. The land embodies the qualities of relationship and interconnection, not in a symbolic way but literally. When stopping to connect with the powers of the land, the Druid stills themselves and turns their direction towards the natural world that surrounds them.

This is perhaps best articulated by example. I am often a leader of pilgrimage and ritual to the sacred lake of Tegid at Y Bala, deep in the mountains of the Snowdonia National Park in North Wales. This is the legendary home of the Welsh goddess of inspiration, Cerridwen, and her family. The lake is the longest in Wales. On its shores are mighty oaks whose roots have long since been exposed by the passing storms of centuries. The lake is surrounded by majestic mountains, each one casting a reflection on the lake's pristine surface. To consider the expression of land here is to stop and take notice of what is around you—to really see it and how everything around you interacts with its environment. Using all the senses, the Druid reaches out and listens, sees, touches, and tastes the world around them.

The Druid is not separate but is a part of that landscape, and the animistic principle within the Druid is able to touch the animistic element in everything around them. We do so by just noticing, observing, watching, hearing, and listening. In some of my own Druid public ceremonies, I will often ask those present—some who may never have attended a Druid ritual previously—to take notice of where they are and pinpoint something in the natural world that they may otherwise have not particularly noticed.

This simple practise hones one's senses to the immediate surroundings and grounds one in the moment.

Often we pass through our environments without giving them a second glance or a bit of notice. Taking notice of where you are and who else lives there moves you from being a passive wanderer to an active participant. On the shores of lake Tegid, the Druids call out to the land and its inhabitants to acknowledge them as well as make ourselves known to them. We may wander into any environment without giving a moment of consideration to those who already live there. By acknowledging the powers of land, we introduce ourselves and state our intention; it is simultaneously demonstrative of good manners and politeness.

We take note of the trees and the grandeur of their presence. On the shores of Lake Tegid, some of the oaks are five to six hundred years old. They have witnessed the passing of time and no doubt were in the company of the medieval storytellers who wrote down the tale of Cerridwen and her magical cauldron of inspiration. All that memory exists in the trees that surround us at that location; to acknowledge them is to become aware of the passing of time and the fleeting nature of human life. Through the land we connect to the various creatures that make this place their home. While anecdotal to some extent, the participants of ritual will often report the presence of animals or birds that pass nearby or over the space the Druids have designated for ceremony. Are they, in fact, engaging with the Druids, or are the Druids simply more aware of their environment? In either case, something is different—something is affected by the power of observation and immersion. This is the glorious face of human beings moving into a conscious and animistic relationship with their surroundings.

The land contains memory, digested into soil; the very fabric of the earth holds the experience of all things that interacted with it, animate or inanimate. History is etched into the contours of the land, its shape manipulated and transformed by the beings that live upon it. The echoes of the past are entwined with the living present landscape. Nothing is truly forgotten, even when it has long since departed from its original form of expression. Our ancestors walked the land; in death their bones have turned to dust within the embrace of earth. When we stop to consider the land, we connect to our ancestors, and we can glean their memory held in the land itself. In death the ancestors exist as an integral part of the song that the land sings, and when we call to the power of the land, we call also to them, to those who have gone before us.

On a spiritual level, the animist considers that all things contain a spark from the divine, the original flicker of life that sings of the origin of the soul itself. And to many, this is enough to consider that *all* things around us are inherently alive and full of the same vital energy that exists within us. To many Druids this spark is the precursor to the individual expression of life, and they are often identified as spiritual entities in their own rights. It is within the concept of sensing the spiritual in nature that we call to the spirits of place and the gods and goddesses that are associated with it. Some of these may be directly connected to the landscape through myth and legends; they are a vital part of the spiritual fabric of the land itself. In ritual we ask that these entities be aware of our presence and our intentions.

The land connects us to all these things and infinitely more, if only we take the time to stop and listen deeply—to do more than simply hear what the world around us has to say for itself. There is a vast difference between hearing something and listening to it.

Hearing is mechanical. It is the receiving of sound by the inner workings of the human ear and its perception in the audible centre of the brain. Listening is the act of hearing with thoughtful attention. Working with the land requires you to move into deeper relationship; you can begin this practise by really looking at your square mile. Not all Druid ritual takes place at ancient monuments or sacred sites. The majority of ritual happens in gardens, on balconies, by a window, in the local park, or anywhere that a moment can be snatched from the day to stop and observe. Your task as a Druid is to get to know the myriad of expressions and moods that your land has. But keep this local and small and stick to your square mile; you will be amazed at what wonders of the natural world might exist as your immediate neighbours. In doing so, learn to appreciate that you are a member of your land's community.

* * * * * *

☞ *What is land?*

....

....

....

☞ *Who lived here before me?*

....
....
....

☞ *What trees and plants thrive in my land?*

....
....
....

☞ *What things do not thrive here?*

....
....
....

☞ *What animals live here?*

....
....
....

☞ *What insects are most prevalent?*

....
....
....

☞ *What are the stories that humans have recorded about this place?*

....
....
....

☞ *Are there any ancestors buried nearby?*

....

....

....

☞ *What places of worship are there here?*

....

....

....

☞ *How does the passage of the sun change the light and shape of this land?*

....

....

....

* * * * * *

The Realm of Sea

Now, don't fret if you find yourself reading this section from a landlocked location that may be a great distance from the nearest shoreline. The influence of the sea is all around us. Symbolically, the sea connects us to profound mystery; physically, the sea connects us to the various life forms that live within it—creatures whose flesh has nourished us since time immemorial, great mammals that instill awe in anyone fortunate enough to see them. Its impenetrable depths can cause us to shiver, wondering what on earth may be down there. What secrets can the sea reveal? From gentle streams to the darkness and crushing pressures of the Mariana Trench, when we call to the powers of the realm of sea, we are inviting so much more than just salt water. In essence, the realm of sea connects us to the function and magic of water. However distant we may appear to be from the sea or any body of water, it is, in fact, quite present.

You may be familiar from your school years of the pictorial representation of the water cycle:

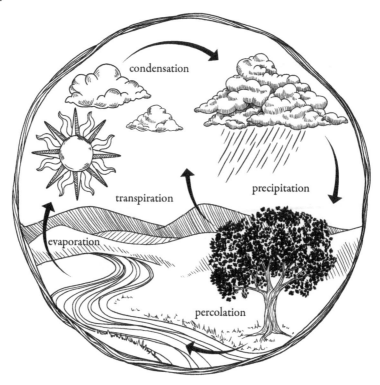

It may well be an aspect of your early education that you paid little attention to; it's just a bit of science, right? To the Druid this science contains a magic that sings of the interconnectedness of all things. In it we can see all three realms in perfect harmony with one another, and yet through it all the realm of sea, in the guise of water, permeates land and sky. None of them exist in a vacuum, and it is the realm of sea that perfectly expresses this mystery. We refer to this realm specifically as "sea" as opposed to "water" for a good reason: 71 percent of the earth's surface is covered by water, and the sea accounts for just over 97 percent of the earth's water. That figure is incredible. It is quite difficult to grasp that so much of our water is held in the oceans; of the remaining 3 percent, 2 percent is held frozen at the poles or in the enormous glaciers of the far north and south. Only 1 percent of the earth's water is fresh and potentially drinkable. To consider one of America's Great Lakes or the vast depth of the planet's largest body of freshwater,

Lake Baikal, it feels quite improbable that so little fresh water exists in comparison to the oceans.

All of that water has come from the sea, transformed by land and sky into a substance that can nurture and sustain life on our planet. Cast your attention back to the water cycle diagram and we can see the relationship between the three realms perfectly clearly. Water falls in the form of precipitation, as either rain, ice, or snow, which then seeps through the earth and runs as streams that become rivers that eventually find their way back to the sea. These waters feed the land and its inhabitants, who in turn exhale that water back into the sky through the process of transpiration. As percolation, water seeps deep into the land as groundwater; rising as springs or accessed through wells, eventually it finds its way back to the sea. Everything is compelled to return to the sea. The sun, as filtered through the realm of sky, heats up our planet and sings the water into air through evaporation. This simple diagram of scientific fact is rich with the magic of relationship and connection, where everything on our planet is reliant on its counterpart for its very existence.

To consider the power of the realm of sea is to be reminded of the triskele of Druid foundations and the spiral of science and magic. As previously explored, the Druid has the ability to perceive the magic in the natural world that expresses not only the wonder of physics and scientific thought, but also the mystery that drives them. This is the beauty of Druid thought. We are not required to believe that this is true; we know it to be so. We have faith in it. We can also see beyond the science and into the magic and wonder that lie at the heart of it. In the Welsh language, the modern word for science, *gwyddoniaeth*, is etymologically constructed from two words, *gwyddon* and *iaeth*. The first term, *gwyddon*, is intimately connected to magic and sorcery and the people who possessed the wisdom of those disciplines. The second term, *iaeth,* refers to an -ism or an -ology. Therefore, our word for science literally means "magicology." It is a fact that never ceases to delight and amaze me, and I often take to musing that perhaps there was a point in my ancestral past where people did not distinguish between science and magic.

Everything eventually returns to the sea. Consider your own physical body: its denseness is indicative of the land, your bones, and the cells that make up your organs, and yet on average your body is 60 percent water. This water is constantly moving in and out of your physical body, either through perspiration, exhalation, or urination. Upon your physical death, the water within you will return to the planet that nurtured you. It will either seep from your physical form into the earth you are interred into or rise as vapour from a crematory. Either way, the water within you will be called home to the sea to begin a new cycle. The water within us sings of this mystery.

You are in constant communication with the realm of sea. The internal mechanisms of your body are governed by tides that emulate the ebb and flow of the oceans. Your hormones react in the same manner: your physical cycles ebb and flow with a pull that is mysterious and intimately connected to the world around you. We may understand the science, yet the science belies a current of magic that has the power to instill awe and wonder. It is this energy, this excitement, that propels the Druid to deepen their connection to the world around them. To know that the water within you has passed through a million life-forms before you offers the opportunity for you to pause and consider that nothing is truly lost; all is remembered by the realm of sea, held in the magic of water.

The human body is remarkable in its ability to produce clear water in the form of tears. Your tears contain sodium, which gives them their salty, seawater-like quality along with some other chemicals like potassium and chloride. An average human being has three forms of tears that they can produce—basal tears for constant lubrication of the eyes; reflex tears that respond to irritants like gas, particles, or onions; and emotional tears that are produced when you are sad or happy or otherwise moved. The scientific community remains uncertain as to the function and purpose of shedding tears when one is moved by emotion, with some arguing that only humans shed emotional tears. Tears are perhaps just an ordinary function of the human experience, but the Druid sees a little more.

Why is it that when we are emotional, we leak water, a water that is purer than the other water we shed through perspiration or urination? Emotional tears contain more protein than basal and reflex tears; the jury is still out on understanding why that may be. One hypothesis has surmised that the additional protein causes the tears to adhere to the skin more effectively, allowing others to clearly see that one is in an emotional state. This implies that crying has a social component that triggers empathy or dispels anger in another individual. The scientific community continues to be perplexed by the function of emotional tears.[79] To the Druid there is profound magic in the shedding of tears, for to do so is to express the quality and mystery of the sea. There is no new water

79 For further reading on the function of tears, read Ad Vingerhoets's *Why Only Humans Weep*.

on earth; we are a closed system, and except for some hydrogen molecules that escape the earth's atmosphere along with some heat, water remains here, on our planet. Long disputed by the scientific community, recent research suggests that water contains the memory of that which has been dissolved into it.[80] To some it is pseudoscience, but to the Druid it poses an interesting enquiry: if water has memory, then any water we are in contact with has the potential to transmit that memory to its surroundings.

From a Druidic and magical perspective, water enables us to feel intimately connected to the world around us. It does so physically by means of the water cycle and metaphysically by means of interconnectedness. To stand barefoot in your nearest body of water is to be connected to all the waters of the earth. To feel and sense the waters within your body is to know that we are not isolated islands but beings connected by molecules of water.

In mythology gods and goddesses of the sea, rivers, lakes, and springs have long since captured the imagination and devotion of humans. From Poseidon of ancient Greece to Neptune of the Romans to Llŷr of the British Celts, there are hundreds of names recorded all over the world that express the human desire to deify water. In Druid ritual we call to the gods and goddesses and spirits that are either present in the landscape itself or indicative of the nearest bodies of water. In the Welsh Druid tradition, the realm of sea is represented by the deities of the house of Llŷr, which includes the great king and god Brân, his brother Manwydan, and his sister Branwen. Through them we are able to connect to the qualities of the sea in its metaphysical or allegorical sense. It is to all the qualities of this discourse that we call when we are in ritual; therefore, it is important that the Druid understands not only the physical makeup of water, but also the metaphysical aspects that sing of its mystery.

* * * * * *

☞ *What do I understand of the water cycle?*

....

....

....

---

80 For further reading, see Kröplin and Henschel, *Water and Its Memory.*

☞ *What is water in a physical sense and as a metaphor?*

....

....

....

☞ *I connect to water by...*

....

....

....

◦ ◦ ◦ ◦ ◦ ◦

The Realm of Sky

If the land holds us and the sea offers us the opportunity to comprehend interconnection and mystery, it is the realm of sky that gifts us the ability to express all that.
When we look up at the sky itself, it is ever changing and constantly moving by forces
that are mostly invisible to the naked eye. Perhaps only meteorologists truly understand
why winds blow and what causes them to happen in the first place. To the ordinary
individual, it is still a mystery. I get that there are low and high atmospheric pressure
systems and jet streams and all manner of invisible stuff that happens in the realm of sky.
Do I understand them? Not entirely—but I certainly am in awe of them. Everything
we can see above our heads—fluffy clouds, rainstorms, lightning, the pristine blue of a
summer sky or the foreboding tumult of a tornado—they all exist and are a phenomenon of our atmosphere, or sky. While we tend to look up at it, in truth sky is all around
us all the time; we are immersed within it. Not only is it essential for our existence, it
also provides us with the mechanism by which we express ourselves. The saying that in
space nobody can hear you scream is true; you can't scream in space, for it is a vacuum
and no sound would arise from your lungs. The medium for sound's transportation does
not exist in the vast emptiness of space. Our planet and its atmosphere enable most life
forms on earth to communicate with each other through energetic means.

Standing on the land and gazing our eyes skywards, we cannot see the approximately six thousand miles of air above us. It is entirely invisible unless it interacts with water molecules in the air, causing them to condense into clouds. When there is so much water in the air, it organises those molecules until such time that a critical mass point is reached and the water falls as precipitation back to the land. A cloud is the way by which the realm of sea kisses the realm of sky. By gazing up at the invisible air and watching whatever clouds are present, we are witnessing the wonder of the three realms in unison with each other. Even though the air around us is invisible, it exerts tremendous pressure on the land; air has volume and takes up space. The closest to the earth the air is, the more pressure it exerts, with the pressure decreasing as the air reaches further from the planet's surface. Eventually there is a vague point where air and space meet. Only the immense powers of gravity (the land) hold this ethereal and invisible realm and prevent it all from floating off into empty space.

We are incredibly sensitive to the pressures that the realm of sky exerts upon us. Meteorologists use terms like low and high pressure to describe the function of weather. During low pressure systems, I am more prone to stress headaches as, I imagine, are countless other individuals. When the pressure is high, usually indicating good weather, I feel lighter and better in myself. We are reacting and responding to the powers of air around us.

To see the pressure for yourself, simply take a glass, fill a sink with water, and push the glass, open end first, into the water. You will feel resistance as the water meets the volume of air that exists within the glass and the forces that are exerted between the three realms, with the glass representing the powers of land. These simple little classroom examples may appear infantile on the surface, yet how often do we stop to perceive the natural powers around us? Sometimes it is worth visiting the little experiments we did as children to reignite our appreciation for the world in which we do not simply live in but exist as vital organisms within a whole.

Weather patterns are the expressive personality of the earth herself; we can glean her moods by the intensity of the weather around us. Everything on our planet is affected to one degree or another by the function of weather. This aspect of the earth's personality is transmitted to sea and land by means of sky. Her moods affect our mood. The manner by which we respond to her moods tells us a lot about ourselves and our inner constitution. Some people may loathe and despise rain or storms, whereas others may bask in them. Some adore sunshine and blue skies, and others may shy away from it and seek the shadows instead. Analysing our moods in accordance to the planet's mood tells us something about our personalities. If given the choice, I will always seek out freezing temperatures, snow, and ice rather than sunshine and blue skies. What does that say about my personality? I was born at the end of November, in a particularly cold and snowy early winter in north Wales. The house I was raised in was always snug and warm, with a roaring fire. I struggle to maintain my composure in heat and hot weather. I am an individual who thrives in situations where the realm of sky causes me to hunker down and be cosy and secure in my environment. I have suffered with body issues my entire life. The cold enables me to disguise my body; heat and warmth expose it and bring about a vulnerability that I find uncomfortable. I can learn so much about myself by meditating and working with the realm of sky.

Having briefly read how sky and the weather affect me, now consider how the planet's moods, expressed by the realm of sky, manifest in your life. Perhaps the easiest manner by which to connect with the realm of sky is to become aware of the air within your body. So many meditations and spiritual techniques will ask for you to become aware of your breath. We can analyse what breath is on a purely physical level by considering the necessity of air for survival and the chemical make-up of it. With your mouth closed, take a deep intake of breath through your nose and feel the sensation of the air as it travels down the area at the back of your nose where it meets your throat, a place called the nasopharynx. If you are indoors or doing this on a warmish day, as the air enters the deepest part of your nasopharynx, you will feel it cool slightly as your body affects the temperature of the air to make its inhalation more effective. On a cold day, you will feel the opposite happening as your nasopharynx warms the air, lest it shocks your lungs. You may have experienced this shock if you have gone outside in severe freezing temperatures and taken a deep breath. Your lungs will shock the air back out, and you will begin to cough involuntarily until you narrow the entry point of air or somehow occlude its impact with something like a scarf. However, unless you are outside in extremely hot temperatures, usually the air entering your body is cooler than the heat of your lungs. By the time the air reaches your bronchi it has been warmed enough for absorption to occur.

This is the magical part, and although explainable by the science of physiology, it is magical nonetheless and worthy of our awe and wonder. To learn a little about how the realms affect our physical bodies is to glean a profound appreciation of the interconnected nature of nature. As the air enters farther into your chest, draw your attention to your lungs. Now, you cannot see your lungs, but you can certainly feel their presence against your chest wall as your rib cage expands and contracts to the rhythm of sky within you. Close your eyes and as you breathe, imagine what is happening in your lungs—that point where sky fuses with the realms of land and sea within you. Those molecules of air need to be pulled down farther and farther into the narrowest and tiniest parts of your lungs, to a place where your body has literally pulled the air apart into single molecules.

These molecules are so small, they can pass through the fabric of your lungs and into the water courses that are also running through them—your blood. The tiny sacks at the farthest reaches of your lungs meet capillaries at this point, tiny little arteries that are so small they have caused your red blood cells, called erythrocytes, to be ordered into single file. These amazing little cells look like disks that are flattened in the middle. You can appreciate what they look like by rolling a little Blu-Tack or plasticine between your fingers into a ball. Place the ball on a hard surface and push your index finger into it until it appears quite flat in the middle with a raised wall around the outside. These disks contain another molecule, called haemoglobin, and their job is to collect a molecule of oxygen from the lungs. A single erythrocyte can contain 300 million individual haemoglobin molecules that in totality can transport a total of 1.2 billion oxygen molecules. At this point the little red blood cell will appear to be bright red as it travels through your body's water courses and feeds your tissues and organs with oxygen. We give names to the corridors that transport these gasses: those rich in oxygen are called arteries. At death they appear totally empty and were called *arteria* by the ancient Greeks, meaning a "windpipe," for the Greeks believed they carried only air through the body. In turn, it will collect carbon dioxide spent from the passage of air and return those to the lungs to be exhaled.

This continuous exchange between land and sea and sky is what enables us to live and experience life. The exchange of gases within us neutralises the immense weight and pressure of the air in the atmosphere that would otherwise crush us. So, when we consider the realm of sky, the most effective initial point of reference should be your breath. Understanding what happens to air within us enables us to connect to it on a level that transcends the mechanics of it and raises it into an experience that is holistic.

By connecting to these realms within us, we are placing ourselves on the stage of existence in a new and exciting manner.

Human nature is not separate to nature; it is an inexorable part of nature. By looking at the sometimes-obvious aspects of sky, we can begin to appreciate another quality of this realm that holds deep value and meaning to the Druid: inspiration.

Inspiration

The function and power of inspiration is equated with the realm of sky, and for good reason. If we look at the word itself and its etymological roots, we will discover something about its nature. The common English term *inspiration* is derived from the Old French term *inspiracion,* meaning "to inhale" or "to breathe in." In turn, this is derived from the Latin word *inspirare,* meaning "to blow into, to breathe upon, or to excite or inflame." There are a lot of wind and sky references there. If we look to the Welsh language, we can glean a little more meaning. The common word for inspiration in Cymraeg is *ysbrydoliaeth*, composed of two words: *ysbrydol* (spirit or spiritual) and *iaeth* (an -ism or an -ology) combined to mean "life-giving or inspirational breath of God."[81] The inclusion of the term "life-giving" is quite amazing in that the word acknowledges that inspiration itself is intimately connected to life and its expression. It animates and sustains. Have you ever been around an individual who is seemingly never inspired by anything or anyone? That energy is dense and can feel as if it is sucking the life force out of you, making you feel heavy and sluggish and drained.

In the Welsh language, inspiration is profoundly connected to the concept of Awen, which as we explored earlier means "blessed or holy breath." Inspiration moves people to create and express themselves in ways that communicate ideas and concepts that sustain the principle of human creativity. In a Druidic sense, the power behind inspiration, Awen, causes us to express the vitality of the universe itself through our expressive creativity: sky.

Our commonly used words in English, Welsh, and other Indo-European languages associate the spiritual with breath and air. In turn, the root word *spirit* is derived from the Latin *spiritus*, meaning "breath." The use of language provides us with clues as to the nature of things; the spirit and all that is spiritual is connected to the realm of sky. In contrast, many Indo-European words for *soul* are linked to the sea and to lakes and bod-

---

81 Bevan and Donovan, *Geiriadur Prifysgol Cymru*, 3827.

ies of water; for example, the Proto-Germanic word *saiwaz* refers to something that originated from or came from the sea.[82] This in itself provides food for thought; ponder on the nature and difference between the spirit and the soul. The realm of sky reminds us that we are constantly surrounded by invisible forces; we can feel them and, on many levels, we can comprehend them. When we call to the powers of sky, it is to all these things and more that we acknowledge. In the Druid traditions, the realm of sky not only holds the winged creatures of our world that are not wholly bound to the land, but it also expresses the qualities of the deities and spirits that represent inspiration, light, lightning, thunder, storms, and the power of the sun as manifested in our atmosphere.

* * * * * *

☞ *What is sky?*

....
....
....

☞ *What does sky represent physically and as a metaphor?*

....
....
....

☞ *Who are the spirits and gods and goddesses of the sky in my locale and culture?*

....
....
....

82 "Soul," Online Etymology Dictionary, accessed July 12, 2022, https://www.etymonline.com/word/soul.

☞ *What does the realm of sky teach me about the way in which I express myself?*

....

....

....

· · · · · ·

The beauty of working with the three realms system is in its ability to heighten the five human senses that we take utterly for granted most of the time. When we hear clearly enough to listen, we move into an orchestra that the environment is conducting. All too often people rarely see what is right before their noses, so to really see your environment and look at the land in a manner that takes notice of everything transforms how you look at the world. In the final part of this book, you will find Druid rituals that incorporate the three realms system, and now that you have a deeper understanding and appreciation of each realm, you are better placed to work with them ritualistically. However, to anyone who has worked with the classical four elements of earth, air, fire, and water, you will obviously note the absence of fire in the three realms system. Its omission is not a denigration of fire, and this requires a little explanation.

The three realms are present and very much tied to planetary forces. While each one contains metaphors and subjective attributes in a spiritual sense, they are ultimately a product of the world itself and how they are interrelated. In the ritual section of this book, you will note that in the central position of the ritual space is a cauldron. This vessel holds the potential for fire. In the natural world fire exists as a potential; it is an energetic force that runs as a current through the other three realms, but a chemical reaction is required to cause fire to burst into existence. For example, a piece of wood (land) needs to be torn apart and heated to release gases that are then ignited into fire. When there is enough heat and fuel, the fire is self-sustaining for as long as there is fuel, air, and heat. Fire does not exist naturally and perpetually on our planet. The viciously hot lava within the earth is not technically fire; it is molten rock that is so incredibly hot it can set other things that are flammable alight, but it is not itself composed of fire. It has the potential to cause fire. In turn, the sun is not fire; it is a different process called nuclear fusion, which does not require oxygen, but the sun can cause fire. It is this potential for fire that is represented by the central cauldron, but it is not fire itself. The cauldron represents the underlying currents within the three realms that have the potential to cause fire but in and of themselves they cannot. In some rituals Druids may light a fire in the central cauldron, which sees them combining the forces inherent in the three realms to chemically initiate fire. Water, of course, will remove the heat required for fire, but the molecules within water, when separated into oxygen and hydrogen, have the potential to be flammable. At the centre of the ritual triskele, the cauldron represents the unmanifested potential of the universe and its finite expression in our world as land and sea and sky.

The Four Elements System

We now turn our attention towards the classical four element system that is predominantly used in Western New Age and Pagan traditions. Based upon the traditional Greek theory of earth, air, fire, and water, the system was developed and adapted by various occultists to eventually form the cornerstone of popular occult ritual. The previous exploration of the three realms will have given you a grounding in elemental forces that can also be utilised when thinking of the four classical elements, with the addition here of fire. The manner by which we consider the four elements shares another commonality with the three realms in that they are not perceived as isolated or independent but rather as interdependent systems that bring about the expression of the world and the nature of humanity.

In a ritual that includes the four elements, there is usually a space that is marked or delineated as a circle; a full ritual example can be found in chapter 22. The outline of a circle might be drawn in sand or by using a length of cord, forming people around its edge, or simply marking four cardinal directions with various items or symbols enabling those present to imagine the circle as it moves from one station to another. The cardinal directions of north, east, south, and west each take on an attribute of an element, namely earth in the north, air in the east, fire in the south, and water in the west. Some Druids may place an item or symbol at each cardinal point to denote which element is present there; examples of this might be a stone for earth, incense smoke or a feather for air, a candle for fire, and a chalice of liquid for water.

In a typical ritual employing the elements, the Druid will move towards each cardinal direction and call to the powers that are represented there. You may hear this referred to by a myriad of different names. Some might refer to it as *calling the quarters*, a reference to the fact that the cardinal directions split the circle into four quarters, or the action may be called *calling the directions* or *calling the elements or elementals*. In some cases, you may even hear a Druid calling to the Guardians of the Watchtowers. These terms may initially sound perplexing or confusing, but they are essentially referring to the same action of intention, which is to call the powers of the four elements at the cardinal points to attend, witness, and protect the ritual itself.

In a group ritual, where several people are present, the usual practise is for a Druid to be preselected to call an element each. This individual will normally position themselves in the circle at or near the cardinal direction they have chosen to call. It is common for the calling to begin at the east, move to the south, then west, and then finally to the north. At the appointed time it is usual for the individual to turn to face outwards, at which point those present will orientate themselves to also face the appropriate direction. When calling, the Druid may raise their arms in a welcoming gesture, and often those present will also stretch out their arms with their palms facing the direction. Using either a memorised set of words or inspired speech, the Druid will call to that element and its qualities to be present. While doing so, the other participants will employ their imagination to visualise the elements arriving in the circle. This is not as tricky as it may sound; it is as simple as imagining the waves on a sea for water or visualising the flame of a candle for fire.

So why do we do this? What is its point? In the same manner as connecting to the three realms, a study of the elements cements their reality as vital aspects of your own existence as well as cogs in the making of the universe itself. They are miniature, bite-size principles that help us sense the whole; the term used for this is microcosm (small) and macrocosm (big). By splitting up the circle and inviting these energies, we are acknowledging their power within and without us, but we do it in such a way they are not so overwhelmingly large that we become undone by their magnitude. We shrink them down so that our amazing yet still relatively small brains can comprehend them enough to form a relationship with them. When we do so, we can assign various qualities to the elements that deepen that relationship, and when we do, we notice ways in which the four elements differ from the three realms system in that a whole hoard of occult correspondences is tied into them. While there is a crossover between the two systems, it is worthwhile informing you of the various attributes that each element represents in the form of a table, below, and how these elements can be seen within the human condition.

Air

Air is considered to be a moist, hot, and light yet active element that influences the human qualities of inspiration, analysis, and communication. People who have a preponderance of air quality to them are inspirational, highly sociable, and funny, but they may sometimes lack attention and are in danger of appearing a little whimsical.

Alchemical Symbol: △

Direction: East

Season: Spring

Hour: Dawn

Colour: Yellow

Spiritual beings: Sylphs

Astrological rulers: Mercury and Jupiter

Natural phenomena: Clouds, wind, the sky

Goddesses: Penarddun, Aranrhod

Gods: Beli Mawr, Lleu

Virtues: Inspiration, communication, intelligence

Vices: Gossip, dishonesty, boastfulness

Fire

Fire is considered to be a hot, dry, and active element that influences the human qualities of passion, courage, and direction. People who have a preponderance of fire element in their personalities are driven and motivated but can burn out very quickly if they are less than attentive to the way in which they spend their energy. They are infectious people who can motivate others into action. Self-driven and ambitious, those with a propensity for fire are enthusiastic and determined; on the other side of the coin, they can be impulsive and easily lose sight of their attention span.

Alchemical Symbol: △

Direction: South

Season: Summer

Hour: Noon

Colour: Red

Spiritual beings: Salamanders

Astrological rulers: Sun and Mars

Natural phenomena: The sun, volcanoes, comets

Goddesses: Brigantia, Braint, Ffraid

Gods: Beli Mawr

Virtues: Passion, motivation, courage, vitality

Vices: Cruelness, greed, revengeful, bitterness, anger

Water

In traditional occultism water is considered to be a cold, moist, heavy, and passive element. In the human condition, water is associated with the emotions; those with a preponderance of water in their personalities are deeply caring individuals who are emotionally expressive. They make brilliant caregivers and are good listeners and tend to put the emotional needs of others ahead of their own. On the flip side, they can be emotionally stunted or unable to deal with the tides of their emotions and become unhinged by them.

Alchemical Symbol: ▽

Direction: West

Season: Autumn

Hour: Dusk

Colour: Blue

Spiritual beings: Undines

Astrological rulers: Moon, Venus

Natural phenomena: Springs, streams, rivers, lakes, oceans

Goddesses: Branwen, Aranrhod

Gods: Llŷr, Manawydan, Brân

Virtues: Kindness, love, compassion, sensitivity

Vices: Cowardice, resentfulness, unkindness, unempathetic

Earth

Earth is considered cold, dry, heavy, and passive. People with a preponderance of this element are stable and secure. They are the kind of individual that you would trust with your life, and they have the ability to make you feel safe. They are good business people and entrepreneurs and are more than happy being at home. They have a tendency to want to look after others and are nurturing and nourishing. The other side of the coin finds them possessive, selfish, and placing too much emphasis on materialism.

Alchemical Symbol: ▽

Direction: North

Season: Winter

Hour: Midnight

Colour: Black

Spiritual beings: Gnomes

Astrological rulers: Saturn, Venus

Natural phenomena: Forests, mountains, valleys, fields

Goddesses: Dôn, Nemetona

Gods: Gwydion, Math

Virtues: Stability, strength

Vices: Stagnation, melancholy

* * * * * *

The above correspondences will provide you with enough base material to conduct your own research into the power of the elements.

Having explored the nature of the three realms and the four elements, consider the following questions:

* * * * * *

☞ *I am drawn to the three realms because...*

....
....
....

☞ *I am drawn to the four elements because...*

....
....
....

☞ *The system I will choose to predominantly work with is...*
   and my reasons are...

....
....
....

☞ *I will happily work with both systems because...*

....
....
....

☞ *I do not feel the need to incorporate either system because...*

....

....

....

☞ *Working with the natural forces of the earth will enrich
my Druidry by...*

....

....

....

21

RITUAL AND ITS FUNCTION

IN THIS SECTION we will be taking a closer look at the rituals that Druids might engage in. Some of them form a foundation of ritual practise while others are indicative of seasonal or daily devotional practises. The reasons for ritual are endless. Performing rituals is timeless. It provides us with the opportunity to step beyond the ordinary and move into the extraordinary persona of the Druid. Before we delve further, it is pertinent that I explore the function and necessity of ritual, which may be something that you are utterly unfamiliar with. Even to a more experienced practitioner, it can often be refreshing to revisit the foundations of why and how Druids engage in ritual activity.

If you want to know anything about a particular culture, look to the manner by which they ritualise elements of their society and you will learn a tremendous amount about the inner constitution of said society. Throughout human history we have had a need, an inherent and often overwhelming desire, to ritualise the components of human life that are significant. Their importance can be joyous in the coming of age or the pairing of people or the celebration of the bounty of summer, or they can mark the traumas in life that enable individuals to emotionally assimilate an experience.

Since the dawn of humankind, evident from the archaeological record, we have engaged in ritual. Ancient graves throughout the world demonstrate a ritualisation of the act of disposing of a dead human body. The presence of grave goods implies that the deceased may need these items in some other existence beyond the veils of death. Rites of passage that demarcate specific points of the human experience continue to this day, and while the old practises of coming-of-age rituals that continue in current tribal practises have changed focus in the developed world, our thirst for them continues. High school proms, college and university official and unofficial initiatory rituals, all hint at a memory of ritual expression that humans are compelled to participate in. According to acclaimed biologist and author Rupert Sheldrake, rituals "imply a kind of continuity, a memory transmitted from past generations to the present generation through the practice of the ritual."[83] Sheldrake continues to elaborate on the function of ritual within society as aspects of cultural inheritance. Rituals are methodologies by which a culture remembers elements of the sacred. While there is an aspect of blind following in many secular rituals, there is also something about them that has the ability to make people feel something deeper than the ordinary. Rituals enable us to touch the sacred, and while we may not be able to wholly articulate what that means, we continue to perpetuate rituals on a spiritual and secular level.

I believe that there is good reason for this. Rituals work, and even those people who do not necessarily believe in their power are often compelled to engage with them.[84] Essentially, the nuts and bolts of a ritual consist of a set of repeated activities, gestures, and words (liturgy) within a particular expression of behaviour. Rituals are an ancient technology, and their effectiveness is demonstrated by their continuous use. If we scratch at the surface of society, we can see how ritual is integrated into the customs and practises of that society. Here in the United Kingdom, we have a prime example of a ritualised function that is ingrained into our society: the monarchy. Charles III is a representative of the sovereignty of our land, the kingdom; he is simultaneously the supreme governor of the Church of England and expresses a religious quality that is part and parcel of his position as monarch. While the faith he represents is Christian, the function of the monarchy continues to maintain the ancient premise of the monarch being the sovereign of the land itself. Except for republican enthusiasts, the kingdom has agreed to maintain the ritual function of the monarchy within British society. The well-being of the kingdom is dependent on the vitality and stability of the ritualised function that serves it. It contains a quality that is purely magical. Other examples of ritualised

83 Sheldrake, *Science and Spiritual Practices*, 110.
84 Gino and Norton, "Why Rituals Work."

function in British society are the Ministry of Justice and its court judges, the coroner, and Freemasons, to name but three; while they are individual human beings, they participate in a ritualised collective that transcends the individual into something "other."

We may, however, use the term *ritual* rather flippantly at times to colour our language with it: "Coffee is my morning ritual," "I have a bedtime ritual." Describing our daily activities in such a way places importance and significance on those events, but in truth they are routines rather than rituals. Routines are often habitual, and we may place huge importance upon them and hate when they are disrupted, but essentially they are a manner by which we create habits that allow us to function as better versions of ourselves. How many of us say, "You don't want to see me if I have not had my morning coffee!"—implying that we are somehow less of ourselves when our routines are disrupted. In contrast, the function of a ritual is to make the ordinary appear extraordinary and is imbued with intention.

We may hear another word that expresses a similar connotation to ritual: ceremony. Often these two words are used interchangeably, with the difference between them being vague or little understood by those who use the words. Usually, a ritual refers to an action that has its foundation in belief, cultural worldview, religion, or spirituality and has assigned to them certain symbolic meanings. A ceremony can be secular, but it may also contain elements of ritual activity that pertain to a set of symbols and meaning that the collective has agreed upon, either through social programming or information. The ceremony can refer to the event as a whole and the ritual to a particular aspect of it that has deep meaning. For example, a secular, non-religious wedding is a ceremony, but within it there are identifiable symbolic rituals such as the exchanging of rings and vows and the proclamation; the majority of people understand those symbols to represent a coupling. No spirituality is present as such, but something sacred is acknowledged as happening—in this case, the symbolic pairing of two people. When something is sacred, we have a propensity to mark it as such, but that sacredness might only be a moment within the entire landscape of a ceremony.

Combined, ceremony and ritual offer a structure that gives form and meaning to human activity in which it emphasises a situation or function as being different from normal everyday activities. By doing this we provide the activity with a depth of meaning that causes it to stand out amongst the mundanity of ordinary life. In essence, a ritual provides the ordinary individual the experience of an extraordinary event that not only enhances their human experience but also has the ability to transform them. When transformation occurs—i.e., the moving across from one state to another—the ritual has served its function and purpose. This transformation can be as subtle as an affirmation or the acknowledgment of the sacred, or it can be deeply emotive as in the emotional relocation that happens during a funeral ritual. In and of itself, ritual does not have an immediate impact on the external world—immediacy is not the point—but to make that statement is not to imply that ritual will not eventually have real-world effects. On the contrary, the true function of ritual is to affect the internal constitution of the individual or individuals that are engaged with it. It affirms and cathartically transforms those who actively engage with ritual, and that can have tremendous impact on the world beyond the moment. I can offer some examples of this.

In a funeral, which is a ceremony that has ritual at its heart, those present are guided through an experience where their emotions are heightened to a crescendo. Its climax is the ultimate removal of the deceased from the world of the living, either by lowering the body into the ground or moving it through a partition and into a crematory. The immediate impact is collective and sends a clear message that a separation has occurred between the living and dead. The deceased individual is acknowledged as being liberated from the responsibilities of life and is no longer active within ordinary society.[85] The eventual effect of the ritual is on the internal constitution of the bereaved individuals. The funeral ritual marks a closure, a moment from which there is no return; psychologically, this initiates the process of emotional relocation, where the deceased is mentally transferred from this world to that of the dead. This ritualistic closure enables the bereaved to begin their personal journeys of assimilating grief. So, the effect is not immediate on the world itself, but eventually it can be seen in the actions of the bereaved as they reintegrate themselves back into the ordinary function of society. Death disrupts the normal everyday workings of society; a ritual—in this case, the funeral—aims to restore what has been disrupted, but it does so gently and over time.

We can see a similar pattern in magical ritual. The individual or group will agree upon the foundation and purpose of the magical act and further elaborate the processes by which they will achieve this. A ritual is designed and then enacted; with the participants imbibing the activity with intent and faith, the energy required to charge the magic is raised and then released to do its work. There is no immediate impact on the

85 Sheldrake, *Science and Spiritual Practices*, 115.

world external to the act, but its trajectory and intent will eventually impact real-world situations. More importantly, the internal constitution of those present has been profoundly affected by the act itself.

An individual Druid sitting at home performing a spell is engaged in ritual. The spell at hand might be a confidence spell for a nervous friend who has a job interview. The Druid will have planned the spell beforehand and prepared the space in which to conduct it. With the appropriate words, intent, and action, the Druid performs the ritual and directs their intention towards the target. The ritual works on two levels: firstly as a psychological affirmation for both the Druid and their friend, affirming that they will be confident, and secondly on an energetic level to magically affect the situation at hand. The ultimate effect will be the result of the interview and its real-world consequences.

The previous examples are energetic and often imbued with emotion, but another example of ritual that is often employed by Druids are seasonal celebrations. These rituals are usually civic or public and are predominantly ceremonies of celebration that contain a set of ritualised structures or actions at their heart. The intent of these rituals is often celebratory and are utilised to strengthen community bonds in a shared experience. On the surface this may seem nontransformative, but on the contrary, an open public ritual of this nature can profoundly affect those present. I have witnessed newcomers to Druid ritual have their entire worldview transformed by their participation, and often leads to them seeing the world through very new eyes. Druids will ritualise the passing of the year to observe and mark the cycles in a way that moves them closer to the natural rhythms of the season. We become active participants in the drama of moon and sun rather than passive observers.

Ritual Energy

In the previous examples of ritual, there is a commonality that was mentioned briefly but is worthy of elaboration; it is energy. The human body mimics and emulates the function of the wider universe. We are a microcosm of the macrocosm; the hermetic-inspired occult phrase "As above, so below" is often used to describe this. Science deals with the material world, and spirituality deals with the ethereal. The human body contains two systems that emulate this quality: a visible material system and an invisible energetic system. They work in union, one with the other, with the energetic system constantly being released from the body as heat, chemicals, or electricity. Druids and other magical workers have an understanding of this potential, there is no separation between the physical and the energetic; they are intertwined. The first law of thermodynamics states that energy cannot be created nor destroyed but is converted or transformed into another form. Druids understand this and use it to their magical advantage. The magical energy they raise in a ritual setting is transformed by the process of ritual to achieve an end result. Magical practise and spirituality is not in diametrical opposition to scientific thought; on the contrary, having an understanding of how energy works assists Druids in their work.

Energy is paramount to effective ritual, and yet that word, "energy," is often used flippantly, with little regard to its actual meaning. In a ritualistic sense, energy often refers to emotion or a fervour of personal energy that is raised by a specific action. The previous funeral example contains an obvious rising of emotional energy; at the climax of the ritual, the participants' emotions are collectively heightened and then released, usually as tears or the process of crying. In a magical ritual, this energy is raised by means of ecstatic chanting, dancing, drumming, or singing. In most cases the action increases in tempo to initiate a form of emotional fervour that causes one to be ultra aware of the energetic systems within the body. The physical symptom of this energy can be felt and seen in the heat that is generated by the participants, who often perspire and appear to glow much in the same way as someone who is engaged in intense physical activity. This same energy is used by motivational speakers, evangelical ministers, entertainers, and preachers, who have the ability to stir the emotional centre of their audience to a palpable level. This palpability is often given a name: hysteria.[86] And for anyone that has experienced it, the energy within that moment is incredibly real and tangible. In either case, the energy is the same: it is emotional energy. In a hysterical situation, the energy is unadulterated and unorganised; in an intentional ritual, the energy is harnessed as a means to an end.

This energy causes the participants to swirl with sensations that can be physically felt in the solar plexus region of the human body. Those butterflies in the stomach that

---

86 *Hysteria* is derived from the Greek word for "uterus," *hyster*, and was used in the nineteenth century as a derogatory term for mental instability in women. The origin of hysteria has its ancient roots in the Proto-Indo-European term *udtero/udero*, meaning "in the abdomen, stomach, or womb."

we feel when in love, lust, or grief is the centre of our emotional being. The reason for this is the magic of our physiology; the brain is not the only nervous system within the human body. Your guts hide another system, called the enteric nervous system, which contains billions of neurons and neurotransmitters in direct communication with the brain. When emotions are perceived by the brain, it sends signals for those to be felt in the region where your gut is most active and hot, which is the place directly underneath your sternum. Think back to when you were disappointed or something immediately intense happened in your life and you will recall feeling it in the pit of your stomach. It is this knowledge that helps the Druid to understand what is happening within the body when energy is being raised in ritual. So, when you hear the phrase "to raise energy" being said, it is this that is being referred to. As a Druid and a scientist, I always encourage those new to Druidry to study the workings of the human body in conjunction with their Druidic studies to deepen the understanding of how we work within the natural world that Druids revere.

EXERCISE

In order to feel this energy and utilise it in ritual, there is a simple technique that you can practise. You may sit or stand to perform this technique. Close your eyes and focus on a period in your life when you felt intense emotional energy or stress; you will invariably collect and sense that memory in the pit of your stomach. As you feel it, immediately stop invoking the memory so that the energy you feel is neutral. The sensation that you are aiming to feel is the butterflies in your stomach. Now take a deep breath through your mouth and follow the journey of that breath directly down the centre of your chest towards the base of your sternum. Obviously the air is going into your lungs, so at this point you need to use your imagination.

Consider the flutters in the pit of your stomach to be a fire that has the potential to burn fiercely. Fire requires air as fuel, so imagine that each breath fuels the sensation, contributing more and more fuel with each intake of breath. To maintain this sensation, you may need to create more thermodynamic energy, and to do that all you need do is move your body as little or as fervently as you desire, or you may feel compelled to beat your hands against your thighs or another surface. As you do, maintain your focus on feeding the fire of your emotions. If done correctly, you will feel the butterflies in your stomach rise and fall in intensity with the pattern of your breath, and the flutters will ripple out through your body as a tingling sensation.

You can further elaborate on this by imagining the fiery flutters in your stomach to be radiating out with tingles towards your hands. Your hands can then be lifted in gestures that direct that energy from you towards your target. Initially the exercise may feel tricky, but as with all good things, perseverance is the key to successful practice. In a magical ritual setting, your mind will also be focused on the goal of the ritual itself, and this again takes practise to master. The trick is to play with this and do it daily so that you get the hang of summoning those butterflies in your stomach whenever you need them.

· · · · · ·

To the Druid, rituals are the practical behavioural framework that allow us to connect with what we believe, and, as previously explored, when that belief raises into faith, we express it by action. In this case, the action at hand is ritual. At the heart of ritual is the desire and need to express connection. It allows us a moment in time to stop and listen to the rhythms of ourselves, our communities, and the world around us. It provides us with a space in which things can be transformed by the powers of magic. It is the acknowledgement of integration between matter and energy, physical and spiritual. The beauty of rituals is in their adaptability and diversity; they can be as simple as lighting a single candle and wishing for something to come to pass or they can be elaborate and full of pomp and circumstance, with the understanding that ritual was the original form of theatre. Rituals do not define a Druid, but they certainly enhance the experience of being a Druid. To me, the function of ritual fills me with wonderment, excitement, and anticipation. I love everything, from the preparation of ritual to its performance, and I do not use that word flippantly, for there is an element of performance in ritual that carries its own magic. We become better versions of ourselves when we stand in ritual. We stand powerful and empowered, moving from mundanity to a place where every cell in our bodies understands that we are a working part of the universe expressing itself. We shift from being individuals to being part of a whole.

I love nothing more than going to the grove near my home either alone or with others to work ritual. The preparation begins at home with the amassing of the tools and items necessary for the purpose of the ritual. I adore the feeling I get when we arrive

at the grove, often at night, and hearing the trees whisper in the darkness as if antici-
pating our arrival. I love how the grove itself, with its mighty beech trees and oaks and
hawthorn, becomes kin as we walk into its presence as our magical allies. The rituals we
perform there, lit only by candlelight and flickering flames, allow us the opportunity to
feel at one with the grove and the wider woodland.

Ritual Etiquette

There are no hard and fast rules when it comes to behaviour and etiquette at a ritual;
your primary duty is to use your common sense. Having an awareness that you are in a
space that is designated as sacred for the purpose of the ritual is often enough to modify
one's behaviour. When something is sacred, it tells us what to do and how to behave, but
this does not imply that everybody should be particularly stiff and retentive. Even the
most intense ritual still has space for laughter and giggles—it would be a travesty if our
deities did not possess a sense of humour! Be mindful of what is appropriate, however;
rituals can be joyous occasions, but it is also easy to overstep the mark into total irrever-
ence and impoliteness.

Keep these points in mind for good ritual etiquette:

- Don't worry if you forget something. We are human; take a
  breath and move on.

- Hold your concentration and intention for the duration of the
  ritual. If your mind wanders off into mundanity, gently rein it
  back into focus again.

- Be mindful of others in a group ritual.

- Do not interrupt others when they are performing their part in
  the ritual.

- Do not grandstand; nobody likes that.

Now that we have explored the function of ritual, it will soon be time to share some
examples with you. What is important at this juncture is that you understand the rituals
included in this book are real examples of working rituals that I and my Druid companions actively work with. I am not a Druid who relishes in creating rituals for the sake of
a book; instead, I believe it is important that you have a glimpse of rituals that actually

mean something to those who perform them. With that in mind, some of the rituals that follow can be seen in some of my other books, while others are in print for the very first time. To say this is not to suggest that these rituals are set in stone; on the contrary, for they can also serve as springboards for your own creativity and inspiration. You may like some of them and yet not connect with certain elements contained within them. If this is the case, then by all means change some of the words or actions to suit your needs. Consider the following rituals to be examples of what you can do and how you might go on to structure your own. The key here is inspiration and how the words that follow inspire you to develop a relationship with ritual that works for you.

The majority of rituals do not just happen on the spur of a moment. Although there is a certain magic to spontaneous ritual, the majority are planned. Your initial preparation would be to write a few lists that capture the essence of the ritual and the intention for it. Next you will list the items, if any, that you need for the ritual and gather them together. I use a wicker picnic hamper and occasionally a large, sturdy supermarket bag with fabric handles to carry my ritual items. Next you will prepare yourself for the ritual. You may wish to do this by either taking a bath or shower with some toiletries that you have selected specifically for special occasions. You may wish to wear a perfume that you might only use in times of ritual. It is important that you change the way your mind is working in the moment and acknowledge that you are consciously moving from the ordinary to the extraordinary.

There are several things we can do to shift ourselves psychologically to achieve this; bathing, clothing, and perfumes are certainly effective. Attire yourself in whatever you are most comfortable or deem the most appropriate for the occasion. Do not fall into the trap of thinking that you must wear a robe or cloak—they have their place, but they are not wholly necessary. The important thing to consider with attire is how they make you feel. Druids tend to dress up for ritual because we are going to interact with the spirits and deities of our tradition. This is a special occasion and akin to the time you would spend getting ready for a wedding, an interview, or a party.

The first two examples are full rituals that involve the three realms system and the four element system, respectively. Their inclusion here is not to suggest that every single ritual you perform must include one of these. Ultimately, your ritual practise, while inspired perhaps by the works of others, must reflect your own connection and not be ruled by assumptions of what is correct or incorrect. There are times when a full-blown ritual with all the bells and whistles is exactly what is needed; at other times, the quiet contemplation of the realms or elements is quite enough. The trick is not to become bogged down or overwhelmed by unrealistic ritual expectations. You might see examples of rituals online or in books that might appear too complex or they may simply just not speak to you. The beauty of the Druid tradition is in its flexibility to allow personal expression and creativity to colour its landscape.

Before we move onto the rituals themselves in chapter 22, it is pertinent to examine the types of rituals that Druids might engage with.

Seasonal Rituals: These connect the Druid to the passing of the seasons and the wheel of the year and will incorporate seasonally appropriate symbols, offerings, prayers, or songs that are indicative of the time of year. Seasonal rituals may also mark the feast days of saints, national holidays, and other celebrations that are locality or culturally specific.

Rites of Passage: These rituals mark the important points that punctuate the human condition. Naming rituals acknowledge a new life and a new addition to a family or community. Coming of age rituals assist the child in acknowledging their transition into adulthood. Marriage and commitment relationships often take the form of a traditional Pagan handfasting, where cords tie the hands of those making a commitment, one to the other. Rituals of parting enable people to consciously separate from situations or relationships that are no longer valid. Maturation rituals acknowledge the power of the elder and honour an individual as they enter the autumnal stage of their living. Death rituals encompass death midwifery and transitional rituals for the dying as well as funeral and memorial rituals.

Magical Rituals: These can be stand-alone rituals for any form of magical working, but they can often be incorporated into the previous categories.

Contemplative Rituals: This is the creating of ritual space for contemplation or meditation or to be in a space for the purpose of finding clarity of direction.

Divinatory Rituals: These are rituals that incorporate methods of divination in a ritualised manner that leads to clarity.

Devotional Rituals: These are rituals created for the sole function of devotion to a particular deity or a number of deities. They usually include prayers, invocations, and offerings and might include specific and repetitive liturgy.

Ritual is a complex and beautiful aspect of Druidry. Having read this chapter, consider and answer the following questions:

• • • • • •

☞ *I define a ritual as...*

....

....

....

☞ *Ritual is or is not important to me because...*

....

....

....

☞ *I plan on incorporating ritual into my practise because...*

....

....

....

☞ *My favourite kind of ritual is or will be...*

....

....

....

☞ *Ritual makes me feel...*

....

....

....

☞ *Solitary rituals and group rituals are different because...*

....

....

....

☞ *The point of ritual is...*

....

....

....

22

PRACTISE

HAVING FAMILIARISED YOURSELF earlier with the concept of the three realms and the four elements, here follows two methods by which we may ritualise those concepts. These are fairly comprehensive rituals with a lot of detail; they can be shortened or lengthened to suit your needs. Primarily these are the rituals that bookend the intent of the ritual or the work itself. You will note that each ritual format has a section delineated at its midway point where the work is performed.

The Triskelion Ritual of Land, Sea, and Sky[87]

This ritual can be performed solitary or in a group. The following text is written as if for a single practitioner; in a group setting, the individual elements of the ritual can be assigned to different people to perform. Keep in mind that in a group ritual setting it is good practise to have a single individual that takes on the role of master of ceremonies; this ensures that the flow of the ritual is maintained. This keeps everything nice and tidy and prevents disruptive breaks.

---

87 This ritual is inspired by the rituals of the Anglesey Druid Order and adapted from
The Book of Celtic Magic by Kristoffer Hughes.

For the most basic version of this ritual, you will need a wand and a cauldron or similar vessel at the centre of your ritual space. Imagine or mark three points of a spiral that radiate out from the position of your cauldron, similar to the image above. Each spiral represents one of the three realms. It is entirely your choice which spiral represents which realm. You may wish to place symbolic markers or items that express each realm; examples would be a stone for land, a chalice of water for sea, and a feather or incense for sky. The choice is entirely yours, and you may be as simple or as elaborate as you wish. You would position the items prior to beginning the ritual. When you are ready and satisfied with your space, you can begin.

As you approach your ritual space, consciously change your demeanour. We are all capable of having a ritual persona; this is where the performance aspect of ritual comes into its own. Be aware of your posture: change the way you hold yourself; stand taller, firmer; become the Druid that you are! Be as tall and sturdy as a tree. As you arrive at your ritual space, walk directly to the centre. Stand with feet shoulder-width apart and arms extended slightly from your body with palms facing outwards. Take a note of where you are and notice as much of your surroundings as possible while breathing steadily and deeply. Gently allow your eyes to close. Feel the firmness of the earth beneath you and take one deep and audible breath with the land beneath your feet; draw the energies of the earth up through your feet to pulsate through your body. Remember the details of the ritual energy section that I covered earlier, and use that breath to actively feel your connection to the land. As you take that deep breath in, hold it for a few seconds and sense the land within you. Exhale fully and audibly.

Now imagine the seas and oceans; see their waves crashing onto the beaches. They may be nowhere in sight or at vast distances from you; in that case, imagine a light in the centre of your being, and then extend that light in an instant, like the flash of a camera, to the shores; take a second deep and audible breath with the seas that surround you. Draw this energy into you and feel the tides of your being moving with the seas. Hold that breath for a few seconds, sensing the sea's ebb and flow within you. Exhale fully and audibly.

Now lift your chin skyward, towards the skies above your head, and take a third deep and audible breath with the sky, pulling that energy down through your mouth and nose and deep into the core of your being. Feel the moistness of sky as it sinks further into your body. Recall the previous examples of working with the realm of sky and any subsequent exploration you have done to really bring that realm into your body in this moment. Hold that breath for a few seconds, sensing the power of sky within you. Exhale fully and audibly.

Take a further three breaths with land, sea, and sky, each time recalling your connection to the three realms. Repeat for a third time and then reach for your wand and hold it in your active hand.

With your wand in your power hand, walk consciously, with awareness of each footfall, to the point of the triskele that you have designated as land. Stand with your feet shoulder-width apart. Stretch your active arm and point your wand towards the ground/land at an angle of approximately 45 degrees. Keep your other arm next to your body with the palm of your hand facing the ground.

Repeat these words or similar with power and conviction, evoking the visualisation and the emotions you encountered in your contemplations with the realm of land.

Songs of the land, I call to you—come by memory of ancestors to this place. By tree and sod, by rock and mountain, I summon the powers of the firmament. Come by molten stone and iron core; hearken to these words I speak. Moon of earth, now hear my call; come by rays of silver light. Material realms both near and far, stir now to this call. Gods and goddesses of the land, O mighty ones [insert names], I call you: bring to this space your wisdom and guidance. Come by means of plant and tree; arise from hill and mound. Spirits and creatures of the land, arise; stir now to these words. Powers of the land, *be here now!*

Take a deep and audible breath with the land as you draw your wand back towards your body, pointing straight down to the ground at all times; held close to the body, this is the wand's neutral position as you transition from one point of the triskele to another. Sense the power of land and what it represents spiralling at the terminus of the triskele arm. As you do, repeat these words three times:

Gods of land, to thee I bow; realm of land, *be here now!*

Slowly, being conscious of every footfall, turn around and walk back towards the centre and then immediately to the point of the triskele that you have designated to represent the sea.

Stand with your feet shoulder-width apart. Stretch your power arm and point your wand directly at the horizon. Hold your free arm close to your body and curl your forearm up, your hand should be just in front of your shoulder with your palm facing the horizon.

Repeat these words or similar with power and conviction, evoking the visualisation and the emotions you encountered during your contemplation of sea:

Songs of the sea, I call to you—hearken to this call! Come by powers of the ninth wave to this place. Songs of ocean's ebb and flow, come and greet thy caller; lunar lover and currents wide pull against thy tide. Creatures of the depths of time, stir and hear my cries; trenches deep that encompass mine, abyss of nothingness shine. Realm of mystery and currents long, come now to this place. From depths of earth to unknown worlds, I call you to this space. Mighty ones, spirits and creatures of the sea, gods and goddesses of the seas within and those without, [insert names], come by wave and tide. *be here now!*

Take a deep and audible breath with the powers of the sea as you draw your wand back towards your body; hold it in its neutral position. Sense the power of sea and what it represents spiralling at the terminus of the triskele arm; as you do, repeat these or similar words three times:

Gods of sea, to thee I bow; realm of sea, *be here now!*

Slowly, being conscious of every footfall, turn around and walk back towards the centre and then immediately to the point of the triskele that you have designated to represent the realm of sky.

Again, stand with feet shoulder-width apart. Stretch your power arm upwards so that it is vertically above your head and point your wand directly at the sky. Position your free arm horizontally to the side, with your palm turned to face the sky.

Repeat these words or similar with power and conviction, evoking the visualisation and the emotions you encountered during your contemplation of sky:

> Songs of the sky, I call to thee—hearken to this call! Lofty place of spirits, come by breath of Awen to this place. Songs of dawn and twilight of vitality and inspiration, hear this call; come be in this space. Winged ones seen and unseen, and those who dwell between, listen to this cry. Place of apparition and bridge of spirit and soul, starlit skies and breath within, I draw one to the other. Gods and goddesses of the skies, O mighty ones [insert names], come by sigh and song. *Be here now!*

Take another deep and audible breath with the powers of the sky as you draw your wand back towards your body; hold it in its neutral position. Sense the power of sky and what it represents spiralling at the terminus of the triskele arm. Repeat these or similar words three times:

> Gods of sky, to thee I bow; realm of sky, *Be here now!*

Slowly, being conscious of every footfall, turn around and walk directly to the cauldron at the centre. It is at this point that you would state the intention of the ritual. Hold your arms out horizontally, with your wand held aloft above the cauldron, and state your intention. For example:

> I come to this place where land, sea, and sky are present, and in the company of [insert deity names]. I come with honour and without malice. My intention is to cause healing for [name]. Spirits of this place, witness and protect this rite.

Sense the spirals of the triskele pulsing to the powers of land, sea, and sky. Now focus your attention on the cauldron as the portal to the otherworld. From its depths bubbles the current of the universe, the Awen; all potential is here. You now summon this force from the depth of meaning.

Hold both your hands over the cauldron, angled so that your wand is pointing directly into its belly. And here comes the tricky bit—a splash of real Celticism. Do not be daunted. Words have power—throw yourself into the moment! Close your eyes and imagine a seething torrent of energy cascading from the cauldron and enveloping everything around you; see it permeating everything.

Speak these words with power and conviction; repeat them in multiples of three until you *feel* the Awen bubbling within you, its currents pulling your atoms and molecules to itself. Know that these ancient words are connecting you by sound and intent back through the mists of time; you speak the words of the ancestors. All the powers of Celtica arise with the uttering of these words:

> *Yr Awen a ganaf—or dwfn y dygaf.* [88]
> (Urr Ah-when A GAN-av—Oh-rr DOO-vun Uh DUG-av.)

If all that is too much for you, then repeat them in English (provided below) or alternate both Middle Welsh and English; the choice is entirely yours. It's the connection that matters.

> The Awen I sing—from the deep I bring it. [89]

As you feel the currents move through you, raise both your arms up to form a wide V shape. Hands to the skies, wand held aloft, chant the three sacred vowels of Awen:

> O, I, W
> (pronounced *oh, ee, oo*)

Allow all three vowels to cascade one after the other in a single breath. Breathe in and repeat in multiples of three. Many Druids also choose to intone or chant the word Awen itself; in that case, instead of the vowel sounds that are particular to the Welsh tradition of Druidry, you would chant the three syllables of Awen three times:

> Ah-oo-en

Breathe deeply at the conclusion of the chant.

The Work

Next you will perform the body of the ritual itself; this may be a celebration of the season, a work of healing or magic, divination, or a rite of passage. Having set the scene, you are now ready to begin your ritual work.

---

88 Haycock, "Angar Kyfundawt" in *Legendary Poems from the Book of Taliesin.*
89 Ibid., my translation.

Conclusion

When the main focus of your ritual reaches its conclusion, it is time to close the space and end the ritual. None of the components that you called will be dismissed as such—they are powers that are continuously present, and we have not summoned them to attend but rather simply acknowledged their presence. Concluding the ritual will be a system of acknowledgement and honouring.

Place your hands over the cauldron, wand aloft in your power hand. Close your eyes and intone the three sacred vowels or the word Awen, again in multiples of three.

See the bubbling essence of the flowing spirit within the cauldron. Imagine your intent sinking into the ever-flowing course of the Awen, working its magic, affecting and changing. Take three deep breaths and acknowledge the power of the Awen within you.

Walk firmly to the point representing sky, assume the position you did when calling it, and say:

> Powers of sky, spirits and creatures of the land, gods/goddesses (name them) of the lofty places, hear these words. Long may you inspire and bring meaning; long may you serve as a bridge between spirit and soul. I give you thanks, sky within and skies without. Blessings to the realm of sky.

Walk swiftly by means of the centre to the point of sea; assume the same position, wand pointed to the horizon, and say:

> Powers of the sea, spirits and creatures of the sea, gods/goddesses (name them) of the deep, hear these words. Sing your songs of unity and current, long may you serve as the flow of the soul. I give you thanks, sea within and seas without. Blessings to the realm of sea.

Return to the centre and move swiftly onto the final position, wand pointed towards the ground, and say:

> Powers of the land, spirits, and creatures of the land, gods/goddesses [name them] of the firmament, hear these words. May you stand firm and your songs forever sing in the smallest parts of being. May you serve to remind us of our place of origin. I give thanks to the land within and the lands without. Blessings to the realm of land.

Return to the centre and, with a sharp intake of breath, see the shield that you extended to the edges of the ritual space shrink. It does so almost like a bubble bursting and returns in a split second to the core of your being.

The ritual is complete.

Grounding

It is imperative that you return yourself fully to the ordinary world, lest a part of you becomes lost in the in-between places, leaving one feeling somewhat beside oneself. Dizziness and a sense of not quite being present are symptoms of not having fully grounded after the experience of ritual. Therefore, ensure that you eat something and have a drink; if you are with friends, laugh and enjoy being with each other. Later, participate in something mundanely human: wash the dishes, do some laundry, clean something, watch TV, anything that will bring you fully back to earth.

The Four Elements Ritual

I present this ritual as if in a group setting where multiple roles are available; a solitary practitioner would perform all roles. This is a pretty full-on ritual, and you are welcome to adapt, edit, and adjust it to your needs and taste. Providing a comprehensive ritual gives you the scope to edit it down to your needs, but know that you can also add as much to it as you feel is necessary and right for your ritual.

All participants arrive at the specified ritual area and prepare the site according to the ritual plan. In a group setting, the ritual coordinator or leader will have preassigned each individual element of the rite to the group members who will be active during the proceedings.

Leader:

> To know truth, to love truth, to maintain truth; let us arrive fully in this place
> with honour and integrity, respect and reverence.

All participants take three breaths: one with the land, one with the sea, and the last with the sky.

All present recite the Druid's Prayer:[90]

> Grant O spirit/god/goddess your protection,
> And in protection, strength;
> And in strength, understanding;
> And in understanding, knowledge;
> And in knowledge, the knowledge of righteousness;
> And in the knowledge of righteousness, the love of it;
> And in the love of it, the love of all existences;
> And in the love of all existences, the love of spirit/
> god/goddess and all goodness.

Now chant the Awen, calling for inspiration to flood into the grove and the circle, by intoning the vowels of the Awen (as seen in the triskelion ritual) or chanting the word Awen itself in a single breath. Repeat three times.

> O, I, W (pronounced *oh, ee, oo*)
> Ah-oo-en

All present focus on the environment that surrounds them, opening their senses to become acutely aware of the subtle energies within the landscape, grounding themselves in this place and this time. The leader then proceeds to declare the intention of the rite and asks that peace be declared within the space. A chosen member of the grove approaches the eastern quarter and speaks:

> Creatures and people of the East, lands of the rising sun, may you strive for peace, may you grow from peace. May there be peace throughout the East.

Moving to the southern quarter:

> Creatures and people of the South, land of the midday sun, may you strive for peace, may you grow from peace. May there be peace throughout the South.

---

90 This was inspired by Iolo Morganwg's Gorsedd Prayer. Williams, *The Barddas of Iolo Morganwg*, 363.

Moving to the western quarter:

> Creatures and people of the West, land of the setting sun, may you strive for peace, may you grow from peace. May there be peace throughout the West.

Moving to the northern quarter:

> Creatures and people of the North, land of the night and cold, may you strive for peace, may you grow from peace. May there be peace throughout the North.

Moving to the centre of the circle:

> May there be peace above and peace below, and peace throughout all the worlds.

The leader then asks the grove if there is peace three times: "Is there peace?" to which they respond, "There is peace!"

The leader now approaches the eastern quarter; the remaining grove should form a circle close to the centre of the space. With a wand or chosen tool, the leader begins to draw the first of the three circles in a clockwise direction. This is the circle of Ceugant; in the Welsh Druid tradition, this circle represents the first principle of life, the place beyond the regions of the gods and the primordial origin of all things.

> From the depth of darkness do we draw this circle round, from the cauldron that made the gods and the darkness before the shining pillars of life.

Moving a few inches inwards, the leader draws the second circle of Gwynfyd. In the Welsh tradition, this realm is the spiritual dimension, the subtle realm that is invisible to mortal eyes, yet its influence can be acutely felt and sensed.

> From the darkness shines the light of spirit. We draw this circle in honour of our ancestors and those who assist us from beyond the veil. Spirits of Gwynfyd, you within the halls of the dead, witness our rite.

The third circle is drawn around the grove itself and represents the here and now, the realm of Abred. This is the apparent world, and its drawing completes the three circles of existence, bringing all into one.

> We draw the circle of life, of stone, of mud and clay, of leaf and bark. Circle of Abred, circle of the tribe, circle of our community, may shining rays of Awen permeate this space.

In my experience, the atmosphere of drawing the circles may be enhanced if the remaining grove whispers a chant. This chant can be as complex or as simple as the grove requires, from the intoning of a single word like "Awen" to entire verses such as "Three circles here entwined; three powers now combined."

Allow your imagination to inspire you. While chanting, the grove should hold the image of the circles within their minds, watching as each one is drawn, contributing their own energy and creative force to their drawing.

Now we honour the spirits of place. Each grove member turns to face the perimeter of the circle with arms outstretched to embrace the spirits of the land.

> Spirits of this place, you of the hidden places and the shadows, hear our call. Shapers of this land, shapers of bark and crystal, of earth and rock, hear us. Know that we come with honour into your kingdom. You of wing and hoof and claw, hear us; creatures and spirits of this place, witness and share in our rite.

Next, we call upon the spirits of our ancestors that echo to us from the trees and hills, from the soft gentle breeze that tantalises our skin and awakens within us ancient memories and songs that stir the spirit.

> Ancestors, you of the hills and the wind, you who walked the fertile plains of our land, hearken to this call. You of memory and heritage and the recent dead, we honour you in our rite. Whisper to us your songs of ancient moonlight through the mists of time. Blessed be the ancestors!

Calling upon the deities of the community and those of the land is a deeply personal process, unique to each grove and individual. Many Druid groves revere a particular deity that may have been revered within their locality for centuries, acknowledged as an integral aspect of that place and that tribe. The following is an example of an invocation that calls to Modron, one of Wales's mother goddesses. After the invocation has been spoken, or during, offerings may be given to the goddess. These can take a variety of forms, from mead that is poured onto the ground or onto a votive that represents the mother goddess to incense that has been specially prepared for her being burned on hot charcoal bricks. The beauty of offerings is in their deeply personal nature that reflects the connection and relationship the Druids have to that particular deity.

Modron, great goddess of this land, you of the shining stars and the silver moonlight, hear us. Milk of the mother, bless this tribe as we honour you in our rite. You who stand at the gates of life and death, great mother of the bounty of our land, hear us now; witness our rite. Blessed be the mother!

Llŷr is the Welsh god of the seas and oceans. He epitomises the deep and profound mysteries of the deep. Suitable offerings would be any form of liquid libation.

Llŷr, our lord of the waters that lap at our islands, hearken to this call. You of the waves and of the wild and forlorn places, hear us. You who guard the doorways to the west and open the portals of death, hear us. Mighty lord of this ocean, we come with honour and reverence; witness our rite. Blessed be Llŷr!

Now we turn our attention to the four cardinal points and the elemental energies of air and fire, water and earth. Tokens to physically represent them may be placed at each point; for instance, incense for air, a candle for fire, mead for water, and a stone for earth. Those chosen to perform this task move to their appropriate quarter. Facing outwards, they begin by calling to their chosen element. Again, offerings can be given if the group deems that appropriate and necessary.

East, air:

Creatures and spirits of the East, powers of air and inspiration, hear us. You of the breath of life from the first to the last, gentle breeze and hurricane, hear us. Flowing spirit of inspiration that calls to us through the breeze, voices of our ancestors, hear us through the winds of the east. Witness and bless this rite. Hail and welcome!

South, fire:

Creatures and spirits of the South, powers of fire and intelligence, hear us. You of the burning midday sun and warmth of the hearth, flickering salamanders of candlelight and molten core of our mother, hear us. Spirits of transformation and destruction, hear us; we ask for your presence to witness and bless this rite. Hail and welcome!

West, water:

Creatures and spirits of the West, powers of water and emotion, hear us. Spirits of bubbling brooks, of wells and sacred springs, hear us; you of the rivers and lakes and oceans, hear us; flowing waters of life, we honour you here in our rite, from the blood that courses through our bodies to the droplets that escape our lungs. We ask for your presence here to bless and to witness this rite. Hail and welcome!

North, earth:

Creatures and spirits of the North, powers of earth and stability, strength of the mother, hear us. Mighty spirits that move and transform our land, raising mountains and hills, hear us. You of the hidden places that lie deep within the womb of the mother, hear us; know that we gather to honour you. Witness this rite. We bid you hail and welcome!

The leader now proclaims, "Our circle is complete; let the work begin." The work or purpose of the ritual happens in this space.

At the conclusion of the ritual work, many groves will hold an *eisteddfod*, or a Bardic sitting, allowing the creative force of the grove to express itself through poetry or song, inspiring the grove and relaying messages from the world beyond the visible.

At the conclusion of the ritual, those who called the individual spirits and elements return to their original position and bid them farewell.

The spirits of place:

Spirits and creatures of this place, thank you for your presence here. May the memory of this rite be held here always. As we return to the apparent world enriched by your presence, we give thee thanks. Blessed be the spirits of this place. Hail and farewell!

The ancestors:

Ancestors, mighty ones, you who have gone before us, we give you gratitude for your guidance and inspiration. As the doors to the halls of the dead close and we return to the apparent world, may your inspiration continue to light our lives. Blessed be the ancestors. Hail and farewell!

To Modron, the great mother:

> Mother of all life, giver and nourisher, we give thee thanks as we walk from this place; we acknowledge your flesh as land and your blood as the flowing rivers. Bestow upon us your blessings as we depart this place. Blessed be the great mother. Hail and farewell!

To Llŷr:

> Lord of the oceans, father of the deep, holder of the mysteries beyond the ninth wave, we give thee thanks. May your waters run deep in our being and your voice be heard in our words. Bestow upon us your blessings as we depart this place. Blessed be Llŷr, our father of the oceans. Hail and farewell!

It is often traditional that the elements are dismissed in reverse order, starting in the North:

> Spirits of earth, we give you thanks for supporting and securing this rite. As we depart may you bless this company with stability and strength. Blessed be the spirits of earth. Hail and farewell!

West:

> Spirits of water, we give you thanks for the stirring of hearts and minds in this ritual. As we depart from this place, may you bless us with clear intent and pure expression of hearts. Blessed be the spirits of water. Hail and farewell!

South:

> Spirits of fire, we give you thanks for the heat of passion and the fire of vitality. As we depart this place, may your warmth and heat radiate from this company in all their tasks. Blessed be the spirits of fire. Hail and farewell!

East:

> Spirits of air, we give you thanks for the breath of inspiration and clear thought. As we depart this place, may the winds of clarity and truth forever blow through us and fall from our lips. Blessed be the spirits of air. Hail and farewell!

The leader who first cast the three circles around the gathering now walks the circle anticlockwise three times, gathering up the circles. The remaining group visualises the circles as streams of blue that are sucked back up into the leader's wand. As they do, they say these words or similar:

Abred, Gwynfyd, Ceugant, three circles round
Here unto my wand return, free and now unbound.
Ceugant, Gwynfyd, Abred, three circles bright
Entwined, combined, three worlds of gleaming light.
Gwynfyd, Ceugant Abred, three worlds deep
Remain within our memory, your wisdom now we keep.

Finally, the Druid's Prayer is recited by all present one more time:

Grant O spirit/god/goddess your protection,
And in protection, strength;
And in strength, understanding;
And in understanding, knowledge;
And in knowledge, the knowledge of righteousness;
And in the knowledge of righteousness, the love of it;
And in the love of it, the love of all existences;
And in the love of all existences, the love of spirit/
    god/goddess and all goodness.

Leader:

This rite ends in peace as in peace it began. It is done.

End.

The Gorsedd Prayer

Within the previous rituals, you will have come across the words of the Gorsedd Prayer, which requires a little note of explanation. The prayer can be found in a book called *The Barddas of Iolo Morganwg*, compiled posthumously in the early part of the nineteenth century. The prayer has been used in cultural and spiritual Druidry ever since. Iolo Morganwg is essentially the father of modern Druidry, and while he is not without controversy, his work went on to inspire the Druids of the future. He was a visionary, a Bardic genius, a stonemason, a polyglot, and a wonder of the early modern Druidic revival. He dreamed a new myth into being, with the result of that dream being the current face of the Gorsedd of Bards of the Island of Britain, which oversees all the ceremonial components of the Welsh National Eisteddfod and modern Druidry. It is not an exaggeration when I say that modern Paganism in its entirety might have a different face had it not been for his influence.[91]

The prayer is said to unite all Druids and is useful as an affirmation or as a general prayer beyond the confines of a full-blown ritual. The beauty of this prayer is that it connects you directly to the inspirational stream of modern Druidry from its first stirrings by Iolo Morganwg as he declared the first new Gorsedd of Bards on Primrose Hill, overlooking the city of London, on June 21, 1792. With that knowledge, it is evident that this prayer is not ancient, but it is centuries old and contains within it the hopes and blessings of generations of people who have loved it. It offers you a Bardic connection to the ancestors of modern Druidry and the magic they seeded for the future.

For the prayer to be effective, it is wise to contemplate the meaning of each line in turn before memorising it. As you read the prayer, consider each line as a gift that arises from the previous line; they act like ripples that emanate from the great spirit or deity at the commencement and return to the original source at its conclusion. Written originally in Welsh, the prayer can be recited or sung, as is traditional in Wales. In the Welsh tradition, the Gorsedd as a song is sung in a call-and-response manner.[92]

In many English-speaking Druid groups, the words are simply recited, but if you feel brave enough to have a go, I encourage you to sing it.[93] In my personal practise, I often recite or sing the prayer when I need a moment to settle myself if I am angry or frustrated or just need to step back from a situation. Rather than the usual "stop and count to ten," I utilise the prayer instead. Its effect is threefold: it grounds me into the moment, it connects me to my ancestors, and it offers me a moment to connect to the spirit of my Druidry. By the time I have concluded the prayer, I have been reset ever so slightly; I take a breath and carry on with whatever was happening that caused me to need a moment out.

In the original Welsh, the prayer looks like this:

Dyro Dduw dy nawdd;

91 For an in-depth exploration of Iolo Morganwg and his influence, read *A Rattleskull Genius* by Geraint Jenkins. Also, an entire chapter in my book *Cerridwen* is dedicated to him.

92 Visit the following page for a sound file example: https://www.peoplescollection.wales /items/24266.

93 For an example of a modern Druid singing the prayer in Welsh and English, visit https://www.youtube.com/watch?v=NyhklF1325k.

Ag yn nawdd, nerth;
Ag yn nerth, deall;
Ag yn deall, gwybod;
Ac yng ngwybod, gwybod y cyfiawn;
Ag yngwybod y cyfiawn, ei garu,
Ag o garu, caru pob hanfod;
Ag ymhob hanfod, caru Duw;
Duw a phob daioni.

Originally Morganwg only referred to *Duw*, meaning "God" in the Christian sense; the prayer was a product of its time, after all. Subsequently, modern Druids tend to substitute that term for something more fitting with their traditions such as spirit, great spirit, or the individual name of a god or goddess. The choice is entirely yours.

An example of the prayer in English with a specific deity name would be thus:

Grant, O Rhiannon, your protection;
And in protection, strength;
And in strength, understanding;
And in understanding, knowledge;
And in knowledge, the knowledge of righteousness;
And in the knowledge of righteousness, the love of it;
And in the love of it, the love of all existences;
And in the love of all existences, the love of Rhiannon and all goodness.

Use the prayer whenever you need a moment to connect to the eternal stream of inspiration that runs through the heart of Druidry. By doing so, you honour all those who have gone before you that dreamed this Druidry into being. This prayer can also be used if you feel the need for protection or before a period of study or practise.

Morning and Evening Salutations to the Sun

These short prayers offer a moment of stillness at the beginning and the end of your day. They are brief enough to not take buckets of time but powerful enough to give pause and reflection. You can perform the salutations in the time it takes to boil an electric kettle. In both cases the prayers acknowledge the Welsh lords of light; these names can be substituted for those of your choosing.

Turn to face the direction of the rising sun and take three deep breaths with the land, the sky, and the sea. Stretch your arms in front of you with your palms facing the sunrise and repeat the following words or similar three times:

> From the gates of darkness, I greet you, O mighty sun.
> I greet thee, Beli, king of the radiant dawn.
> I greet thee, Lleu, in your splendour.
> I greet thee, lords of light.
> Bless my day with your radiancy.
> Let the light of truth shine on my actions;
> Let my truth be a guiding light for others.
> Blessed are you, lords of light.

At eventide and the close of the day, in the same manner as the morning salutations, turn to face the direction of the setting sun and say these words or similar:

> At the threshold of night, O mighty sun, I give you thanks.
> I praise you, O Beli, king of the sun.
> I praise you, O Lleu, and your splendour.
> I praise you, lords of light.
> May your light remain with me;
> May your light guide me;
> May your radiancy shine from within me.
> Blessed are you, lords of light.

Ritual Invocation of the Awen

Create a sacred space using the three realms system or four elements system, and in the work/purpose section stand in the centre of your space with your feet slightly apart, but only enough to give you a stable footing. With your arms stretched out before you and your palms facing the earth, imagine the land beneath you pulsating with the powers of Awen. It is in everything—all things sing inwardly of its power; imagine what that might sound like. Imagine a light streaming from the land itself and up into your hands and say:

Awen of earth and land, arise and come into me!

Stretch your arms directly in front of you with your palms facing the horizon and imagine all the water courses of your region and the seas that surround your land shining with the light of Awen. From the water in your faucets to the distant oceans, imagine the sound of the song of Awen within them; that song carries through moisture molecules in the air. Imagine them streaming towards you and into your body and say:

Awen of sea and water, arise and come into me!

Now raise your arms towards the sky in a wide V formation and turn your face and palms upwards. See or visualise iridescent clouds speeding through the skies as the wind of Awen blows them hither and thither. Imagine the pristine blue of a summer sky and breathe in all that light and breath into your body and say:

Awen of sky and air, arise and come into me!

Pause momentarily to feel the flow and Awen held in land, sea, and sky as they move within your being, and then position yourself to mimic the pattern of the three rays thus: standing with feet shoulder-width apart, extend your arms at 30-degree angles from your sides with hands open and palms facing outwards.

Breathe deeply three times, and as you do imagine above your head a swirling vortex of silvery clouds. From the clouds a silvery-blue beam of light bursts forth and penetrates the top of your head, passing through your body, between your legs, and into the ground between your feet. As you visualise it, intone the vowel O (*oh*) a minimum of three times, seeing the lights shining through you.

Cast your attention to the clouds once more and see another beam of light burst forth to penetrate your right shoulder and pass down your arm, out through the tips of your fingers and on into the ground. As you do, intone the second vowel, I, whose sound is *ee,* a minimum of three times.

Next, see a beam of light pass from the cloud, through your left shoulder, down your arm, and into the ground. As you do, intone the final vowel, W, whose sound is *oo*, a minimum of three times.[94]

Now see yourself glowing with the light of the Awen; imagine a gentle breeze accompanying it, teasing your hair and clothing. Take to standing in this position, visualising the light and singing the vowel sounds over and over, until you lose track of yourself and the sounds that you are making. Remain in this space for as long as you are able to, basking in the light and breath of the Awen. Imagine what your body looks like penetrated by the rays of light, or /|\, with the center ray aligned with your spine and the side rays aligned with your arms. As you sense the completion of the work, allow the clouds above you to slowly melt away, but keep the image of your body filled with the light of Awen. Know that you are inspired; know that you are inspirational.

Now, return to the three realms or four elements system and close your ritual space.

Prayers to the Parent Deities of Land, Sea, and Sky

Dôn, Llŷr, and Beli Mawr are the presiding parent deities of land, sea, and sky, respectively, in the Welsh tradition. These prayers are simply offerings of praise to them and their realms. They are usually orated in multiples of three and optionally with accompanying offerings. Consider locations within your vicinity that might be suitable for performing and presenting your prayers and the giving of offerings. If you are choosing to do them at home, consider items or symbols that represent the deities and place them on your working altar or sacred space. These deities are specific to the Welsh Celtic tradition, which may not sit perfectly well with you; in that case, consider if there are equivalent deities in your locale or culture and substitute the names. In any form of prayer or petition, it is relationship that matters most; therefore, foster and nurture relationship with the deities that represent these powers in your square mile.

Another Prayer to Dôn, the Earth Mother[95]

---

94 If it is your preference, you can intone the word Awen itself broken down into three sounds: *ah, oo, en.* Either is fine and traditional as long as you are comfortable with the sounds you are making.

95 You may recall that there's a prayer to Dôn on page 203 too.

Suitable offerings are water, wine, or other liquid offered as a libation.
In Welsh:[96]

> Dôn, arglwyddes y fam ddaear, faethlon, croth pob enaid byw,
> A'u gorffwysfa ar ddiwedd einioes,
> Fe alwaf arna ti.
> Dôn, mam y tir, Duwies y ddaear,
> I ti rhow'n foliant,
> Caraf dy fynyddau, dy afonydd,
> Bryniau a chreigiau,
> Moliannaf ti—o fy Nuwies.
> Dyro dy fendithion arna'i.

Translation:

> Dôn, lady of earth, great nourisher, the womb of all living things,
> And our rest at the end of living,
> I call to you.
> Dôn, mother of the land, goddess of earth,
> To you I sing praise,
> In the love of your mountains and rivers,
> Your hills and rocks,
> I give you, my goddess, my praise.
> Bestow upon me your blessings.

---

96 Spoken versions of this prayer can be heard online; see the resources section.

A Prayer to Llŷr, God of the Seas

Suitable offerings are water, wine, or spirits. Do not offer plant material or items with man-made fabrics into the sea.

In Cymraeg:

> Llŷr, tad y tonnau, arglwydd y môr,
> Y ti yw dirgelwch tu hwnt ir nawfed don,
> Y ti yw dirgelwch y dwfn,
> Fe alwaf arna ti.
> Duw y moroedd,
> I ti rhow'n foliant,
> Y ti biau'r moroedd,
> A'r dyfroedd pob dafn,
> Moliannaf ti—O fy Nuw.
> Dyro dy fendithion arna'i.

Translation:

> Llŷr, father of the waves, lord of the seas,
> You who are the mystery beyond the ninth wave,
> You who are a mystery of the deep,
> I call to you.
> God of the ocean,
> To you I sing in praise,
> You are the oceans wide and deep,
> You are in every drop of water,
> I give you, my god, my praise.
> Bestow upon me your blessings.

A Prayer to Beli Mawr, God of the Sky/Sun

A suitable offering is incense smoke.

> Dwyfol Beli Mawr, duw y teyrnas uchel,
> Argwlydd yr awyr,
> Y cymylau a'r ddrycin,
> Fe alwaf arna ti.
> Beli Mawr, Tad yr awyr, brenin yr haul,

Penarglwyddiaeth yr Awen,
Bendigaid bu dy oleuni,
Awel a gwynt yw dy gân,
Moliannaf ti O fy Nuw.
Dyro dy fendithion arna'i.

Translation:

Blessed Beli Mawr, god of the lofty places,
Lord of the skies,
The clouds and tempests,
I call to you.
Beli Mawr, father of sky, king of the sun,
Sovereign of Awen,
Blessed be your light;
The breeze and winds are your songs,
I give you, my god, my praise.
Bestow upon me your blessings.

A Chant to Charge any Spell or Work of Magic

When creating a spell, called a *swyn* in Cymraeg, it is made particularly effective if you use your voice to enchant or charge the intention of the work. The most effective are those that you create yourself. In doing so, try as best as you can to get the chant to rhyme so that you will remember it more easily, and it will act as a repetitive mantra that will affect your mind and attention as you use it. The chant that follows in Welsh is one that I use the most in my personal practise. I created it in a fashion that can be used for the majority of magic that I perform. It rhymes perfectly in Welsh, but alas, the rhythm is lost in translation. You are, of course, welcome to use it, but I encourage you to create your own.

In Welsh:

Coed, tân, blodau, fflam,
Dyfroedd, awyr, daear fam,
Codwch, dewch, clywch fy nghri,
Rhowch i'm swyn eich pwêr chi.

Literal translation:

> Trees, fire, flowers, flame,
> Oceans deep, sky, and earth mother,
> Arise, come, hear my call,
> Lend to my spell your power.

Rhyming translation with some nuance lost:

> Fire, flowers, flame, trees,
> Earth mother, sky, and oceans deep,
> Arise, come, I call to you,
> Your powers to my spell imbue.

Ritual examples have the potential to fill countless books. The previous suggestions are indicative of actual practise; for more examples, see the suggested reading and resources sections of this book.

23

A DRUID Q AND A

HAVING READ THE previous chapters, it will be evident to you that there may well be things that lie outside the scope of this book to address. You may have had certain questions arise as you read this book. Therefore, what follows are a series of questions and answers that attempt to fill in some of the gaps you may have in your understanding of Druidry. They are by no means exhaustive, but they do offer a wider perspective on some Druid practises and principles that may not have warranted entire chapters.

Do I need tools to practise Druidry?

In short, no, but you may decide that you fancy physical items that may deepen or add to your practise. In my own practise, the only true tools that I have are wands, but even these are unnecessary to be a practising Druid. The reason I choose to work with wands is twofold; the first is that wands appear in the myths of Cymru, and the second is they act as a bridge to connect me to my magical allies. I have a range of wands that enable me to work with the specific energy of different trees for the purposes of my rituals or magical work. Each wand has been handcrafted either by myself or a Druid companion. They offer a powerful way by which I can continuously connect with the wisdom of the trees and incorporate their qualities into my Druid practise.

Do I need a new wardrobe of robes and cloaks?

No. Special clothing is not a requirement nor an expectation; however, many Druids do wear ritual clothing when they are practising. The primary function of ritual attire is to subtly change the way you feel by wearing something that is slightly out of the ordinary. This is not an alien concept to people; we will dress in special clothes to attend a party or a special occasion. The same is true for ritual clothing, which further cements the fact that something extraordinary is about to take place. This does not suit everybody, and you may be equally as comfortable in your own everyday clothing.

Do I need an altar?

Altars are sacred spaces set aside for religious or spiritual activity. They can be seen as portals between worlds and can be considered places that give us space by which to pause, contemplate, and practise one's spiritualty. While an altar is not a requirement of Druidry, many Druids do have them, and some may have several altars within their homes and garden spaces. An altar can be anything from a designated table top or shelf that is set aside for sacred work. They may be adorned with symbols that represent their function. An altar does not define your Druidry, but they can provide organic spaces that grow with you and reflect your practise. In my personal practise, I have several altars in my home; some are dedicated to the various deities I am devoted to, another is for the spirit of the house itself. They punctuate my home in a way that gives me pause for reflection and are spaces where I can focus my devotion and practise my spirituality.

Do Druids engage with politics?

Druidry has always been a political statement, and many of our Druid ancestors were active on the political scene, either as politicians themselves or as activists. In modern Druidry, environmental politics and ecological issues are first and foremost for many Druids, who strive to make changes within their local, national, or global political landscape. Engaging in political activity is ultimately a choice of the individual and their compulsion to be involved; not all Druids are drawn to the political spectrum. When it comes to matters of peace and the maintaining of peace, Druids have a tendency to do what they can to stand up for it. The degree of political action is individually dependant on what that Druid can do or feels inclined to do. Some Druids give their time to charities and organisations that operate within a particular political spectrum, while others who feel they are unable to be physically active may give of their energy through donations.

What are the ethics of Druidry?

Modern Druid ethics arise from the concept of sacred relationship. There are no strict rules in Druidry that define how a Druid should or should not behave or conduct themselves. It is a free and liberal tradition. Many Pagan practitioners will adhere to the rule of three: what you give out will return to you threefold. No such rule exists in Druidry. The tradition places responsibility firmly on the practitioner and their ability to respond to ethical issues. When we are in relationship with something or someone, our actions are tempered and moderated by the quality of that relationship. Deeming whether an action is good or bad or neutral is solely the responsibility of each individual. Many Druids will subscribe to the principle of cause and effect, or whatever you throw into the ocean will return on the tide, however transformed. This asks us to be mindful of our choices and know that our actions have consequences; if we are able to morally and ethically live with those consequences, fair enough. If we can't, then it's best not to proceed with that action. Druidry is a tradition that honours personal choice and expression of self. By honouring oneself, one should be more able to honour others. Druidry does not judge people on lifestyle choices unless those actions upset the peace or cause harm to another. Consent is paramount to good, decent human behaviour. We use honour and sacred relationships as gauges to moderate our individual behaviour.

Do I need to be Celtic?

No. Celticity is defined by cultural expression, and Druidry is an aspect of that culture, but it is not a closed practise. The various constitutions described earlier in this book may capture the reasons why you are drawn to Druidry. Because it is a facet of culture, it is important that you follow that with education. By arming yourself with knowledge and information about the Celtic cultures that thrive today, you will be compelled to serve those cultures in meaningful ways, contributing to them and not taking from them. For the past fifty years or so, Druidry has been flavoured by the English language and English culture, but it does so while honouring its Celtic origins. You can be in active relationship with what it means to be Celtic by learning elements of language, history, and the demographics of current Celtic-speaking peoples.

I am a [insert religious affiliation]; can I also be a Druid?

Yes, you can. Druidry is inclusive of any worldview or thought, and the majority of early modern Druids from the Romantic era were Christians. If the religion you adhere to offers the flexibility and freedom to explore another spiritual practise, then there is no reason why you cannot incorporate both. Look to the doctrine, elders, and teachings of your current religion for guidance and advice.

Do I need to join a group or an order to be a Druid?

No. There is no requirement for you to become a member of a group, a grove, or an order. The path of the solitary Druid is just as viable. There are several books on the market today that are written specifically for the solitary practitioner. Druids who are inclined to join groups do so for community and for structured teaching within a particular tradition.

Can I start my own group or grove of Druids?

Yes, you can. If you decide that you would like to be a part of a larger community of Druids and there are no such groups in your vicinity, then maybe you should be the Druid who starts one. Before you do, it is important that you consider the reasons for such a group to exist and what it will offer to those who may join it, and how they in turn will contribute. When beginning a group, it is necessary that you have some understanding of group dynamics and that you set some boundaries or rules to contain and steer the group's energy. Decide if your group is to be a study group or one that engages and practices ritualistically or both. If you decide to run a study group, be consistent in what you study and see it through to its conclusion before moving on to something else. A good idea is to study a particular myth, technique, or idea for a set duration of time, allowing time at its conclusion for feedback and group sharing. Running a group or a grove can be exhausting; learn techniques to look after and preserve your energy.

I identify as LGBTQ+; am I welcome in Druidry?

Yes. Druidry welcomes any and all sexualities, genders, and expressions thereof. Individuals are not judged by who they choose to love, have physical and sexual relations with, or how they choose to express their inner nature. From a Druid perspective, all beings are expressions of the universe singing in praise of itself. Druidry tends to not be dualistic and can be practised in a non-binary fashion. Sexuality is celebrated in Druidry with the emphasis on consent as a primary rule.

I am a witch; can I also be a Druid?

Yes, you can; as this book has demonstrated, there are parallels between the development of Druidry and the modern religion of witchcraft, Wicca. The craft of the witch can be seen emulated in the qualities of the Ovate. There are aspects of Druidic magical practise that are indistinguishable from witchcraft and folk magical practise. Many witches choose to learn about Druidry to deepen their devotional practises and their relationships with Celtic deities.

Is Druidry an animistic tradition?

Predominantly, yes. Animism is the concept that all things are expressions of the divine or have a spark of the creative force within them. According to Dr. Graham Harvey in his Animist Manifesto, the world is populated by other-than-human persons. He goes on to explain that all that exists is alive and living, and that all of those lives are worthy of respect. In turn, you don't have to like what you respect, but not liking them is no reason for not showing them respect.[97] Many Druids acknowledge this principle of a world full of other-than-human persons. To nontheistic Druids, those who do not believe in the gods, it offers another method of connecting to the natural world that is not deity specific.

I have disabilities; does this limit my experience of being a Druid?

No. In the modern world, and effectively demonstrated during the COVID-19 pandemic, our technologies have enabled less-abled Druids to engage in community, education and ritual from the comfort of their own homes. I am personally aware of several Druids with various disabilities who have never been able to attend an open ritual or a conference; when these events moved online during the pandemic, that dynamic changed. A person with limited internet access could access books on Druidry to further their studies and practise. Druidry is not solely a nature-based spirituality; it also operates on the subtle and magical realms, and no access to the natural world is

---

97 Harvey, "An Animist Manifesto," https://www.animism.org.uk/HarveyAnimism%20flyer.
    pdf.

necessary for that to occur. If a connection to the natural world is something that the Druid desires, even those who are unable to leave their homes can maintain garden spaces, window boxes, and indoor plants to offer the opportunity to connect with the non-human world.

Do Druids believe in an afterlife?

This is not an easy question, and there is no one cover-all answer. If we look to the accounts of the classical authors, there is a suggestion that the Druids believed this life to be one point along a very long line of existence. Celtic mythology and the Bardic tradition imply a continuation, but it does not necessarily convey in precisely what form. The otherworld in Celtic myth is not synonymous with the land of the dead. If there is any consistency in the Celtic world, it is the implication of continuation. In my experience of Druidry and from having been a death services professional for over thirty years, I believe this life to be only one phase along an eternal existence that is not defined by my experience in this lifetime but does embrace it. Upon my death, I believe that the apparent persona of Kristoffer will die as he is a product of this world and the relationships forged here. But the permanent persona that has always existed will maintain its course, carrying the memories of Kristoffer with it forever. Other Druids may tell you something completely different.[98]

Do I need psychic or similar skills to be a Druid?

No. These are not skills that are necessary for practising Druidry, but you may find that your intuitive skills are heightened as you progress and develop your practise. This can often lead to an increased sense of the subtle and energetic, which may in turn heighten your psychic abilities.

98 See my book on death and dying, *As the Last Leaf Falls* (previously titled *The Journey into Spirit*).

CONCLUSION

CONTINUING YOUR JOURNEY

A BOOK OF this nature is limited by the sheer scope of potentiality within Druidry. My hope is to have offered you a place from which to start your personal exploration. Druidry has not only changed and transformed my life, it has brought to it significant joy and a profound sense of wonder and awe. There have been many times when the path has been difficult and overwhelming, but I have maintained to the best of my abilities my Pwyll, Pryderi, and Lleu qualities. There have been times when I have failed at all three and acted in ways anathema to their virtues, but I have persevered, taken responsibility for my actions, and found a way to bring those virtues back into focus. I hasten to imagine that your path may mirror my own at times, but when those moments of doubt occur or when direction seems to elude you, hold on to the wonder that initially drew you. Revisit your moment of wild awakening and evoke the Lleu within you. A book is a guide, a friendly hand that takes yours and whispers to you as we walk together across a midnight meadow towards a distant forest. A book of this nature contains the hopes and dreams of its author, and their deepest desire to inspire.

My hope is that my words will offer you the same sense of wonderment and enchantment that Druidry brings to my life, or at least a sense of their potential. The forest of Druidry has many paths that meander through the dappled groves, but there is no single destination; instead, it is a path that meets innumerable groves along its course. It is a journey into wisdom that serves to plant seedlings of that wisdom for others to touch and be inspired by long after you have left this earth. Druidry is truly a call to action for being oak-wise and standing as a beacon of Awen in a world that can, at times, be difficult and troublesome. I hope that this book has gone some way into helping you answer the questions that were posed to you at the beginning of this book. In time, look back at the other questions asked of you, now held within this book, and reevaluate them; have they changed? If so, how? What does that change say about your spiritual journey into the grove of the Druids?

With that, it is time to revisit those initial questions and see whether they have changed since you first encountered them.

∙ ∙ ∙ ∙ ∙ ∙

☞ *I think a Druid is...*

....

....

....

☞ *Can someone be a Druid in the modern world?*

....

....

....

☞ *This is what I think a Druid does:*

....

....

....

☞ *The function of a Druid is...*

....

....

....

∙ ∙ ∙ ∙ ∙ ∙

In addition, perhaps you might take a fancy and attempt to answer these questions:

* * * * * *

☞ *I am a Druid because...*

....

....

....

☞ *As a Druid, I shall...*

....

....

....

* * * * * *

Where do you go from here? Read as much as you can about the subjects that bring meaning and value to the Druid tradition. Speak with others within the wider Druid community, for it is as diverse as there are trees in the forest. Look to the other Celtic nations for inspiration. But above all, do your Druidry, and do it in a way that causes you to crackle with light and inspiration. Share your Druidry, and bask in the Awen of others who choose to share their Druidry with you. Be a novice, a student, and a teacher all at once, and never pause in your learning.

To be a Druid is to be an agent of the Awen in this world. It is to stand upon the shoulders of giants whose legacy stretches back into the furthest recesses of time. To be a Druid is to speak the language of trees and share their wisdom with a world whose thirst for sagacity and enchantment can be quenched by your ability to be oak-wise.

I wish you a journey of awe that is Awen filled and truly fabulous.

Bendithion. Yours in the grove of the Druids,

Kristoffer

ACKNOWLEDGMENTS

Writing a book is a difficult task, and it is particularly tricky when English is not one's first language. I am thankful to the countless friends who help keep my English on course. Writing a book of any nature does not happen in a vacuum, and several people have helped in one way or another to bring this book to life. I am indebted to many members of the Anglesey Druid Order who endured my endless questioning and probing and to the kind authors who agreed to read advance versions of this book. My editorial team at Llewellyn Worldwide, in particular Elysia and Becky, always strive to steer my work onto the right tracks and help me become the best writer I can be; thank you.

A GUIDE TO WELSH PRONUNCIATION

THERE ARE A lot of Welsh words and phrases in this book. To help you with their pronunciation, I offer this simple guide to the Welsh language; in addition, video files are also available on my YouTube channel—see the resources section for direction. In contrast to English, there are no silent letters in the Welsh alphabet; every letter is pronounced phonetically. Every letter has a sound, and the sound is vocalised in spoken Welsh. The stress of any word almost exclusively stands on the penultimate syllable. The sound of a vowel is elongated if it appears with a circumflex above it; in Welsh this is referred to as a *to bach* (a "little roof"). As an example, one appears thus: ô, e.g., Don without the circumflex would be pronounced as Donn, as in to *don* a coat. With the addition of a circumflex—Dôn—it would be pronounced in the same manner as the English word *dawn*.

The modern Welsh alphabet appears thus and contains twenty-eight letters, some of which are not present in English:

a, b, c, ch, d, dd, e, f, ff, g, ng, h, i, l, ll, m, n, o, p, ph, r, rh, s, t, th, u, w, y

Welsh Vowels

The Welsh language has seven vowels, in contrast to the five common vowels in English. In some instances, the letters I and W may act as consonants.

a	short as in *mat*	long as in *farmer*
e	short as in *let*	long as in *bear*

i	short as in *pit*	long as in *meet*
o	short as in *lot*	long as in *lore*
u	short as in *ill*	long as in *limb*

- U is a tricky sound to mimic and sounds different between north and south Wales. In south Wales it is similar to the sound of the letter *i*, while in the north it resembles the French *u* and is often described as a sound one makes to express repulsion. This is perhaps one of the most difficult letters to articulate phonetically in written English.

w	short as in *look*	long as in *fool*
y	short as in *hiss*	long as in *under*

- If present in the final word or syllable, it will sound similar to the letter u. Otherwise, it sounds like *uh*.

Welsh Consonants

Some may be similar in sound to their English counterparts but with emphasis on heavy aspiration of sound.

b	as in *bin*
c	as in *cat*
ch	as in *loch*, never as in *chin*
d	as in *dad*
dd	as in *them*, never as in *thin*
e	as in *elephant*
f	as in *van*
ff	as in *off*
g	as in *gate*, never as in *gem*
ng	as in *song*, never as in *linger*
h	as in *hit*; it is never silent
l	as in *lit*
ll	no counterpart; voice by placing tip of tongue in *L* position and exhaling voicelessly through the sides of the mouth

m	as in *mat*
n	as in *nit*
p	as in *part*
ph	as in *phrase*
r	trilled by the tip of the tongue, as *ravioli* in Italian
rh	no counterpart; voice by placing tongue in *R* position and exhaling quickly and harshly but voicelessly through the narrow gap the lips form
s	as in *sit*, never as in *kiss*
t	as in *tap*
th	as in *thick*, never as in *them*

GLOSSARY

Abred (AB-redd): the material world

Alban—(AL-ban): a quarter, solstice, or equinox

Annwfn (Ann-OO-vn) also Annwn (ANN-oon): Welsh term for the indigenous otherworld of the Welsh Celts

Aranrhod (Ar-ANN-rhod): goddess, daughter of the mother goddess Dôn and Beli Mawr

Awen (Ah-when): blessed, holy breath; the spirit of creative transformation and inspiration

Awst (OUST): Lammas

Beli Mawr (BELL-ee MAH-oor): Ancestor deity of the British pantheon. Literally means "big fire or light." In the Welsh tradition of the Anglesey Druid Order, he is perceived to be a god of the sky and the sun.

Blodeuedd/Blodeuwedd (Blod-AYE-edd/Blod-AYE-wedd): Woman created from flowers in the Fourth Branch of the Mabinogi. Her name changes into the second form when she is transformed by magic into an owl.

Brittonic (BRIT-tonic) (also Brythonic): the predecessor to Welsh, also classified as the P-Celtic group of languages

Calan Gaeaf/Nos Galan Gaeaf (KAL-ann GAY-av/NOSS GAL-ann GAY-av): the calends of winter, with the second example being the designation for All Hallows Eve

Cerridwen (kerr-ID-when): the mother of Awen, goddess of inspiration

Ceugant (KAY-gant): the infinite world

Cymreag (KUM-ra-eeg): the language of Wales

Cymru (KUM-ree): the land of Wales

Cymry (KUM-ree): the people of Wales

Derwydd (DARE-with): Welsh translation of Druid

Derwyddiaeth (DAR-with-yay-th): Welsh term meaning Druidry

Dôn (DAWN): Welsh mother goddess

Dryw (DREE-oo): Welsh name for a wren

Duw (Dew): Welsh for the Christian concept of God

Eisteddfod (ais-TEDD-vod): a festival of Welsh culture and Bardism

Gorsedd (GORE-sedd): a seat or collective noun for Bards

Gwyddoniaeth (gwee-THON-eeayth): the modern word for science

Gwyl (GOO-ill): meaning a feast

Gwynfyd (GWIN-vid): the spiritual world

Hanes (HAN-ess): history

Heddwch (HEH-dd-ooch): the action of bringing peace

Hudoliaeth (HID-all-yay-th): translation of magic

Lleu Llaw Gyffes (LL-ay LL-aw GUFF-ess): Abandoned son of Aranrhod, central figure in the Fourth Branch of the Mabinogi. His name means "light one of skillful hand or hands."

Llŷr (LL-ir): Welsh god of the sea

Mabinogi (mab-INN-ogee): Small tales or tales of youth; the collective name given to a series of native Welsh myths. Mabinogion (mab-INN-ogee-on) refers to the collection of eleven tales that include the Four Branches of the Mabinogi.

Mai (my): Beltane

Math (MATH): Druid king of the Fourth Branch of the Mabinogi

Pryderi (PRUD-air-ee): the son of Pwyll and Rhiannon

Pwyll (PWEE-ll): the main character of the First Branch of the Mabinogi and consort of Rhiannon

Rhiannon (rhee-ANN-on): Welsh goddess of sovereignty

Swyn (ZOO-in): Welsh word for spell, charm, magic, enchantment, witchcraft

Taliesin (tal-YES-inn): a portmanteau meaning "one with a radiant brow"

Teyrnon (TAY-rr-non): the man who adopts Rhiannon's stolen child

Traddodiad (traa-DDOD-iad): tradition

Y Nod Cyfrin (UH NOD KYV-reen): a term for the symbol of the three rays, meaning the mystic mark /|\

Ynys (UN-is): island

Ysbrydnos (us-BRID-nos): spirit night

Ysbrydoliaeth (us-brid-ALL-eeaeth): inspiration

SUGGESTED READING

The Awen Alone, Joanna van der Hoeven (Moon Books, 2014)

The Bardic Book of Becoming, Ivan McBeth (Red Wheel/Weiser, 2018)

Blood and Mistletoe, Ronald Hutton (Yale University Press, 2011)

The Book of Hedge Druidry, Joanna van der Hoeven (Llewellyn Publications, 2019)

Caesar's Druids, Miranda Aldhouse-Green (Yale University Press, 2010)

Contemplative Druidry, James Nichol (CreateSpace, 2014)

The Druid Magic Handbook, John Michael Greer (Red Wheel/Weiser, 2008)

Druid Mysteries, Philip Carr-Gomm (Rider, 2002)

The Druid Path, John Michael Greer (Sterling, 2022)

The Druid Way Made Easy, Graeme K. Talboys (O Books, 2011)

The Druid's Primer, Luke Eastwood (Moon Books, 2012)

Druidcraft, Philip Carr-Gomm (CreateSpace, 2013)

Druidry and Meditation, Nimue Brown (Moon Books, 2012)

Druidry and the Ancestors, Nimue Brown (Moon Books, 2012)

The Druidry Handbook, John Michael-Greer (Red Wheel/Weiser, 2021)

Pagan Paths, Pete Jennings (Rider, 2002)

The Path of Druidry, Penny Billington (Llewellyn Publications, 2011)

SUGGESTED READING

Rethinking the Ancient Druids, Miranda Aldhouse-Green (University of Wales Press, 2021)

Urban Druidry, Brendan Howlin (Moon Books, 2014)

Urban Ovate, Brendan Howlin (Moon Books, 2016)

What Do Druids Believe, Philip Carr-Gomm (Granta Books, 2006)

Wild Magic, Danu Forest (Llewellyn Publications, 2020)

RESOURCES

ONLINE VERSION OF *Geiriadur Prifysgol Cymru* (Dictionary of the Welsh Language): www.welsh-dictionary.ac.uk.

For sound files of rituals and glossary of words, visit www.youtube.com and search for the Kristoffer Hughes channel or type in https://www.youtube.com/user/dynmarw1.

• • • • • •

There are dozens of Druid orders, groups, and networks in existence. This list is not exhaustive, and locality- or interest-specific orders and groups can be found online.

The Order of Bards, Ovates and Druids. The largest of modern Druid orders, it offers a correspondence and online course that progresses through the three grades of Bard, Ovate, and Druid: www.druidry.org.

The British Druid Order. Offers a similar structure to the OBOD with emphasis on shamanic and visionary techniques and skills: www.druidry.co.uk.

The Anglesey Druid Order. Based in the ancestral home of the ancient British Druids, Anglesey, this order offers an in-person and online programme with emphasis on mythology and magic: www.angleseydruidorder.co.uk.

Ár nDraíocht Féin: A Druid Fellowship. A predominantly USA-based Druid organisation that promotes the study and further development of Druidry. It encompasses all Indo-European religions and actively encourages scholarship: www.adf.org.

Reformed Druids of North America. The oldest Druid organisation in the USA, which started as a protest in the late 1960s. They have a vast website with hundreds of articles and journals: www.rdna.info.

Druid Clan of Dana, also known as the Fellowship of Isis. Formed by Olivia Robertson, this Irish-based organisation offers teaching and initiation into their clan system: www.fellowshipofisis.com.

The Druid Order. The oldest of modern Druid orders offers an online teaching programme: www.thedruidorder.org.

Ancient Order of Druids in America. A traditional Druid order rooted in the revivalist movement of the eighteenth and nineteenth centuries, they offer a comprehensive study programme and membership: www.aoda.org.

The Druid Network. An information and sharing network with lists of celebrants and other service providers: www.druidnetwork.org.

BIBLIOGRAPHY

Aguiar, William, and Regine Halseth. "Aboriginal Peoples and Historic Trauma."
Prince George: National Collaborating Centre for Aboriginal Health, 2015.
https://www.ccnsa-nccah.ca/docs/context/RPT-HistoricTrauma
-IntergenTransmission-Aguiar-Halseth-EN.pdf.

Aldhouse-Green, Miranda. *Caesar's Druids: Story of an Ancient Priesthood.*
London: Yale University Press, 2010.

———. *Rethinking the Ancient Druids.* Cardiff: University of Wales Press, 2021.

Aldhouse-Green, Miranda, and Ray Howell. *Celtic Wales.* Cardiff: University of
Wales Press, 2017.

Antic, Ivan. *The Physics of Consciousness.* London: Samkhya Publishing, 2021.

Barnhart, Robert K., ed. *Chambers Dictionary of Etymology.* Edinburgh:
Chambers, 2008.

Beckett, John. *The Path of Paganism.* Woodbury, MN: Llewellyn, 2017.

Bevan, Gareth A., and Patrick J. Donovan, eds. *Geiriadur Prifysgol Cymru:
A Dictionary of the Welsh Language.* Cardiff: University of Wales Press,
1987–1998.

Billington, Penny. *The Path of Druidry.* Woodbury, MN: Llewellyn, 2011.

Brady, Maggie. "Culture in Treatment, Culture as Treatment. A Critical Appraisal
of Developments in Addictions Programs for Indigenous North Americans and
Australians." *Social Science & Medicine* 41, no. 11 (1995): 1487–98. https://
doi.org/10.1016/0277-9536(95)00055-C. https://pubmed.ncbi.nlm.nih
.gov/8607039/.

Braithwaite, William Stanley, ed. *The Book of Restoration Verse*. New York: Brentano's, 1910.

Bromwich, Rachel, ed. *Trioedd Ynys Prydein: The Triads of the Island of Britain*. Cardiff: University of Wales Press, 2006.

Celtic Life International. "The Chinese Celts." https://celticlifeintl.com /the-chinese-celts/.

Chadwick, Nora, and Myles Dillon. *The Celtic Realms*. London: Weidenfeld and Nicolson, 1972.

Crowley, Aleister. *Magick in Theory and Practise*. Secaucus: Castle Books, 1991.

Cunningham, Scott. *Magical Herbalism*. St. Paul, MN: Llewellyn, 1983.

Davies, Janet. *The Welsh Language: A History*. Cardiff: University of Wales Press, 2014.

Davies, Sioned. *The Mabinogion*. Oxford: Oxford University Press, 2018.

DiZerega, Gus. *God Is Dead, Long Live the Gods*. Woodbury, MN: Llewellyn, 2020.

Donne, John. *The Works of John Donne, Vol. III*. Henry Alford, ed. London: John W. Parker, 1839. 574–5. http://www.luminarium.org/sevenlit/donne /meditation17.php.

Edwards, Hywel Teifi. *The Eisteddfod*. Cardiff: University of Wales Press, 2016.

Elbert, Thomas, Frank Neuner, and Maggie Schaur. *Narrative Exposure Therapy*. Cambridge, MA: Hogrefe Publishing, 2011.

Evans, Gwenogvryn J., ed. *The White Book Mabinogion*. Pwllheli: privately published, 1909.

Fortune, Dion. *The Mystical Qabalah*. Milton Keynes: Aziloth Books, 2011.

———. *The Sea Priestess*. York Beach, ME: Red Wheel/Weiser, 2003.

Frankl, Viktor E. *Man's Search for Meaning*. London: Rider, 2004.

Gerald of Wales. Lewis Thorpe, trans. and intro. *The Journey Through Wales*. London: Penguin Classics, 1978.

Gino, Francesca, and Michael I. Norton. "Why Rituals Work." *Scientific American*. May 14, 2013. https://www.scientificamerican.com/article/why-Rituals-work/.

Gone, Joseph P. "Redressing First Nations Historical Trauma: Theorizing Mechanisms for Indigenous Culture as Mental Health Treatment." *Sage Journals Online: Transcultural Psychiatry* 50 (2013). https://doi.org/10.1177/1363461513487669.

Gramich, Katie, ed. & trans. *The Works of Gwerful Mechain*. Peterborough: Broadview Press, 2018.

Harvey, Graham. *Animism: Respecting the Living World*. London: Hurst, 2005.

———. "An Animist Manifesto." PAN: Philosophy, Activism, Nature no. 9, 2012. https://www.animism.org.uk/HarveyAnimism%20flyer.pdf.

Haycock, Marged, ed. & trans. *Legendary Poems from the Book of Taliesin*. Aberystwyth: CMCS, 2007.

Henry, John. "Magic and the Origins of Modern Science." *The Lancet* 354, SIV23 (December 1999). https://doi.org/10.1016/S0140-6736(99)90366-5.

Hughes, Kristoffer. *As the Last Leaf Falls*. Woodbury, MN: Llewellyn, 2021.

———. *Cerridwen: Celtic Goddess of Inspiration*. Woodbury, MN: Llewellyn, 2021.

———. *From the Cauldron Born*. Woodbury, MN: Llewellyn, 2012.

Hutton, Ronald. *Blood and Mistletoe: The History of the Druids in Britain*. London: Yale University Press, 2009.

———. *The Druids*. Hambledon: London, 2007.

———. *Stations of the Sun: A History of the Ritual Year in Britain*. Oxford: Oxford University Press, 1996.

———. *The Triumph of the Moon: A History of Modern Pagan Witchcraft*. Oxford: Oxford University Press, 1999.

———. *Witches, Druids and King Arthur*. Hambledon: London, 2003.

Ifans, Dafydd, and Rhiannon Ifans, trans. *Y Mabinogion*. Llandysul: Gomer, 1980.

Jenkins, Geraint H, ed. *A Rattleskull Genius: The Many Faces of Iolo Morganwg*. Cardiff: University of Wales Press, 2009.

———. *Y Digymar Iolo Morganwg*. Talybont: Y Lolfa, 2018.

Jones, Horace Leonard, trans. *The Geography of Strabo*. New York: Loeb Classical Library, 1923.

Julian the Apostate, trans. Wilmer C. Wright. *The Complete Works of Julian the Apostate. Illustrated: Orations, Letters to Themistius, To the Senate and People of Athens, To a Priest, The Caesars and Others.* N.p.: Strelbytskyy Multimedia Publishing, 2021. https://www.google.com/books/edition/The_Complete _Works_of_Julian_the_Apostat/cfREEAAAQBAJ.

Koch, John T., ed. *The Celtic Heroic Age.* Aberystwyth: Celtic Studies, 2000.

Kröplin, Bernd, and Regine C. Henschel. *Water and Its Memory.* Auflage: AT Verlag, 2017.

Lachman, Gary. *Aleister Crowley: Magick, Rock and Roll, and the Wickedest Man in the World.* London: Penguin, 2014.

Lewis, Gwyneth, and Rowan Williams, trans. *The Book of Taliesin.* London: Penguin, 2019.

Miles, Dilwyn. *Secrets of the Bards of the Isle of Britain.* Llandybie: Gwasg Dinefwr Press, 1992.

Muller, Sylvie. *The Irish Wren Tales and Ritual. Béaloideas / The Journal of the Folklore of Ireland Society* 64/65 (1996/1997).

O'Driscoll, Dana. *Sacred Actions.* Atglen: Red Feather, 2021.

Order of Bards, Ovates and Druids. "Peacemaking in Druidry." https://druidry .org/get-involved/peacemaking-in-druidry. Accessed July 12, 2022.

Owen, Trefor M. *The Customs and Traditions of Wales.* Cardiff: University of Wales Press, 2016.

Parker, Will. *The Four Branches of the Mabinogi.* California: Bardic Press, 2005. http://www.mabinogi.net/translations.htm.

Parry, John Jay, trans. *The Life of Merlin; Vita Merlini by Geoffrey of Monmouth.* Marston Gate: Forgotten Books, 2008. Reprint from 1925 edition.

Radin, Dean. *Real Magic.* New York: Harmony Books, 2018.

Ridley, Sir Edward, trans. *Pharsalia, M Annaeus Lucanus.* London: Longmans, 1905.

Roberts, Gwyneth Tyson. *The Language of the Blue Books: Wales and Colonial Prejudice.* Cardiff: University of Wales Press, 2011.

Ross, Anne. *Everyday Life of the Pagan Celts.* London: Batsford, 1970.

Sala, Luc. *Ritual: The Magical Perspective*. New Delhi: Nirala Publications, 2014.

Selcon, Harold. *The Physicians of Myddfai*. Marston Gate: Createspace, 2018.

Sheldrake, Rupert. *Science and Spiritual Practices*. London: Coronet, 2017.

———. *Ways to Go Beyond: Spiritual Practises in a Scientific Age*. London: Coronet, 2019.

Stavrakopoulou, Francesca. *God: An Anatomy*. London: Picador, 2021.

Thomas, Gwyn. *Y Traddodiad Barddol*. Caerdydd: Gwasg Prifysgol Cymru, 2012.

Vingerhoets, Ad. *Why Only Humans Weep*. Oxford: Oxford University Press, 2013.

Williams, Ifor. *Pedeir Ceinc y Mabinogi*. Caerdydd: Gwasg Prifysgol Cymru, 1978.

Williams, John ab Ithel, ed. *The Barddas of Iolo Morganwg*. Boston: Weiser Books, 2004. Reprint of original 1862 and 1874 editions by the Welsh MSS Society.

Williams, Mark, and Danny Penman. *Mindfulness: A Practical Guide to Finding Peace in a Frantic World*. Piatkus: London, 2013.

Williams, Mark. *The Celtic Myths that Shape the Way We Think*. London: Thames and Hudson, 2021.

Zakroff, Laura Tempest. *Weave the Liminal: Living Modern Traditional Witchcraft*. Woodbury, MN: Llewellyn, 2019.

INDEX

NOTES